INDIGENOUS AUTOCRACY

Indigenous Autocracy

POWER, RACE, AND RESOURCES IN
PORFIRIAN TLAXCALA, MEXICO

JACLYN ANN SUMNER

STANFORD UNIVERSITY PRESS
Stanford, California

Stanford University Press
Stanford, California

© 2024 Jaclyn Ann Sumner. All rights reserved.

No part of this book may be reproduced or transmitted in any form or by any means, electronic or mechanical, including photocopying and recording, or in any information storage or retrieval system, without the prior written permission of Stanford University Press.

Printed in the United States of America on acid-free, archival-quality paper

Library of Congress Cataloging-in-Publication Data
Names: Sumner, Jaclyn Ann, author.
Title: Indigenous autocracy : power, race, and resources in Porfirian Tlaxcala, Mexico / Jaclyn Ann Sumner.
Other titles: Power, race, and resources in Porfirian Tlaxcala, Mexico
Identifiers: LCCN 2023017955 (print) | LCCN 2023017956 (ebook) | ISBN 9781503636279 (cloth) | ISBN 9781503637399 (paperback) | ISBN 9781503637405 (ebook)
Subjects: LCSH: Cahuantzi, Próspero, 1834–1915. | Governors—Mexico—Tlaxcala (State) | Water-supply—Government policy—Mexico—Tlaxcala (State)—History. | Racism against indigenous peoples—Mexico—History. | Tlaxcala (Mexico : State)—Politics and government. | Mexico—Politics and government—1867–1910.
Classification: LCC F1366 .S86 2024 (print) | LCC F1366 (ebook) | DDC 972/.47—dc23/eng/20230519
LC record available at https://lccn.loc.gov/2023017955
LC ebook record available at https://lccn.loc.gov/2023017956

Cover design: Martyn Schmoll
Cover art: Próspero Cahuantzi, 1885, Instituto Nacional de Antropología e Historia, Fototeca Nacional. *Carta de las cuencas hidrográficas del Estado de Tlaxcala*, 1910, CONAGUA-AHA, Aprovechamientos superficiales, Caja 3487, Expediente 47891, Legajo 1, Foja 2.

CONTENTS

Maps, Figures, and Tables	vii
Acknowledgments	ix
Introduction	1
ONE The Appointment of an Indigenous Governor	15
TWO Claiming the Past	32
THREE Building a State, Building a Regime	52
FOUR Litigating Water	72
FIVE The Political Currency of Water	92
SIX The Price of Progress	116
Conclusion	135
Notes	145
Bibliography	193
Index	219

MAPS, FIGURES, AND TABLES

Maps

1	Tlaxcala, Mexico, 1900	xiv
2	Topography and Hydrology of Tlaxcala	xv
3	*Carta del Estado de Tlaxcala*, 1881	59
4	*Carta de las cuencas hidrográficas del Estado de Tlaxcala*, 1910	89

Figures

1	Próspero Cahuantzi, 1885	7
2	"Borrascas en las Alturas" ("Storms brewing above"), August 11, 1901	23
3	"Así Gobernamos" ("This is how we govern"), February 25, 1906	24
4	"Las Prosperidades de Tlaxcala" ("Prosperity in Tlaxcala"), May 28, 1899	26
5	*El Senado de Tlaxcala*, Rodrigo Gutiérrez, 1875	36
6	Mexicano rail line, 1877	56
7	Mexicano rail line running over the Zahuapan River near the San Luis textile factory outside Apizaco, Tlaxcala, 1911	57

8 Deviation dam "San Diego" over the Zahuapan River, 1911 — 87

9 Iron water pipeline leading to textile factory San Luis, 1911 — 90

10 Pipeline down La Malintzin mountain to the San Luis textile factory, 1911 — 95

11 Waterfall from the Zahuapan River, 1911 — 99

12 Hydroelectric pipeline located on the Hacienda San Diego Apatlahuaya — 100

13 Canal and reservoir from the Zahuapan River and location of the hydroelectric plant on the Hacienda San Diego Apatlahuaya — 101

14 Sketch of the Zahuapan River near the rancho San Isidro and towns of Panotla, Tepehitec, and Totolac, September 23, 1903 — 104

15 Iron bridge over the Zahuapan River in Tlaxcala City, 1894 — 124

Tables

1 Governors reelected two or more times, 1877–1911 — 18

2 Textile factories in Tlaxcala, 1905–1906 — 75

3 Petitions from water users in Tlaxcala state to the Secretaría de Fomento, 1888–1910 — 84

ACKNOWLEDGMENTS

Many people have shaped this book and provided the support and friendship that made it possible. Although this book began at the University of Chicago, the idea that I could even be a historian was sparked by countless conversations with Josef Barton, Brodwyn Fischer, and Frank Safford in the basement of Harris Hall at Northwestern University. I wrote my first paper on caudillos for Frank, who will be greatly missed. Joe introduced me to the archives, and culinary delights, of Mexico City. Joe and Brodie taught me to think critically about how structures of power shape history. Brodie is one of few women role models I have had in the field of Latin American history; I am grateful to have learned from her so early in my career. Joe and Brodie, along with my advisors at Northwestern, Jeff Rice and Christopher Hager, encouraged me to combine my interests in politics and social justice, and my Spanish skills, to apply for a Fulbright Institute of International Education/García Robles Award. My experiences conducting research and living in Veracruz, Mexico, on a Fulbright IIE changed the trajectory of my career from law to history.

At the University of Chicago, Emilio Kourí constantly pushed me to answer, "so what." I am grateful that Emilio hired me to work at the Katz Center for Mexican Studies some fifteen years ago and that he has encouraged and shaped my work ever since. Mauricio Tenorio first gave me the idea to explore an Indigenous governor he had heard of during the Porfiriato. Dain Borges pushed me to read and think broadly. I was lucky enough to be among the last students to take Friedrich Katz's History of

Mexico course and to hear his magnificent stories. I am grateful to Jaime Gentry, Josh Beck, Christelle Marpaud, and the rest of the staff in the Center for Latin American Studies for their administrative adeptness and friendship. Participants in the Latin American History Workshop commented on many chapter drafts and offered support and advice. These include Amanda Hartzmark, Aiala Levy, Matt Barton, Casey Lurtz, Stuart Easterling, Nicole Mottier, José Luis Razo, Patrick Iber, María Balandran Castillo, C. J. Álvarez, Patrick Kelly, Julia Young, Antonio Sotomayor, Carlos Bravo Regidor, Mikael Wolfe, Ananya Chakravarti, Diana Schwartz, Sarah Osten, Tessa Murphy, Luis Fernando Granados, Romina Robles Ruvalcaba, Ben Johnson, Marcel Anduiza Pimentel, Chris Dunlap, José Juan Pérez Meléndez, Marco Torres, and Emilio de Antuñano. My friendships with Diana Schwartz, Casey Lurtz, Natalie Belsky, and Tessa Murphy helped me to survive graduate school—our bonds have only deepened as we have become professors and mothers together. Casey has done more for this book than anyone. I am so lucky that one of my dearest friends also happens to study nineteenth-century Mexican history.

Raymond Buve, Tim Henderson, and Guy Thomson facilitated my initial revision process by giving me advice about the archives in Puebla and connecting me with scholars there. In Mexico, conversations with Graciela Márquez Colín and Luis Aboites helped me to think about the big arguments of the book. Moisés Mecalco López provided friendship and help navigating Tlaxcala when I first arrived, and in the years since. Carlos Bustamante López and Mark Morris first introduced me to the Archivo Histórico del Estado de Tlaxcala and pointed me to many invaluable secondary sources written by scholars in Tlaxcala and Puebla. Mark also facilitated an introduction with Jaime Sánchez Sánchez, who talked to me for hours about the Revolution in Tlaxcala. Jeff Bortz introduced me to Mariano Torres, who offered valuable advice about doing research in Tlaxcala-Puebla, and who in turn introduced me to Evelyne Sánchez. Evelyne generously shared with me a treasure trove of documentation that she collected in Tlaxcala over many years of research. She also introduced me to her research assistant, Willy Méndez, whose familiarity with the archives in Tlaxcala and Puebla allowed him to find documentation that I would not have found on my own. I owe a huge debt of gratitude to the staff at the Archivo Histórico del Estado de Tlaxcala, especially the former director, Liliana Zamora Poiré. Thank you also to Sergio Sanluis Hernández at the Casa de Cultura Jurídica in Tlaxcala. In Mexico City, staff at the

Acknowledgments

Archivo Nacional del Agua, the Porfirio Díaz archives at the Universidad Iberoamericana, and the Hemeroteca Nacional at UNAM were so helpful. Laura Peláez and her family and Maricarmen Tenorio Fernández and her family made research a much less lonely endeavor during my months in Tlaxcala. Although he passed away before I got to know him, I am grateful to Ricardo Rendón Garcini and his *equipo* for their archival sleuthing that made research in uncataloged archives easier.

At Presbyterian College, I have been fortunate to have the support and friendship of my colleagues in the history department, Roy Campbell, Anita Gustafson, Will Harris, Rick Heiser, Michael Nelson, and Stefan Wiecki. They have encouraged me to say no—to overloads, summer school, and service—so that I could finish this book. Provost Don Raber allowed me to reduce my course load so I could dedicate more time to finishing the book. Sarah Burns, Erin McAdams, Brooke Spatta, Evelyn Swain, and Emily Taylor have been my faculty role models and female comrades while teaching at a small liberal arts college. Emily, my fellow academic mama and confidante, has cheered on this book since the day I met her. I owe gratitude to the staff at the Presbyterian College library, especially the library director, Betsy Byrd, for helping me to hunt down sources that were difficult to access at our small college. Betsy and Emily, along with Lindsay Howerton-Hastings and Heather Love, have supported me and my family in many ways since moving to South Carolina nine years ago. I am so grateful for their friendship.

The Southeastern Council of Latin American Studies (SECOLAS) and many of its affiliated members—including Jürgen Buchenau, Angela Willis, Monica Rankin, Greg Crider, Steven Hyland, Lily Balloffet, and Lisa Covert Pinley—became my Latin Americanist family after moving to the South. Jürgen has become an invaluable mentor to me as he has for so many new faculty and graduate students. Since meeting her at the SECOLAS conference in Cartagena, Christina Bueno has led me toward some key sources and provided generous feedback on my article in *Mexican Studies/Estudios Mexicanos*, a revised version of which comprises chapter two of this book. Jürgen, Lisa, and Lily, along with Vanessa Freije, Corinna Zeltsman, and Casey Lurtz, connected me with editors and helped me to navigate the publishing process. Sarah Osten had impeccable timing when, in the middle of the pandemic, as I was finishing up the manuscript, she revitalized the UChicago Latin American History Workshop for the women who had once participated. Sarah, Julia Young,

Ann Schneider, Ananya Chakravarti, Diana Schwartz, Nicole Mottier, Casey Lurtz, and Romina Robles Ruvalcaba read and commented on manuscript chapter drafts, offered publishing advice, and created a much-needed sense of online community. It is still so sad, and hard to believe, that we lost Romina months ago.

Margo Irvin has believed in and supported this project ever since I first presented it to her. I am grateful to her; her editorial assistant, Cindy Lim; my production editor, Chris Peterson; and all the staff at Stanford University Press. Two reviewers offered sharp and valuable criticisms of the manuscript. One of my reviewers, my friend Mikael Wolfe, kindly revealed himself to me. Mikael read the manuscript carefully and provided pages of insightful commentary. My developmental editor, Megan Pugh, provided a roadmap for revisions. Her feedback was crucial for sharpening my arguments and clarifying my writing. Dawn Hall copyedited the manuscript thoroughly, and Jacqueline Ly produced a comprehensive index. An earlier version of chapter two appeared as "The Indigenous Governor of Tlaxcala and Acceptable Indigenousness in the Porfirian Regime," *Mexican Studies/Estudios Mexicanos* 35, no. 1 (Winter 2019): 61–87.

Material support for this book was made possible by the Department of History, the Katz Center for Mexican Studies, the Center for Latin American Studies, and the Center for the Study of Race, Politics, and Culture at the University of Chicago, which funded exploratory research trips. The bulk of the research for this book was funded by a Fulbright-Hays Doctoral Dissertation Research Abroad Fellowship. At Presbyterian College, faculty development funds and the Orr Faculty Research Fellowship allowed me to complete my research and present various chapters at conferences. An American Council of Learned Societies Project Development Grant allowed me to reduce my course load and bought me precious time to finish the manuscript.

The challenges of finishing this book, with a heavy teaching load and a small child, during a pandemic, were daunting sometimes. I am grateful to my family and friends for seeing me through these challenges as well as those that came before. My sister, Jenna, and my grandmother, Barbara, have given me so much love. They always believed I would finish the book, no matter how difficult. The Avgerins, Bill, Chris, and especially my mother-in-law Judy, have encouraged my career for almost two decades. My grandmother and my grandfather, Kay and Bill Sumner, instilled in me a love of learning and curiosity. They would have read every word of this book. I have shared decades of travel, laughs, and love with Kim Lacker and Lara Tilley. I am also indebted to the many women who have provided our family with childcare so that I could have time to write, especially Hayley Small and Lucy Hayes. The loves of my life are Billy and Harrison. Billy has nourished my career, and my stomach, for two decades, as he followed me from Chicago to Mexico City to South Carolina. I am grateful for his companionship and unwavering support. Harrison has given us a new reason to live and to fight for a more equitable world.

My parents, Denise and Jim Sumner, worked day and night—literally—to provide me, a first-generation college student, with incredible educational opportunities. This book is dedicated to them, for my mom who will read it, and for my dad who would have—and handed out copies to everyone on the golf course. Thank you, Mom. Miss you, Dad.

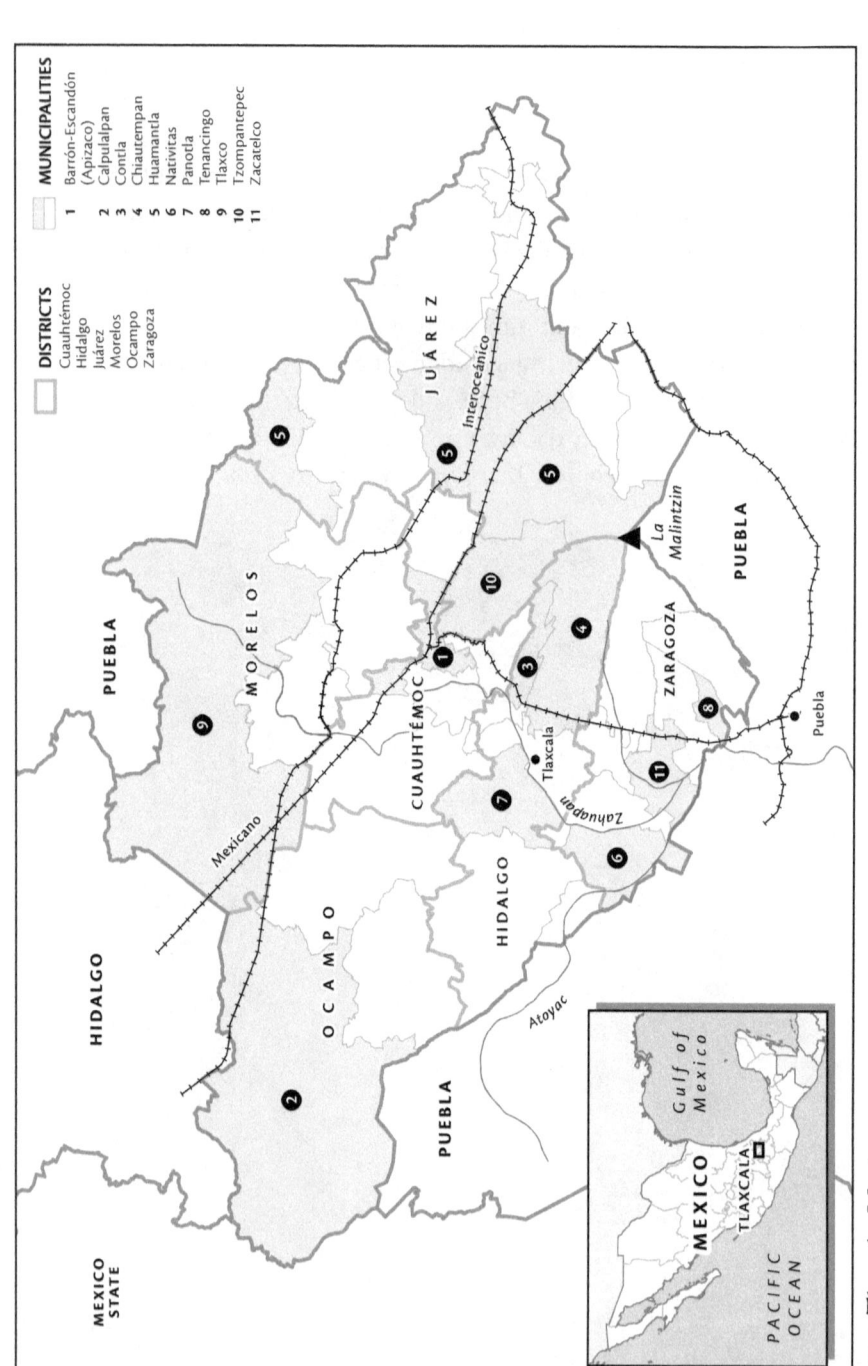

MAP 1. Tlaxcala, Mexico, 1900.

Map by Erin Greb Cartography; boundary data provided by Casey Lurtz

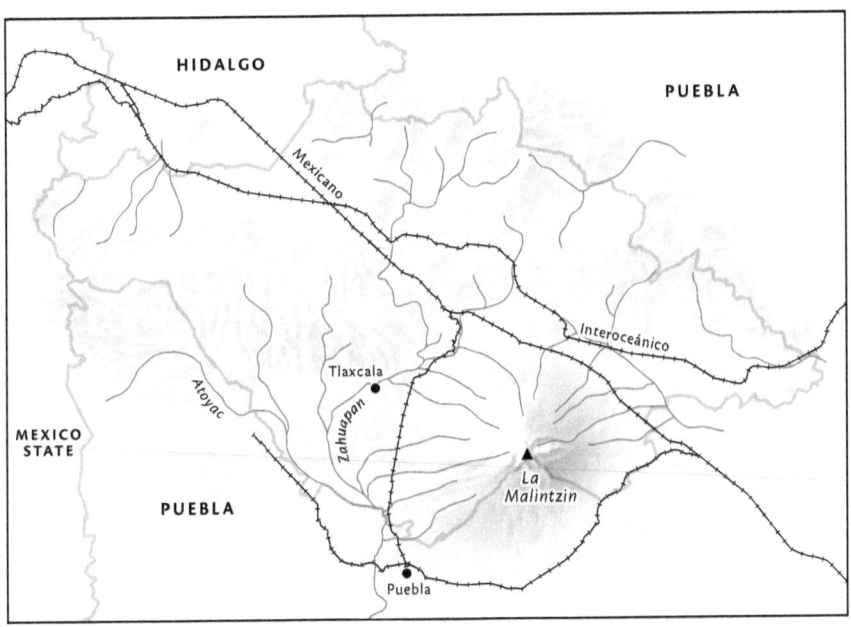

MAP 2. Topography and Hydrology of Tlaxcala. Source: Adapted from *Carta de las cuencas hidrográficas del Estado de Tlaxcala*, 1910. Comisión Nacional del Agua/Archivo Histórico y Biblioteca Central del Agua (CONAGUA-AHA), Aprovechamientos superficiales, Caja 3487, Expediente 47891, Legajo 1, Foja 2; *Memoria de la administración pública del estado de Tlaxcala presentada a la H. Legislatura del mismo, por el gobernador constitucional Coronel Próspero Cahuantzi, el 2 de abril 1893*. Tlaxcala: Imprenta del Gobierno, 1894.

Map by Erin Greb Cartography

INDIGENOUS AUTOCRACY

Introduction

On December 11, 1901, the Minister of Foreign Relations (Secretaría de Relaciones Exteriores) in Mexico City received an angry plea from the Minister of France in Mexico. The French minister was writing on behalf of Clement Manuel, a French citizen who owned a hacienda (*estate*) in the small central province of Tlaxcala, among other properties in Mexico.[1] Manuel had fled his hacienda in Tlaxcala after the governor there, Próspero Cahuantzi, ordered the district judge to charge Manuel with "kidnapping." According to the arrest warrant, Manuel had detained a worker whom he caught stealing tools and sacks of wool from a storehouse on his property. The French minister pleaded with the Mexican Minister of Foreign Relations to "urgently intervene" in the matter and to "suspend" the warrant to arrest Manuel, which, the minister insisted, was the result of one worker's "simple complaint."[2]

Witness testimonies bely the French minister's facile explanation of what transpired that December day. Witnesses, including workers and the governor, Cahuantzi, explained how Manuel had been using "degrading methods" on his workers, that he had "mistreated" them, and that his "behavior" was "irregular."[3] The worker whom Manuel accused of robbery, Juan González, was a shepherd from the nearby village of Tocatlán, one of numerous *vecinos* (residents) from Tocatlán who Manuel insisted had been stealing from his hacienda for years. This time, it appeared that Manuel was determined to hold González, "a resentful Indian," and Tocatlán residents, "his clear enemies," accountable.[4] In González's testimony, he described how Manuel pressed a "gun against his chest" while threatening to shoot if González did not "confess the truth."[5] After refusing to confess, the hacendado locked González in a storehouse. Sometime in the middle of the night, the purported thief escaped. Bypassing the district judge and the *prefecto político* (district boss), González went directly to the governor to tell him what happened. Manuel also fled, absconding to Mexico City, per his lawyer's advice, until "the situation was sorted out."[6] It was good for Manuel that he left. The next morning, the prefecto político, members of the local constabulary (*rurales*), and some twenty Tocatlán residents, showed up on Manuel's property to arrest him.[7]

Manuel believed he knew why Governor Cahuantzi took the worker's word over his own. Cahuantzi accused Manuel of failing to pay off his peons' debts to the estate owners who previously employed them, as was customary in Tlaxcala. Manuel denied these charges. He further insisted how Cahuantzi "favors the indigenous race and believes whatever they tell him, [and he] does not care when these persons violate the laws."[8] He continued, "all of the sensible people in the state [of Tlaxcala] are aware [of the] great fondness the governor has for indians [*sic*] and their bad inclinations."[9] In his letter to the Mexican Minister of Foreign Affairs, the French minister alluded to previous "complaints" that had been "brought to his attention" about the "attitude of the Governor of Tlaxcala."[10] He suggested to "your excellency [the Minister of Foreign Affairs]" that he attend to these.[11] In light of the preeminent social Darwinism of the era, the xenophobia the French hacendado exhibited toward Indigenous peoples was hardly shocking. And yet some of those who Manuel thought of as "Indians" with "bad inclinations" likely disagreed with the Frenchman's assessment that the governor somehow preferred them. When small landowners in Tlaxcala, whom Manuel no doubt saw as Indians, protested the governor's property tax hike in 1897, Cahuantzi threw them in jail. Later, as protests grew more vociferous, the governor had the leader of these protests assassinated. No further information about the incident between Manuel and his workers can be found in the historic record, though Manuel does not appear to have returned to Tlaxcala.

Against the backdrop of early twentieth-century Mexico, the outcome in this case is unusual. During Porfirio Díaz's nearly continuous reign over Mexico from 1876 to 1911, Díaz and his gubernatorial appointees prioritized development over the rights of the agricultural working majority. Examining the different strategies that Cahuantzi used to endure in office—as this book does—helps to clarify why the governor stood up for local workers' rights and held a foreign landowner accountable for mistreating his workers. He did so in this case, as well as in others. Some of the strategies Cahuantzi used to rule—patronage, electoral corruption, suppression of dissent—echo countless histories that have been told about the caudillos, caciques, and *coronéis* (political strongmen) who dominated the political landscape of postindependent Latin America.[12] But while Cahuantzi was a strongman appointed by the national dictator, he also used the political tools that were available to him as one of the few governors who had recognizably Indigenous heritage and was native to the state he ruled. Because of his background, Cahuantzi realized that, for both he and Díaz to remain in power, he had to occasionally conciliate, rather than repress, dissent.

This book uses Próspero Cahuantzi's governorship as a window into the complex and diverse regional political practices that underpinned Díaz's authoritarian rule. The so-called Porfiriato lasted from 1876 until the Mexican Revolution broke out in 1911. Following five decades of foreign invasions, civil wars, and presidential turnover, Porfirio Díaz ushered in Mexico's first prolonged period of stability as a nation. Historians have thoroughly probed how Mexico was transformed under Díaz, paying particular attention to how Porfirian administrators facilitated liberal capitalist development. Under Díaz, the nation became more fiscally solvent, and its economy grew prodigiously. Railroad networks, dams, and irrigation systems were built to facilitate the domestic and especially the international sale of sugar, coffee, henequen (sisal), and other exports, and new regulations and laws were enacted to enable export-oriented growth. Although Mexico's development was uneven, and its effects disparately experienced throughout the nation's thirty-one states, Mexico's growth during the Porfirian period was remarkable as compared to the decades that preceded it.[13]

To beget this growth, the political practices that Díaz and his regional representatives used were often decidedly undemocratic and became more so as the regime aged. Díaz remained outwardly committed to liberal democracy. National and state elections were nearly always staged, and the press was permitted to scrutinize certain aspects of the regime. But on the ground, throughout Mexico's vast and diverse provincial landscape, practices such as controlling electoral outcomes, establishing new and co-opting old patronage networks, and stifling dissent through nondemocratic means frequently mirrored those used by Latin America's authoritarian strongmen, past and present. Porfirian leaders' overt coercion and corruption is encapsulated by historians through the old phrase "*pan o palo*"—bread or the stick. Essentially, conform, or else.[14]

Próspero Cahuantzi remained in office longer than any other gubernatorial appointee under Porfirio Díaz's transformative, yet highly repressive and inequitable, dictatorship. Whereas Díaz's other gubernatorial appointees either died, took on a new position, or were pushed out of office by Díaz, Cahuantzi persisted as Tlaxcala's governor for twenty-six years, from 1885 until 1911. Cahuantzi was one of the dozens of General Díaz's former military allies who had assisted Díaz with the coup he staged in 1876 (Plan de Tuxtepec) to overthrow the existing government, whom Díaz, now president, awarded with a state governorship.[15] Like all governors, Cahuantzi came to power via Díaz's appointment, rather than election. He was subsequently "reelected" six times, more than any other gubernatorial appointee under Díaz.[16] Cahuantzi remained steadfastly devout to Díaz even after revolutionaries toppled the Porfirian regime and Díaz sailed off to Paris in exile.

Like Díaz, Cahuantzi engaged with practices that were typical of political bosses in Latin America and throughout the world. Cahuantzi's politics were highly personalistic. The governor often suppressed dissent in person, riding out on horseback to put down strikes at factories and mills. He intervened in residents' natural resource disputes even though it was not legal for him to do so. Like Díaz, Cahuantzi installed loyalists in key administrative posts and pushed them out when he feared their deference waned. He also used political patronage to conciliate those who opposed him. Though rare, Cahuantzi had people—including former allies—killed.[17] Cahuantzi was a sycophant and a strongman, but he was also a pragmatist. The governor's political practices reflected his extensive knowledge about local history, environmental conditions, and political culture. The governor's familiarity with his region's past was useful when it came to making Tlaxcala known to nation-builders and investors. This knowledge was similarly useful when it came to defending Tlaxcalan state sovereignty against its much larger and wealthier neighbor, Puebla. As with the imbroglio with the French landowner Clement Manuel, Cahuantzi sometimes defended small landowners' and villagers' demands over those of foreign landowners and developers. This was especially true when it came to residents' access to water, which Cahuantzi knew to be a precious and limited local resource. The governor allowed some Tlaxcalans to continue to farm their lands communally as they had for centuries, despite national laws that prohibited communal property ownership. Contradictorily, he took advantage of the same national laws to attempt to usurp village lands and expand his personal estate.

Cahuantzi's longevity in office, his acknowledged Indigenous heritage, and his nativeness to Tlaxcala set him apart from many other Porfirian governors. But the ways in which Cahuantzi exploited the schisms between national dictates, laws, and policies, on the one hand, and local practices and expectations, on the other, resonate well beyond Porfirian Mexico. In this book I build on the work of scholars who have shown how diverse, sometimes noncoercive measures at the regional levels buoyed authoritarian regimes in Latin America.[18] More than a regional political history, I analyze different dimensions of politics and how they intersect, including the politics of race, nation-building, modernization, and the environment. National autocrats like Díaz and their regional representatives like Cahuantzi used political tools such as corruption and repression to maintain political control. However, focusing on these strategies by themselves obfuscates, first, the diversity of societal experiences under authoritarianism; second, the regional spaces where residents pressed their claims—even if their votes mattered little; and third, how authoritarian rulers' political practices changed over time and according to local circumstances.

The argumentative premises of this book—that different regions experienced authoritarian rule differently, and that regional actors and circumstances shaped national projects—are informed by the historical canons on Indigenous and mixed race interlocutors in Latin America.[19] Historians within these canons push against nationally centered narratives by showing how, in Mexico, Porfirian rule was an ongoing and constantly changing political dance among national, state, and local actors.[20] Historians of popular liberalism in Mexico have reinforced these ideas by examining how regional interlocutors in the early national period appropriated liberal political discourse to make claims and assert their rights as national citizens.[21] If popular liberalism's legacy was that "Mexico's subsequent leaders . . . realized that in Mexico even an authoritarian state had to be inclusive," this book offers proof that this assertion, made by Peter Guardino, holds true in certain spaces during the Porfirian era.[22] Moreover, within these spaces, political peace was not brokered through coercion alone. Scholars of popular liberalism emphasize how the influence of regional interlocutors waned under Díaz's stable, yet dictatorial, rule.[23] But

Cahuantzi's loyalty and ties to Díaz did not preclude him from influencing how Díaz's laws and policies were implemented in his state.

Indigeneity and Pragmatism

Cahuantzi's early life, though unusual for a Porfirian governor, was typical of most Tlaxcalans. Próspero Cahuantzi (1834–1915) was from Santa María Ixtulco, a small town in the populous Nativitas or Zahuapan Valley of Tlaxcala.[24] Like many Tlaxcalans, he spoke Nahuatl (the Aztec language) in addition to Spanish.[25] Although he received only a rudimentary primary education, many sources attest to his skills as an autodidact.[26] Cahuantzi hailed from a family of landless peasants. As such, his only opportunity for advancement was through the military, which he joined in 1856 at the age of twenty-two.[27] Cahuantzi presented many of the physiognomic and cultural signifiers that marked Indigenous difference during this period.[28] Cahuantzi's surname, multilingualism, peasant background, and low level of education signaled to many Mexicans and non-Mexicans alike that he had Indigenous heritage.[29]

In Mexico, legally, all men were equal regardless of their race. This had been true ever since the nation wrote its first constitution in 1824. Yet few nation-builders anywhere in Latin America in the nineteenth century believed that Indigenous peoples were worthy of equal rights. The attitudes of Latin American elites toward Indigenous peoples ran from ambivalence to disdain, tending more toward the latter than the former. At best, politicians and statesmen disregarded their Indigenous populations. At worst, they displaced them, usurped their natural resources, and abused their labor.[30] In Mexico, this was especially true for Indigenous peoples living in frontier areas away from Mexico City, in the north and in the Yucatán Peninsula, key export production sites.[31] During the Porfiriato, nation-builders were strongly influenced by social Darwinism. Porfirian intellectuals and policy makers had diverse opinions about why Indigenous peoples were degraded, as well as what to do about them.[32] But they rarely saw Indigenous peoples as modernizing actors. Practices that were traditionally ascribed to Indigenous peoples, communal landholding and Catholicism in particular, were viewed by Porfirian elites as hindrances to national progress.[33] To be sure, Mexico's Indigenous populations were highly diverse. Moreover, Mexico was a majority mestizo (mixed race) nation. Most Mexicans—including those who held prominent offices—

FIGURE 1. Próspero Cahuantzi, 1885. Source: Instituto Nacional de Antropología e Historia, Fototeca Nacional. Reprinted with permission.

had Indigenous lineage. This included President Díaz, and, more famously, President Benito Juárez (1806–1872, in office 1858–72), a Zapotec Indian from the southern, predominately Indigenous, state of Oaxaca. However, given extant racial hierarchies of the nineteenth century, few Mexicans who hoped to ascend to, or who held political power, outwardly claimed their Indigenous heritage. They were much more likely to try to hide it. What distinguished Cahuantzi from most other Mexican leaders was that he claimed his identity as an Indigenous Tlaxcalan and used it selectively and strategically over the course of his career.

Cahuantzi crafted an image of himself and his region as representing one of the great Indigenous groups of Mexico. He aligned himself clearly with his state. He also touted a specific historical narrative about Tlaxcala, one that appealed to Porfirian nation-builders who believed that, whereas contemporary Indigenous peoples stymied progress, Indians of the pre-Hispanic era were enthralling. Nation-building elites used ancient American civilizations—the Aztecs, Inca, and Maya, especially—to build patrimonies for their young countries and evince their deep and proud histories. They juxtaposed ancient American civilizations with foundational civilizations of the West such as the Greeks and Romans. As with racialization—defining who was an Indian and who was not—composing a uniform national history was fraught with incongruities. Nation-builders often made arbitrary decisions about what to include in Latin American nations' official pasts, and what to omit. The great pyramids of the Aztecs and the Maya were a wonder, but the bellicose Apache, to name one example, were deemed unworthy of nation-builders' reverence.[34]

Cahuantzi supported nation-builders' efforts to create a national Mexican patrimony. Moreover, he marshaled a usable Tlaxcalan past, one that emphasized the region's exceptionalism as compared to other Indigenous groups as well as Tlaxcala's proximity and importance to the center of Mexican power. Pre-Hispanic Tlaxcalans had been enemies of the imperial Mexica (Aztecs), against whom the Tlaxcalans constantly warred to defend their sovereignty. When Hernán Cortés and his men arrived in the Valley of Mexico, Tlaxcalans provided the Spanish with manpower and information that were vital to invading and toppling the Aztec capital city-state of Tenochtitlán (1519–1521).[35] Tlaxcalan elites were among the first to convert to Catholicism. They assisted the Spanish in colonial campaigns to pacify and Christianize more "rebellious" natives in the Mexican north and in modern-day Central America.[36] Colonized Tlaxcalans were consequently exempt from encomienda—the institution that forced Indigenous peoples to give tribute and labor to the Spanish crown—and had direct parlay, or communication, with the monarchy.[37] They also kept their pre-Conquest political system—four *cabeceras* (in Nahuatl, *altepetl*) and various barrios, towns or neighborhoods (in Nahuatl *tlaxilacalli*)—intact.[38] Over the course of centuries, many Tlaxcalans had acculturated to "Hispanic" signifiers and adopted "Hispanic" practices.[39] Many Tlaxcalans did indeed speak Indigenous languages. But many, including Cahuantzi, also spoke Spanish. By the 1870s, goods and people from all over the Atlantic world passed through Tlaxcala by rail line, Mexico's first, to reach Mexico City. Emblems of modernity, textile factories, dams, paved roads, electric lights, followed. Even in the present day, as theatre scholar Patricia Ybarra explains, Tlaxcalans continue to celebrate their ancestors' roles in the "Spanish Conquest" and in forging the eventual Mexican nation.[40]

Cahuantzi's actions in the Porfirian era presaged those of present-day Tlaxcalans who perform and honor their history. Cahuantzi exploited elements from Tlaxcala's past and present to make himself into the kind of Indian that Porfirian elites could accept—one who was assimilable and whose region, insofar as Cahuantzi portrayed it, had a glorious past and welcomed modernization in the present. Cahuantzi drew attention to Tlaxcala's history to enhance his region's reputation, to attract investment, and to defend Tlaxcala's political and economic sovereignty from its larger and more populated central Mexican neighbors. The governor used his region's patrimony to make material political claims in the modern era. He argued, for example, that Tlaxcala's territorial claims over a textile factory predated those of Puebla state, since Tlaxcala existed during the pre-Hispanic era, whereas Puebla did not. Cahuantzi used his identity as an Indigenous Tlaxcalan as a political instrument through which he ingratiated himself to Díaz and other Porfirian nation-builders, and to convince them that he was worthy of long-term rule and capable of modernizing his state. He spoke in Nahuatl at public events that commemorated the nation's ancient Indigenous civilizations. Toward the end of his rule, as Cahuantzi's and Díaz's grips on power were slipping away, Cahuantzi and his supporters reminded Tlaxcalans that they were "lucky" that Cahuantzi was a "native son" and a "genuine representative of his intelligent race," as if he had been elected democratically.[41]

By examining how Cahuantzi claimed his Indigenousness selectively, this book offers new insight into the racist milieu of turn-of-the-century

Mexico and Latin America. During a period in which national actors' policies and practices scuttled Indigenous peoples' agency, Cahuantzi played an important role in the politics and modernization schemes of the national authoritarian regime in Mexico. At the same time, Cahuantzi only identified with Indigenous signifiers in specific spaces that elite nation-builders codified as acceptable for celebrating "civilized" indigeneity. The governor understood how indigeneity was a diverse, mutable, and contextually dependent category, one that could be engaged when politically useful and dropped when not.[42]

One of the main ways that Cahuantzi dissociated himself and his home state from Mexico's *indios bárbaros* (barbarous Indians) was by advancing modernization projects. The latter chapters of the book examine Cahuantzi's politics on the ground and how Tlaxcalans propelled and reacted to these politics. I focus on how the governor managed modernization in his state, especially the management of natural resources, infrastructure, and public works. Whereas Díaz wanted a loyal governor who advanced the national modernization project, the people of Tlaxcala wanted a leader who addressed their daily material concerns. These concerns included land and water access, dams, bridges, safe and passable roads, and fair taxes. The French landowner from the opening vignette, Clement Manuel, alleged that the governor "favor[ed] the Indigenous race." Manuel's claim irrefutably reflected his own racism toward Indigenous Mexicans. However, careful analysis of documentation in national, state, and local archives in Mexico make clear that the outcome in that case was not atypical in terms of how Cahuantzi implemented and managed modernization projects.

In contrast to other examinations of modernization under Díaz that focus primarily on how the regime's development policies spurred dissent, I examine how Cahuantzi managed modernization to help Porfirian rule endure in Tlaxcala. Water, I argue, was key to Cahuantzi's management strategies. Because of its hydrological geography and high population density, water, both accessing and controlling it, had been a problem that only grew worse over the centuries in Tlaxcala.[43] As factories were built in the region during the Porfiriato, demand for water increased and water-related problems worsened. Governor Cahuantzi's understanding of the local waterscape allowed him to mediate gaps between federal modernization demands and laws, on the one hand, and usufruct resource practices, on the other, to maintain a degree of resource equity in Tlaxcala.

By elucidating the connections between modernization, hydrology, and regional politics, this book brings the Porfirian era and the region of Tlaxcala into critical conversations taking place about water and environmental politics in Latin America.[44] To rule Tlaxcala, even as an autocrat, Cahuantzi could not altogether ignore locals' concerns about their often-unlivable environmental circumstances. In the absence of free and fair elections, petitions were valuable means through which residents pressed Cahuantzi to meet their material needs and make their voices heard.[45] Tlaxcalans wrote to the governor and other officials to protest how a factory or large landowner nearby was building yet another dam or artificial water deviation. When Cahuantzi abided residents' demands, even occasionally, he tempered regional power brokers' economic ambitions and placated the small landowning and village majority. In other words, by selectively conciliating residents' demands, he maintained local-level political order, a key charge Díaz bade of his governors. Through these arguments, I challenge the framework of paternalism that historians often use to explain how Porfirio Díaz and other caudillo figures held lasting power in Latin America.[46] More than a benevolent patriarch, Cahuantzi was a pragmatist. He was someone who understood the historical, environmental, political, and economic circumstances of his state, and he used that knowledge to his advantage. Over time, Cahuantzi's rule, like that of Díaz, became increasingly despotic and violent. The escalating demands Cahuantzi placed on residents—to fix water infrastructure and roads with their own funds, to pay higher property taxes—coupled with state encroachment on the political and economic autonomy of municipalities, undermined Cahuantzi's and Díaz's rule in Tlaxcala. But despotism alone does not explain how either Díaz, or Cahuantzi, maintained power for decades.

Organization and Overview

The book contains six chapters. In each chapter I examine a different dimension of the book's central question—how did Cahuantzi's governorship endure longer than any other state regime under Mexican dictator Porfirio Díaz? Chapters are organized by theme rather than by chronology. As such, their timelines sometimes overlap. In the final chapter as well as the conclusion I engage most directly with Cahuantzi's demise and the coming of the Mexican Revolution in Tlaxcala.

In chapter one I situate Cahuantzi within the panoply of Díaz's governors. Cahuantzi's background as an Indigenous Tlaxcalan differentiated him from most other gubernatorial appointees. There were seventy-one Porfirian governors in total, excluding dozens of interim governors. For most of these, reputational, economic, or sociocultural privilege shored up their claims to power. And yet Díaz chose Próspero Cahuantzi—a landless, undereducated, and recognizably Indigenous person—as his main ally in Tlaxcala and longest-serving state representative overall. Díaz chose Cahuantzi not despite but rather *because* of his distinct background. Thus, I argue that neither their privilege nor loyalty to Díaz were exclusive paths to Porfirian governors' political longevity.

In chapter two I explain the role that Cahuantzi played in nation-builders' efforts to create a national patrimony, and how and why the governor turned his identity as a Tlaxcalan into political power. Cahuantzi embraced his Indigenous ancestry and promoted Tlaxcala's pre-Hispanic legacy to bolster his political station and to ingratiate himself to Díaz and other nation-builders. The governor fed nation-builders' obsession with the pre-Hispanic past and consecrated himself as the modern forebearer of Tlaxcala's ancient legacy. He donated local artifacts to World's Fairs, presented in Nahuatl at nation-building forums, and endorsed chronicles that foregrounded Tlaxcala's role in making the Mexican nation. Yet Cahuantzi also distanced himself and his region from Mexico's "primitive" Indians. Thus, while the governor promoted Tlaxcala, he concurrently reinforced anti-Indigenous discrimination.

In chapter three I examine the different political strategies that Cahuantzi pursued to establish his regime in Tlaxcala. Some of these strategies—administrative centralization, patronage, electoral fraud—mirrored those used by Díaz and by caciques and caudillos throughout Latin America, as well as in any place where bosses subjugated democratic rule. Others, however, required Cahuantzi to have extensive local knowledge. Chapter three explains how Cahuantzi used his local acumen, especially about his region's past, to create a cohesive, sovereign state, secure state borders, and forge a sense of what it meant to be Tlaxcalan in the modern era, even if not all Tlaxcalans agreed with these meanings.

In chapters four and five I explain why water management was important for Cahuantzi's political longevity. Water—whether too little, or more often, too much—had been a problem for centuries in Tlaxcala. With the 1888 Federal Waters Law (*Ley sobre vías generales de comunicación*), the nation's first law regulating water usage, the federal government hoped to overcome the nation's modernization challenges by facilitating large landowners' access to water. Where water had been the purview of municipalities since colonial times, the 1888 Waters Law federalized waterways that were navigable or made up state borders. By enacting the 1888 Waters Law, Porfirian administrators aimed to diminish local actors' influence over waterways and expedite development. However, as I explain in chapter four, Cahuantzi found ways to keep water management in state, rather than in federal or municipal, hands, both before and after the 1888 Waters Law was passed.

In chapter five I examine the effects of land privatization and disentailment on water rights in Tlaxcala, and how Cahuantzi brokered between unclear federal resource laws and local customary resource practices to adjudicate residents' water disputes. Federal resource laws—the Ley Lerdo of 1856 and the Federal Waters Law of 1888—aimed to increase developers' access to land and water. Yet the laws failed to treat land and water as part of a symbiotic whole, and their terms contradicted significantly. Cahuantzi exploited these contradictions and fashioned water into a political tool through which he mediated between Tlaxcala's socioeconomically diverse residents. Tlaxcala's small landholding and village majority also used the ambiguities embedded in federal resource laws to press federal, state, and local officials to protect their customary water rights.

In chapter six I trace how Cahuantzi attempted to modernize his state through public works and infrastructural improvements. From bridges and roads to lighting and potable water to schools and administrative buildings, the governor leveraged public works and infrastructure as physical manifestations of his power and worthiness of enduring rule. Locals, too, saw value in these projects. Tlaxcalans of all stripes pressured the governor to consider how modernization could and should improve their daily lives. Through infrastructure improvements, Cahuantzi conciliated and negotiated between the diverse demands of the national dictator and his residents. The fiscal challenges the governor faced while trying to make these improvements happen, however, and the demands of time, money, and labor he imposed on municipalities and individuals to carry out his vision of modernity, were pivotal to the regime's demise.

By way of conclusion, I discuss the different actors and interests that shaped the coming of the Mexican Revolution to Tlaxcala. The actors who participated in the Revolution were a diverse lot with diverse interests, making it difficult for Tlaxcalans to form a coherent revolutionary movement. But it was precisely their differences that had allowed Cahuantzi to selectively placate residents' demands and to remain in power for twenty-six years. In the conclusion I emphasize the need to examine the Porfiriato on its own terms—not merely as a precursory period that preceded the Mexican Revolution—so as not to confound the local origins of Porfirian stability or the challenges that Tlaxcalans continued to face in its wake.[47]

ONE

The Appointment of an Indigenous Governor

State governors were President Porfirio Díaz's most essential regional interlocutors. Governors helmed the cadre of leadership that helped Díaz to unseat or lessen the autonomy of provincial families who had dominated the vast, complex, and diverse regional landscape of Mexico, some since independence.[1] Reputational, economic, or sociocultural privilege shored up the claims of most governors. Out of the 165 total men who held a gubernatorial post between 1876 and 1911, most were well-educated, from prominent families, or financially advantaged.[2] Most formidable political actors during the Porfirian period, governors included, did not engage with markers of Indigenous identity even when they descended from mixed race ancestry. In this chapter I examine why, then, Díaz chose Próspero Cahuantzi—a landless, undereducated, and recognizably Indigenous person—as his main ally in Tlaxcala and longest-serving state representative overall.

In common with all governors, Próspero Cahuantzi's political career hinged on his fealty to the national authoritarian regime. State elections were held regularly in Tlaxcala as in other states during the Porfiriato. But electoral outcomes reflected the affirmation of Díaz and his political network (*camarilla*) rather than the will of the people. States amended their constitutions accordingly to legalize consecutive gubernatorial appointments. At the same time, Cahuantzi differed from most other state-level appointees in that he was born in the place he governed and engaged with Indigenous signifiers. Cahuantzi's ties to Indigenousness—specifically and singularly as an Indigenous Tlaxcalan—influenced Díaz's decision to keep Cahuantzi in power for twenty-six years. Analyzing why Díaz installed Cahuantzi—who in some ways conformed to, yet in other ways diverged from, other gubernatorial appointments—challenges the historiographic (and popular) notion that Díaz followed a "formula" to select his governors.[3] Neither their privilege nor their loyalty to Díaz guaranteed governors' political longevity. When making gubernatorial appointments, Díaz carefully considered appointees' personal circumstances as well as the conditions of the region where they would rule. Governors who lasted were those who could effectively carry out Díaz's modernizing agenda while also maintaining peace in the provinces.[4]

Próspero Cahuantzi, Homegrown Governor

Born into a family of landless peasants in a small town in Tlaxcala, Próspero Cahuantzi, like many men with similar backgrounds, joined the military in 1856 at the age of twenty-two. Cahuantzi fought on behalf of the liberals during the Reform Wars and the Republic during the French intervention under General Porfirio Díaz's direction. In 1871, he fought against Díaz's first attempt at insurrection. Then, like many other eventual Porfirian loyalists, Cahuantzi switched allegiances and helped Díaz and the Tuxtepecanos to execute the Plan de Tuxtepec, which thwarted the reelection of President Lerdo de Tejada in 1876. While climbing the military ranks, Cahuantzi earned the title of colonel and formed a close friendship with Díaz. Cahuantzi was a municipal official (*regidor del Ayuntamiento de Tlaxcala*), a state representative (*diputado*), and commander of the local armed forces (*Cuerpo Rural de Caballería*) before accepting the governorship in 1885.[5]

Cahuantzi was initiated as one of what historians deem "the President's Men" or "compromise candidates" when Díaz appointed him to neutralize infighting between two opposing factions in Tlaxcala.[6] On one side of the local political divide stood Miguel Lira y Otera. A former military colonel, Lira y Otera was a key campaigner for Tlaxcalan statehood in the late 1850s. Following the French occupation, he became governor from 1868 to 1872. After Melquiades Carvajal—a hacendado from the prominent Carvajal family of the Tlaxcala-Puebla region—took the state reins from 1873 to 1877, Lira y Otera ruled again from 1877 to 1881. Like Cahuantzi, Lira y

Otera fought against Díaz during his first attempt at insurrection; Lira y Otera was President Benito Juárez's choice for governor. Opposing Lira y Otera was José Mariano Grajales, a hacendado who governed from 1881 until 1885. Grajales's term was cut six months short after he participated in a local religious procession, thus violating the Reform Laws that separated church and state in Mexico. Grajales's antiliberal actions and the incipient controversy they sparked opened the door to Cahuantzi's candidacy in 1885.

Cahuantzi was more of an insider among the Tuxtepecano set than among local politicos—he owned no lands and had dashed off to the military in his early twenties. In 1884, the year of Cahuantzi's appointment, Díaz's power had just been assured by his reelection following the presidency of Manuel González (1880–1884), who was, by all accounts, a Porfirian puppet. Newly reelected, Díaz was well positioned to impose his chosen candidate in Tlaxcala's state seat and to override regional elites who in previous decades had sided with either Juárez or Lerdo de Tejada. Cahuantzi was Díaz's man.[7]

When he first came to power, Díaz needed dependable and faithful underlings—military allies met those qualifications most immediately.[8] Cahuantzi was one of many former military comrades whom Díaz rewarded with a governorship after they helped him to win the Tuxtepec revolt and seize the presidency. In 1876, colonels or generals led in eighteen out of thirty-one states.[9] Promoting military personnel also allowed Díaz to dramatically reduce the size (and cost) of the armed forces by militarizing civilian politics. It was only after the Porfirian administration began to slowly and unevenly consolidate that Díaz was able to move away from military appointees and the "patchwork" of relationships he forged with local leaders during his first term in office.[10]

As Díaz's goals and policies shifted, and as he grew more confident and autocratic in his rule, so too did the qualities he sought out in his governors. After his reelection in 1884, the president began to target younger, civilian statesmen who were more adept at carrying out national liberal policies that endorsed free trade and private property.[11] Díaz appointed civilians in geopolitically and economically valuable states such as Oaxaca, Chihuahua, and Yucatán.[12] The rising influence of positivism and the *científicos* likely also impelled Díaz to replace military governors with civilians.[13] Guided by Latin America's distinct form of positivism, Porfirian científicos were technocrats based in Mexico City who insisted on measuring and managing Mexico's national "progress" through scientific

TABLE 1. Governors reelected two or more times, 1877–1911. Source: Bravo Regidor, "Elecciones de gobernadores durante el Porfiriato," 277–79.

Governor	State	Total elections	Total reelections	First election	Reelections	C.R.	N.C.R.
Próspero Cahuantzi	TLX	7	6	1885	1889, 1893, 1897, 1901, 1905, 1909	6	0
Francisco González de Cosío	QRO	7	6	1880	1887, 1891, 1895, 1899, 1903, 1907	5	1
Francisco Cañedo	SIN	7	6	1877	1884, 1892, 1896, 1900, 1904, 1908	4	2
Bernardo Reyes	NL	6	5	1889	1891, 1895, 1899, 1903, 1907	5	0
Teodoro Dehesa	VER	5	4	1892	1896, 1900, 1904, 1908	4	0
Mucio Martínez	PUE	5	4	1893	1897, 1901, 1905, 1909	4	0
Luis E. Torres	SON	5	4	1879	1883, 1891, 1899, 1907	0	4
Juan Manuel Flores	DUR	5	4	1877	1884, 1888, 1892, 1896	3	1
Carlos Díez Gutiérrez	SLP	5	4	1877	1885, 1889, 1893, 1897	3	1
Aristeo Mercado	MICH	5	4	1892	1896, 1900, 1904, 1908	4	0
Rafael Cravioto	HID	4	3	1877	1889, 1893, 1897	2	1
Manuel Alarcón	MOR	4	3	1896	1900, 1904, 1908	3	0
José Vicente Villada	EDOMEX	4	3	1889	1893, 1897, 1901	3	0
Joaquín González Obregón	GUA	4	3	1897	1901, 1905, 1909	3	0
Jesús Aréchiga	ZAC	4	3	1880	1888, 1892, 1896	2	1
Alejandro Vázquez del Mercado	AGS	4	3	1887	1891, 1903, 1907	2	1
Abraham Bandala	TAB	4	3	1895	1899, 1903, 1907	3	0
Francisco Santa Cruz	COL	4	3	1879	1893, 1897, 1901	2	1
Simón Sarlat Nova	TAB	3	2	1877	1887, 1891	1	1
Pedro L. Rodríguez	HID	3	2	1901	1905, 1909	2	0

					C.R.	N.C.R.
Miguel Cárdenas	COAH	3	2	1897	1901, 1905	2	0
Miguel Ahumada	CHIH	3	2	1892	1896, 1900	2	0
Manuel González	GUA	3	2	1884	1888, 1892	2	0
Luis C. Curiel	JAL	3	2	1893	1895, 1899	2	0
Genaro Garza García	NL	3	2	1877	1881, 1885	0	2
Francisco Arce	GUE	3	2	1885	1889, 1893	2	0
Emilio Pimentel	OAX	3	2	1902	1906, 1910	2	0
Antonio Mercenario	GUE	3	2	1894	1897, 1901	2	0

C.R. = Consecutive reelections
N. C. R. = Non-consecutive reelections

and otherwise quantifiable means.[14] Over time, the president also began to oust appointees who he feared had amassed too much regional authority. Such was the case in Chihuahua when Díaz replaced Gerónimo Treviño with Bernardo Reyes, an outsider from Jalisco, in order to wrest power from the Treviño-Naranjas clan.[15] Other times, Díaz tempered governors' growing regional influence by offering them a different political appointment. Although gubernatorial turnover was not always based on Díaz's mandate, many politicians used the position of governor as a rung on the ladder to higher office.[16]

Considering his lack of education and connections to erstwhile ruling circles, Cahuantzi was not likely to rise to a higher office or to challenge Díaz's power. Most gubernatorial climbers like Emiliano Rabasa in Chiapas (in office 1891–95), the governor turned jurist, were relatively well educated, as were most ministers, governors, and congressional representatives who held political posts during the Porfiriato.[17] Of the seventy-one Porfirian governors (excluding interim governors), fifty-five had degrees in law, medicine, or engineering, while only ten had not advanced past primary school and two were autodidacts, including Cahuantzi.[18] Cahuantzi was one of the few governors whose educational and economic status (at least at the beginning of his gubernatorial career) more closely mirrored that of most Mexicans, 80 percent of whom were illiterate with only some basic primary school education.[19] Cahuantzi's durability in office indicates that while preferred, an observably elite background was not a prerequisite for remaining in Díaz's good graces.

In general, turnover at the state level was more common than not during the Porfiriato. Most states saw at least two or three, or even upwards of twelve state leaders, excluding interim officeholders of which there were dozens more.[20] Whether because of ruptures with local elites or other local political groups, estrangements from Díaz, ascent to another office, or ailment or death, most Porfirian governors did not endure alongside the national dictatorship.[21] Indeed, Cahuantzi's longevity in life was just as remarkable as his longevity in office.[22] The American writer John Kenneth Turner, one of first foreigners to indict the Porfirian regime publicly, was not entirely wrong when he assessed that "the chief reason why the states are not governed by men who have been in office for thirty-four years is because those who were first put in have died. . . . As it is, Colonel Prospero Cahuantzi has ruled the State of Tlaxcala for the whole Porfirian period."[23] By 1903, only eight of the once eighteen military governors remained, including Cahuantzi.[24] Próspero Cahuantzi "won" the governorship in 1889, 1893, 1897, 1901, 1905, and lastly in 1909. Only two other Porfirian governors—Francisco González de Cosío in Querétaro and Francisco Cañedo in Sinaloa—achieved this feat.[25] Bernardo Reyes in Nuevo León was reelected five times, and in the states neighboring Tlaxcala, Teodoro Dehesa in Veracruz, Mucio Martínez in Puebla, Rafael Cravioto in Hidalgo, and Manuel Alarcón in Morelos were all reelected for three or four consecutive terms.[26]

In addition to his longevity in office, Cahuantzi stood apart from most of Díaz's gubernatorial appointees in that he was born in the state he had been appointed to rule. Most so-called compromise candidates appealed to Díaz because they were outsiders and thus presumably less enmeshed in local politics. Díaz installed and kept a local man like Cahuantzi in office only when their devotion to him was assured and they could effectively stymy local conflicts, a task that became increasingly hard to do over time.

One of the few other governors who met these qualifications was Manuel Alarcón of the central state of Morelos (in office 1895 to 1908).[27] Alarcón grew up working on a hacienda and, like Cahuantzi, advanced through the military as soon as the opportunity presented itself at the age of fifteen. Described by historian John Womack as "stern but benevolent," Alarcón negotiated between large planters and small landowners who in turn respected the governor's hard-working, local roots.[28] After Alarcón died, Díaz replaced Alarcón with his own chief of staff at the time, Pablo Escandón. Womack surmises that "Alarcón must have turned over in his grave. A man less like him could not have been found in the whole Republic."[29] Escandón was from a prominent financier family whose national influence was in decline. He swiftly installed outsiders as jefes políticos, forged alliances with sugar hacendados, and, most detrimentally, according to Womack, raised taxes in Morelos.[30] Although it is impossible to know, had Alarcón lived, how his leadership would have affected the rise of the Zapatista movement, Womack makes clear how Díaz's substitution of "native son" Alarcón with Escandón precipitated discord against the Porfirian regime in Morelos.[31]

Díaz's appointment of Escandón in the wake of Alarcón's death helps to elucidate how regional conditions shaped Díaz's decisions to oust some governors while allowing others to remain in office. Tlaxcala and Morelos, though located close to each other, had vastly different economies. The wealth, expanse, and national market-impact of Tlaxcala's haciendas paled in comparison to Morelos's expansive sugar and rice estates. Díaz's appointment of Escandón reflected his fear that he was losing his grip on an economically critical region. In Tlaxcala, by contrast, Díaz likely allowed Cahuantzi's leadership to abide in part because of the state's relatively low impact on the national economy. Alarcón's death in 1908 and political chaos that ensued afterward also reveals the limitations inherent to governance based on personalism and nondemocratic rule. When Alarcón died, so too did the tenuous deals he had presumably made with residents.[32]

Because Cahuantzi and Alarcón were both native sons of their states, people, especially foreigners, made racialized assumptions about them. English chronicler and Cuernavaca resident Rosa E. King depicted Alarcón as an "Indian . . . a popular man," conflating the governor's local origins with his racial background.[33] Similar presumptions were also made about fellow Morelos resident and revolutionary Emiliano Zapata. Mexican anthropologist Manuel Gamio, for example, saw the Zapatistas as representing "Indianism," even though most contemporary scholars understand Zapata and his followers to have been, like Alarcón, Spanish-speaking mestizos.[34] Cahuantzi was believed by foreigners and nationals alike to be an Indian. Cahuantzi's birthplace, background, and socioeconomic status no doubt shaped racialized assumptions about the Tlaxcalteco. Indubitably, descriptions of Alarcón and Cahuantzi as "Indians" reflected the deeply embedded anti-Indigenous racism that pervaded Mexico during this period.[35] However, Cahuantzi differed from Alarcón and other prominent Porfiristas in that he purposefully and publicly engaged with Indigenous signifiers. In specific spaces and on specific occasions, Cahuantzi *wanted* others to see him as Indigenous.

This overview of a profuse literature on Porfirian governors highlights why Díaz chose Cahuantzi as governor of his home state and kept him in office for twenty-six years. Cahuantzi was a military *Tuxtepecano*. He had deep local knowledge, yet he was not entrenched in Tlaxcala's political scene. Because his political career was tethered entirely to the national regime rather than to well-connected or privileged backgrounds, Cahuantzi was not likely to rebel or contest Díaz's power. Moreover, because the economic stakes in Tlaxcala were lower than in other regions, Díaz worried less about economic production there and could therefore let his old military compadre hold onto power longer. Yet none of these reasons adequately explain why Díaz appointed a self-marked Indigenous person to a governorship and kept him in power longer than any other governor during an era of staunch anti-Indigenous racism. It is to this question the chapter now turns.

"A Delightful Aztec Gentleman": Cahuantzi as an Indian

Over the course of his rule, Cahuantzi became a nationally known, and often racialized, figure. Political cartoons depicted the governor as typifying the sycophancy and oppression associated with Don Porfirio's governors. They also portrayed him as having darker skin than the figures shown alongside him. In a cartoon titled, "Borrascas en la Alturas" ("Storms Brewing Above") published in *El Hijo del Ahuizote* in August 1901, Cahuantzi kneels in the foreground alongside other governors groveling like children at Díaz's feet (figure 2).³⁶ Cahuantzi's physiognomic difference is clear: his skin appears darker than other governors and darker than that of Díaz. In another cartoon published in *El Colmillo Público*, Cahuantzi is similarly darkly hued, as well as portly, as compared to Díaz whose hand he shakes (figure 3). The illustration in *El Colmillo Público* satirizes professed Porfirian ideals of "peace" and "law and order." Cahuantzi and

FIGURE 2. "Borrascas en las Alturas" ("Storms brewing above"). Source: *El Hijo del Ahuizote*, August 11, 1901. Hemeroteca Digital, Universidad Autónoma de Nuevo León.

FIGURE 3. "Así Gobernamos" ("This is how we govern"). The caption reads: "I [Díaz] am peace . . . and I [Cahuantzi] am law and order." Source: *El Colmillo Público*, February 25, 1906. Hemeroteca Nacional de México.

Díaz are shown to represent these ideals. The two men shake hands while people in the background—including Yaqui Indians—lay slaughtered.[37]

The juxtaposition of Cahuantzi and the slain Yaqui Indians behind him succinctly captures the hypocritical attitudes held by Porfirian intellectuals and administrators about their nation's Indigenous peoples.[38] On the one hand, nation-building elites glorified ancient Indigenous civilizations at world's fairs, going so far as to construct a replica of the Aztec palace that was displayed at the Exposition Universelle in Paris in 1889.[39] Yet they also displayed overtly racist attitudes toward contemporary Indigenous persons and championed abusive and violent policies toward them.[40] Díaz's treatment of the Yaqui Indigenous people of northern Mexico was particularly egregious. After forcibly removing Yaquis from their lands, the Porfirian government seized and sold Yaqui territories to agricultural and mining investors. They then sold many Yaqui into slavery, most to henequen barons in the Yucatán Peninsula.[41] Like most Latin American nation-builders during the nineteenth century, Porfirian elites divorced the Indigenous past from the Indigenous present.[42]

The complex and contradictory ways that Cahuantzi engaged with indigeneity mirror this hypocrisy. Cahuantzi fulfilled foreigners' and nation-builders' arbitrary and discriminatory ideas of Indigenous presentation during the late nineteenth century.[43] Cahuantzi's surname, bilingualism, physiognomic features, and socioeconomic origins led many people to recognize Cahuantzi as Indigenous.[44] US social scientist Frederick Starr depicted Cahuantzi as a "pure blood indian, whose native language is Aztec . . . a large well-built man, with full face and little black eyes that are sunken deeply into the flesh . . . [and] a man of some force and energy."[45] Henry Baerlein, a traveler, likewise portrayed Cahuantzi as a "delightful Aztec gentleman," a statement that was incorrect in both pre-Hispanic and contemporary contexts.[46] American writer John Kenneth Turner described Cahuantzi as "an Indian . . . illiterate but rich."[47] To Turner, Cahuantzi's illiteracy as an Indian was expected, but his wealth, which Cahuantzi had begun to accumulate only after assuming office, was not. Turner also noted how Díaz sent Cahuantzi a teacher so "that he might learn to sign his name to documents of the state."[48] Later, in 1914, when the *New York Times* reported Cahuantzi's capture at the hands of Francisco "Pancho" Villa, they described Cahuantzi as "a full-blood Tlaxcalan Indian," assigning a more correct characterization than "Aztec" yet one that nevertheless relied on a biological understanding of Indigenous difference.[49]

In addition to his Indigenousness, foreign accounts emphasized Cahuantzi's outsized presence, conflating the governor's corpulent stature with his persuasion throughout the region. The ever-bombastic American traveler Carleton Beals remarked that at "Seventy-seven years old in 1910, [Cahuantzi] had become so obese he could not keep awake when spoken to more than fifteen minutes, but 'if the operatives of a local cotton-mill were out on strike, he took [to] the field in person, on a horse, and after that the strike was never serious.' "[50] Other accounts explain how Cahuantzi kept a daybed in his office and that he passed out frequently, even in front of an audience.[51] In sum, Cahuantzi's public persona was that of a sycophantic, illiterate Indian, "delightful" to some yet slovenly, especially in his old age.

In Mexico, Cahuantzi's Indigenous heritage was sometimes defamed. Take for example a letter in which a Tlaxcala City resident wrote to Díaz to protest Cahuantzi's reelection in 1900, insisting that "Tlaxcala City . . . is in a state of misery . . . because Cahuantzi is an ignorant Indian, lacking education, lacking proper ways of behaving, and he does not have the '*luces*' to help Tlaxcala to progress."[52] During the incident discussed in the

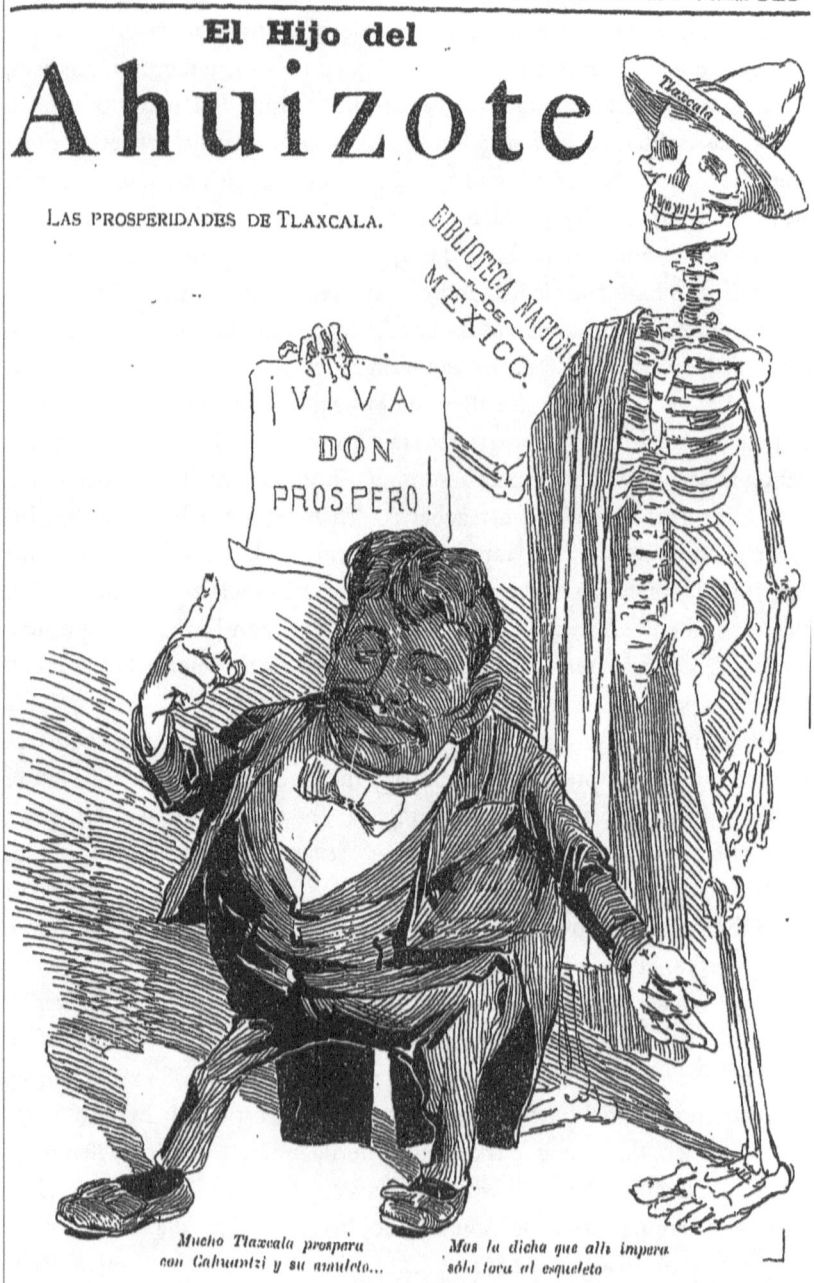

FIGURE 4. "Las Prosperidades de Tlaxcala" ("Prosperity in Tlaxcala"). Source: *El Hijo del Ahuizote*, May 28, 1899. Hemeroteca Nacional de México.

introduction to this book, a landowner from France who owned properties in Tlaxcala and quarreled with Cahuantzi claimed that the governor "always sided with the Indigenous race [and] . . . believed whatever they told him," and likewise that "all sensible people in the state . . . are aware [of the] great esteem the Governor has for the Indians and their bad inclinations."[53] The Frenchman contrasted Cahuantzi with the state's "sensible residents," thereby inferring Cahuantzi's inferior status as an Indian.[54]

Yet there were also sources—especially pro-Porfirian sources—that exalted Cahuantzi's Indigenous heritage. A biography that appeared in Tlaxcala's state-sponsored newspaper *La Antigua República* in 1905 linked Cahuantzi to the "men who have produced our *raza india* (Indian race)," naming "the great Tlahuicole" and "Xicohténcatl," pre-Hispanic Tlaxcalteco warriors, as well as "the illustrious Indian named Benito Juárez."[55] In another edition in 1908 *La Antigua República* wrote that "Mr. Cahuantzi is from very humble origins, [the] son of the defeated and enslaved race, [who] has come to power by his own merits [and who] has drawn the attention and great esteem of the high classes; [Cahuantzi] has been chosen by the most important men of this state to govern them."[56] Published in the state newspaper, these articles are grossly obsequious and reflect the yellow journalism of the Porfiriato; the biography that ran in *La Antigua República* was six pages long and circulated just as Cahuantzi had "won" reelection. Nevertheless, the descriptions of Cahuantzi as "Indigenous" with a "humble class" background, introduced by the newspaper as the governor's most approbatory attributes, are noteworthy during an era in which those terms were rarely used to venerate a living Indigenous person.[57] Because the biography ran in the state-sponsored newspaper, Cahuantzi almost assuredly approved of the depictions of himself contained within it.

To be sure, Cahuantzi was far from the only person who had Indigenous ancestry and held political office in Mexico. There were innumerable jefes políticos, caciques, and other regional administrators who came from Indigenous backgrounds—acknowledged or not—and played important roles in the Porfirian political world. Juan Francisco Lucas, a Nahua Indian and regional cacique in the Sierra Norte of Puebla, influenced politics there and was well regarded by national officials.[58] Among Porfirian governors, two-term Governor Martín González in Oaxaca (in office 1894 to 1902) was chided by Oaxacan high society for his "humble origins" and called "*caclito*," an insult meant to invoke a huarache-wearing Indian.[59] Other recognizably Indigenous governors included Governor Policarpo

Valenzuela in Tabasco, an "Indian of plain beginnings" who became a prominent timber hewer in his state and briefly served as governor before the Revolution broke out.[60]

President Díaz himself was generally recognized as a mestizo with Mixtec origins. The president hailed from Oaxaca, a predominantly Indigenous state in the south. Although the extent to which Díaz had Mixtec ancestry is debated by historians, in his portraits, Díaz was often represented with whitened skin.[61] Depictions of Díaz that whitewashed his probable Mixtec background attest to the anti-Indigenous discrimination that was rampant throughout Mexico—and all Latin America—in the nineteenth century. Despite that the Mexican Constitution of 1824 abolished the separate legal caste of "Indian," being acknowledged as an Indian in Porfirian Mexico was rarely advantageous to the bearer of that designation.

More so than Díaz, the most famous Mexican leader to have overcome anti-Indigenous discrimination and ascend to the nation's highest office was Benito Juárez.[62] Juárez was a Zapotec Indian, and, like Díaz, he was from Oaxaca. Unlike Díaz, however, Juárez did not attempt to obscure his Zapotec heritage. Juárez was acknowledged as an Indian both during and since his rule and was often compared to other mythologized Indigenous figures including those from the pre-Columbian era.[63] Juárez became a lawyer, governor, minister of justice, and head of the Supreme Court before winning the presidency. To this day, Juárez is revered alongside other great Mexican leaders as the Indian who vanquished the French, reasserted Mexican nationalism, and set the nation on a path toward being a modern Republic.[64]

The success that Juárez and Cahuantzi enjoyed as Indigenous peoples in official positions of power underscores how the terms "Indigenous" or "Indian" were contextually contingent: their meanings were altered by the historical or geopolitical contexts in which they were employed.[65] Juárez was and is remembered by Mexicans as a national Indigenous hero, someone who represented "authentic" Mexican nationhood during a critical period in which the country's sovereignty was under attack by foreign invaders.[66] Yet modern hagiography obfuscates the complexity of Juárez's politics, as well as the complexity of Indigenousness in general. Juárez was a staunch liberal. The policies he pursued—particularly the expansion of private property and secularism—often undermined the political, economic, and cultural values held by Indigenous groups. Although the president tried to attenuate the effects of land privatization on Indigenous villages, Juárez's policies were devastating overall for the rural Mexican majority.[67] Juárez's geographic origins were also vital for his success. Oaxaqueños were often involved in national politics. Even the region where Juárez was from within Oaxaca, the sierra, afforded him more opportunities for upward mobility than had he been born in another part of the state.[68] Juárez's ideologies, as well as the specific circumstances in which he grew up and ruled, made it possible for Mexicans to accept, and even to venerate, a Zapotec Indian from Oaxaca.

As with Juárez, Cahuantzi's ability to claim Indigenousness were predicated on fluid determinations of ethnic difference related to time, place, and other factors. Cahuantzi had two advantages that distinguished him from other identifiably Indigenous peoples during the Porfirian period. First, he had close ties and was deferent to the national authoritarian regime. Second, Cahuantzi was Tlaxcalan. More than other Indigenous groups, Porfirians saw the Tlaxcalans as exceptional and even "civilized" Indigenous peoples. Their viewpoint was shaped largely by mythologized understandings of Tlaxcala's past, a past that enabled Porfirian nation-builders to advance their goal of creating a uniform national patrimony. In brief, the ancient Tlaxcalans aided the Spanish to invade the Mexica (Aztec) capital of Tenochtitlán (1519–21). After Tenochtitlán fell, Tlaxcalans had some privileges under Spanish colonial rule relative to other Indigenous groups. They had a relatively large territory, maintained a centralized Indigenous-led government, and were exempted from encomienda, the early colonial system whereby the Spanish crown coerced Indigenous labor. The Tlaxcalans were also early Christian converts and helped the Spanish to colonize more peripheral Indigenous groups.[69] As historian Sean F. McEnroe writes, "Spaniards considered the Tlaxcalans ideal emissaries for transmitting the emerging Hispano-Indian civilization to the north: they were expert agriculturalists, skilled craftsmen, reliable soldiers, and enthusiastic converts to Christianity."[70]

Tlaxcala's history—as a place that was rewarded for its alliance with the Spanish during and after their invasion of Tenochtitlán—appealed to dictatorial Porfirians who believed that Indigenous peoples ought to be similarly accommodating in the modern era.[71] The Aztec Empire had long since fallen. Yet the physical space called "Tlaxcala" endured and its "descendants"—like Cahuantzi—could still be honored, even though nearly four hundred years had radically transformed that space and the people who resided within it. Unlike the Maya, for whom the same argument could be made, present-day Tlaxcalans were not actively waging war against Díaz's regime.[72] Cahuantzi, then, was accepted by Díaz and other Porfirian nation-builders because he made himself into a modern personification of Tlaxcala's exceptional past, an Indian who deferred to and implemented national authoritarian ideals and projects. Contemporary scholars have elucidated a much more complex and contested picture of Tlaxcalan history than the overly romanticized, racist, and inaccurate portrayals that Cahuantzi and other nineteenth-century nation-builders used. To many Indigenous peoples during and after the Spanish invasion, Tlaxcalans were race traitors who gave themselves and their culture up willingly when they teamed up with the Spaniards, eventually giving rise willingly to *mestizaje*.[73] Tlaxcalans were not simply granted privileges by the Spanish. Historians have shown how they fought fiercely to retain their "special" status under Spanish rule and how their communities were beset by deep class divisions.[74] And of course, Tlaxcalans were just as—if not more—devastated as other Indigenous peoples in central Mexico by the Europeans' most deadly weapon, endemic diseases.[75]

But the nation-builders of nineteenth-century Latin America did not set out to tell nuanced accounts of the past. The purpose of the Porfirians' patrimonial project was to root the young Mexican nation in a common cultural heritage. Porfirian intellectuals often manipulated pre-Columbian and colonial texts to suit the Porfirian state's propagandistic and nationalistic needs. This was also true of Tlaxcala's historical texts.[76] Porfirians' understandings of the past, and the public's perception of Cahuantzi as an Indian in general, was based on ahistorical and discriminatory understandings of indigeneity. Cahuantzi's selective engagement with Indigenous signifiers underscores this argument. While touting Tlaxcala's Indigenous antiquity, Cahuantzi disassociated himself and his region from Indigenous peoples who Porfirian elites thought of as "primitive," such as the Yaquis and the Maya, who resisted the nation-state's encroachment and exploitation.[77] Cahuantzi made strategic decisions about how and in which spaces he engaged with Indigenous signifiers. These decisions were crucial for Díaz to keep Cahuantzi, a recognizably Indigenous person, in office.

Conclusion

Like many other Porfirian governors, what landed Próspero Cahuantzi a governorship was his military preparation and his loyalty to President Díaz. However, Cahuantzi's military experiences and allegiance to the national regime do not sufficiently explain why Díaz supported Cahuantzi—a native of his own state and a recognizably Indigenous person, rare qualities among prominent Porfiristas—in office longer than any other gubernatorial appointee. Díaz chose to support a native *Tlaxcalteco* as governor for twenty-six years because he could tether Cahuantzi to Tlaxcala's exceptional legacy, a legacy that lent itself to the sort of patrimony that Díaz and Porfirian nation-builders wanted to sculpt. Keeping Cahuantzi in office allowed Díaz to boast that a "real" Tlaxcalan governed in a place that the Porfirian administration touted as embodying "real Mexico."[78]

Yet Cahuantzi also tethered himself to Tlaxcala's past. Cahuantzi was well apprised and proud of his region's pre-Hispanic and colonial histories. The governor drew on, spoke about, and even glorified Tlaxcala's ancient past to justify his leadership to Díaz and other Porfirian elites. He also used his historical acumen to defend Tlaxcala's state borders and to propel state-level modernization projects. If Díaz and metropolitan nation-builders understood how to exploit the ambiguities and contradictions inherent to processes of racialization and making national history, so, too, did Cahuantzi, an Indian who used Indigenous signifiers to make political claims in the modern era.

TWO

Claiming the Past

On October 1, 1895, attendees of the Eleventh International Congress of Americanists gathered in Mexico City. Since the inauguration of the meetings twenty years earlier, international delegates—a myriad sort of intellectuals, archaeologists, and politicos—communed biennially to deliberate advancements in the field of "Americanism," with a particular focus on the ancient Americas.[1] When Mexico was selected as the first place outside of Europe to host the congress, President Porfirio Díaz and his administrators saw it as a critical opportunity to highlight the nation's Indigenous past on a global stage.[2] Próspero Cahuantzi attended many congressional events. During the congress's "highly animated" opening banquet, the Tlaxcalteco gave a toast entirely in Nahuatl, the modern Aztec language.[3] The next day, Cahuantzi helped lead congressional attendees on a tour of the recently commissioned Gallery of Monoliths at the National Museum.[4] The gallery housed some of the most impressive artifacts discovered during excavations of archaeological sites, including Teotihuacán, the Plaza Mayor in Mexico City, and Chichén Itzá.[5] At the tour's conclusion, Cahuantzi stood in front of three major artifacts—the Aztec calendar stone, the colossal head of the Aztec god Xipe Totec, and a statue of the Maya god Chacmool—to deliver another speech, this time in Spanish. The congressional record captures his address as follows: "Mr. Colonel D. Próspero Cahuantzi, Governor of the State of Tlaxcala, read a speech that paid tribute to the importance of studying archaeological monuments to advance the history of the ancient peoples of the Americas, especially those of Mexico during ancient times."[6]

In the wake of independence, Latin American nation-builders began to consider and commemorate their pre-Columbian pasts.[7] They saw creating national patrimony—a common cultural heritage—as essential to demonstrate their nations' progress to the world, and to prove themselves to, and distinguish themselves from, the European civilizations they emulated. Latin American nation-builders wrote patrimonial chronicles, collected Indigenous relics to display at home and abroad, and organized ceremonies of all kinds, from parades to congresses, to elevate the Aztec, Inca, and Maya civilizations and liken them to the ancient Greek and Roman civilizations of the West. Along with erecting railroads, renegotiating national debts, and expanding into international trade markets, nation-builders believed that creating a national patrimony would improve Latin America's global repute and build worldwide trust in their feeble institutions.[8]

In Porfirian Mexico, the coordinators of patrimonial projects were dubbed the "wizards of progress."[9] Díaz's wizards of progress were administrators and intellectuals of all kinds, in the president's close circle, with varied levels of professional experience.[10] They were heavily influenced by scientific positivism—the idea that national progress could be quantifiably measured through scientific, technological advancement over time.[11] For the wizards of progress, venerating Indigenous antiquity was a way to show the world how Mexico's path to modernity and progress had begun long before their time. Under their direction, tributes to the nation's pre-Columbian past became more frequent, elaborate, and expensive. Mexico spent tremendous sums of money—likely more than any other foreign country—on their contributions to world's fairs.[12] After all, endeavors such as building a replica of the Aztec Palace, as they did for the World's Fair in Paris in 1889, were costly. At home, Porfirian nation-builders made museums into spaces that enshrined linkages between antiquity and progress. Porfirian officials enacted laws to protect "ancient objects" and appointed key statesmen and archaeologists to collect and guard them in Mexico City's National Museum and at international expositions.[13] As historian Christina Bueno argues, "the very act of protecting [artifacts] was thought to give Mexico the coveted aura of a scientific, civilized, modern nation."[14]

Próspero Cahuantzi fashioned Indigenous antiquity into a political opportunity, one that he used to secure his political position and to enhance the reputation of his small state. Cahuantzi was the rare Porfirian governor who was a native of the state he ruled. He had a genuine interest in Tlaxcala's history, as well as disseminating that history. Although Cahuantzi was recognized by many in and outside of Mexico as having Indigenous ancestry, once he became governor, Cahuantzi could have attempted to drop all Indigenous signifiers, as many Mexican leaders, such as President Díaz, did before him. Instead, Cahuantzi embarked on a mission to publicize his region's rich past and position himself as a modern exemplar of that past, delivering a toast in Nahuatl at the Congress of Americanists in 1895 among other acclaimed roles. Cahuantzi's efforts to celebrate Indigenous patrimony offer a rare but significant exception to historian Rebecca Earle's argument that "preconquest Indians were good to build nations with, but contemporary Indians were not."[15] At the same time, however, Cahuantzi disassociated his public identity from pejorative Indianness. When Cahuantzi came up for criticism for participating in a Catholic funerary ritual in 1896, the governor and his supporters framed such rituals as essential to the functioning of *"pueblos civilizados"*—civilized towns, which Cahuantzi claimed to represent.[16] Meanwhile, to the people of Tlaxcala, debates about their governor's heritage and public persona mattered much less than his day-to-day governing practices.

Tlaxcala's Patrimony

Porfirian technocrats were intent on creating a coherent national patrimony. But there was no singular vision for how the Indigenous past should inform Mexico's present.[17] Compiling a national history involved contradictory and contested processes.[18] The wizards of progress debated, for example, which of Mexico's ancient civilizations had been the most advanced and whether scientific "evidence," such as dental and cranial measurements, could be used to prove their assertions. They disputed which artifacts and modern-day resources met their criteria to represent Mexico's past and contemporary "popular culture," the emblems that would be examined by archaeologists and anthropologists and admired by global cosmopolitan elites.[19] Whereas nation-builders believed that the Indigenous past was exotic and intriguing, most concurrently thought that Indigenous peoples had become degraded over time and were unassimilable into Mexico's present-day population.[20] Yet as to why Indigenous peoples were degraded, they disagreed. Many liberals, who prized secularism, blamed

Spanish Catholicism for Indians' backwardness. They also disparaged the Spanish for allowing Indigenous peoples to keep their communal lands, which they thought made Indians recalcitrant to private property laws in the modern era.[21] Still others alleged that because of their "communal" nature, Indians were unable to understand patriotism and were thus incapable of becoming citizens of liberal nation-states.[22] Regardless of how they came to hold them, nation-building elites' beliefs about Indigenous peoples in the nineteenth century produced the same result: the erasure of Indigenous diversity, past and present.[23]

Ironically, the contradictions and contestations inherent to creating a national patrimony, as well those involved with defining Indigenousness at any given time, opened the door for Cahuantzi to imprint Tlaxcala's history into the patrimonial narrative that nation-builders wanted to craft. Tlaxcalans had long seen themselves, and been recorded by historical accounts, as exceptional compared to other Indigenous groups. Tlaxcalans traced their status as an exceptional Indigenous people as far back as the pre-Columbian era, when they remained one of the few Nahua groups in the Valley of Mexico whom the Aztecs could not conquer. They then played a unique role as allies of the Spanish, both during and after the Spanish invasion of the Tenochtitlán. Their distinguished legacy continued during the colonial era, when Tlaxcalans were exempted from encomienda and retained the right to self-rule—even during the Bourbon Reforms of the late eighteenth century when the Spanish government tightened its grip on the colonies' political and economic autonomy.[24] Tlaxcalans and non-Tlaxcalans alike reinforced the narrative of exceptionalism through historical chronicles, performances, and art. Rodrigo Gutiérrez's 1875 painting, *El Senado de Tlaxcala* (figure 5), depicts Tlaxcalan elites debating whether to ally with the Spanish during the Europeans' planned Aztec invasion. Unlike other artistic representations of the conquest, "this scene is peopled entirely by Indians" who are positioned in classical form to mimic a Roman senate deliberation, foregrounding Tlaxcalans' ancient supremacy.[25] *El Senado de Tlaxcala* depicts the ancient Tlaxcalans as "noble" and therefore as worthy of comparisons to Rome, yet also disengaged from conflict.[26] *El Senado de Tlaxcala* became a mainstay at international exhibitions, an exemplar of honorable Indigenous peoples who assimilated into "civilized" society.

Cahuantzi reinforced the legacy of Tlaxcalan exceptionalism and nobleness displayed in *El Senado de Tlaxcala*. He did this by facilitating the publication of historical chronicles and geographic works, encouraging ar-

FIGURE 5. *El Senado de Tlaxcala*, Rodrigo Gutiérrez, 1875. Source: Museo Nacional de Arte, INBA Acervo Constitutivo, 1982.

chaeological digs, sending artifacts from Tlaxcala to international exhibitions, and participating actively in the Congress of the Americas in 1895 in Mexico City. Cahuantzi's contributions to patrimonial campaigns encouraged Porfirian nation-builders to see Tlaxcalans of past *and* present as acceptably Indigenous, thereby challenging their entrenched ideas about Indigenous degradation.[27] To be sure, when Governor Cahuantzi spread a romantic vision of his region's past, and suggested that he could represent that vision in the modern day, he was being thoroughly pragmatic. As with the wizards of progress, Cahuantzi hoped to draw attention and money to his small state and improve its national and international repute. An editorial that ran in the state newspaper in 1885 lamented how ancient Tlaxcala was revered, yet contemporary Tlaxcala was ignored:

> It causes us real and profound grief to see the little or nonexistent regard given to our state, so notable [as it is] for its historical memories, for its momentous past, for the heroism of its valiant sons who have always fought, [who were] always the first ones [to arrive] where there was a

right to defend, a freedom to protect, . . . Tlaxcala is motivated by the incessant desire for progress. . . . The great Xicoténcatl's belligerent descendants [Tlaxcalans] have become humble shepherds and peaceful farmers.[28]

This editorial, which ran in the official state newspaper in September 1885—the year Cahuantzi became governor—presented modern-day Tlaxcalans as "valiant" sons and "descendants" of once "belligerent" peoples who were now "humble" and "peaceful." The editorial, as well as Cahuantzi's contributions to national patrimony, make clear how Tlaxcalans, not just the elite wizards of progress, understood the value of historical patrimony as propaganda and how to use it to prove their region's capacity for progress.

Chronicles, Artifacts, and Geographic Publications

Cahuantzi pursued various opportunities to record and propagate his region's history. Although his connections to Díaz and other administrators facilitated these opportunities, Cahuantzi insisted that Tlaxcalans—not just Mexico City elites—ought to control how the stories of Tlaxcala's past were told. Soon after taking office, the governor wrote to Díaz to request that *Historia Oficial de Tlaxcala* housed in the Archivo General de la Nación in Mexico City be sent to Tlaxcala to be copied, so that Tlaxcala could build its own patrimonial collection.[29] In 1896 he wrote to Secretary of Finance José Y. Limantour to ask for money in order to complete "printing a series of historical laminates [*láminas históricas*]," a project that the governor feared was in "danger" of not being finished.[30] Cahuantzi also wrote accounts of Tlaxcala's recent history, such as *Memorias de un Tlaxcalteca*, that according to the Tlaxcala state newspaper, "narrate[d] local events . . . between 1854 and 1876."[31]

None of these works achieved the national or global notoriety of the *Lienzo de Tlaxcala*, however, a historical chronical that Cahuantzi helped to reproduce and recirculate. The *Lienzo de Tlaxcala* was one of numerous painted cloths that told the stories of ancient Mesoamerican peoples from their perspectives. Originally authorized in 1552 by the Cabildo, or council, of Tlaxcala, the *Lienzo* contained mostly images—the Indigenous method of communicating. The captions on the *Lienzo* were printed in alphabetic Nahuatl, a script that was developed by Spanish priests, in concert with Indigenous peoples, after their arrival in New Spain. The top of the *Lienzo* showed the political structure of ancient Tlaxcala, followed by rows of smaller images portraying how the Tlaxcalans and the Spanish defeated the Aztecs.[32] The original *Lienzo* cloths were lost, believed to have disappeared in transit from Tlaxcala to Mexico City during the French intervention of the 1860s. However, a very accurate paper copy had been recreated by Tlaxcalans, then stored in Tlaxcala.[33]

In 1890, Cahuantzi ordered a reproduction of and wrote an introduction for Tlaxcala's copy of the *Lienzo*.[34] Cahuantzi intended to present the work as an "homage to his state" at the Columbian Historical Exposition in Madrid in 1892.[35] Yet the *Lienzo* that inevitably circulated at most international exhibitions was not Cahuantzi's version. Instead, another reproduction was shown, one that was drawn by a different artist and had originally appeared in the *Descripción de la ciudad y provincia de Tlaxcala* (1585), recommissioned as *Historia de Tlaxcala* in 1892.[36] The commissioner and editor of this latter reproduction was Alfredo Chavero, a Porfirian intellectual, director of the National Museum, and author of the pre-Hispanic volume of Mexico's first comprehensive historical narrative, *México a través de los siglos* (1887–89).[37] *Historia de Tlaxcala* included the *Lienzo* reproduction. It also included a copy of *Descripción*, the first known history of Tlaxcala, written in narrative prose by Diego Muñoz Camargo, a mestizo chronicler who descended from a noble Tlaxcalan mother and a Spanish father. The narrative and images contained in *Descripción* explained how migrating P'urhépecha and Chichimecas founded Tlaxcala in the tenth century. It described Tlaxcalans' role in the Spanish invasion, their privileged status during the early colonial period, and their religious and warfare customs. A Tlaxcalan delegation had personally delivered the original *Descripción* to King Philip II between 1584 and 1585.[38]

It was a boon for Cahuantzi and Tlaxcala that Tlaxcala's pictorial and narrative histories appeared at international exhibitions in Madrid and Chicago. Yet it was also telling of Cahuantzi's status relative to other, more elite, nation-builders that Chavero took credit for reproducing the *Lienzo*, even though Cahuantzi had done so first. Chavero dismissed the artist who produced Cahuantzi's version of the *Lienzo* as "incorrect."[39] Chavero included his version in other publications on Mexican "antiquities," including in an "Homage to Christopher Columbus."[40] He wrote additional introductions to, and commentaries on, these versions, separate from the one that Cahuantzi had authorized in 1890.[41]

Fifty years later, in 1939, the version of Cahuantzi's *Lienzo* was finally published as a stand-alone work, Cahuantzi's introduction included. It also listed Cahuantzi as editor. In the prologue that precedes Cahuantzi's introduction, the author emphasizes how "specialists prefer the 'Cahuantzi' edition [over Chavero's edition] because [it] has more Indigenous characteristics, the yellow ochre background helps the images stand out, and because the explications below . . . the images are helpful for interpreting the codex."[42] The same author had harsh words for Chavero, writing that it was because of Chavero's "carelessness" and "egotism" that Cahuantzi's "edition remained forgotten in Tlaxcala's Government Palace, condemned to suffer [and] wear away from neglect."[43] In her analysis of the two *Lienzo* versions, literary scholar Jannette Amaral-Rodríguez confirms that there are, in fact, subtle yet nevertheless significant discrepancies between the images in Cahuantzi's and Chavero's versions. These discrepancies, as well as Chavero's commentaries on the images, downplayed Tlaxcalans' historical viewpoint. Amaral-Rodríguez thus concludes that Chavero's *Lienzo* reproduction "silences and erases fundamental aspects of that local historical narration."[44]

That Chavero elided Cahuantzi's contributions to the recirculation of the *Lienzo de Tlaxcala* is unsurprising; Chavero's cunning and selfishness were well-known. Chavero's attempts to silence him notwithstanding, Cahuantzi's connections to national elites and his desire to make Tlaxcala more well-known helped to ensure that Tlaxcala's history was included in Mexico's patrimonial narrative. The version of the *Lienzo* that Cahuantzi commissioned that more accurately portrayed ancient Tlaxcalans' viewpoint stands in contrast to Chavero's more propagandistic and Hispanicized version. The differences between these two *Lienzo* reproductions, though subtle, underscore the purpose of the patrimonial project, which was to romanticize, thereby distort, Mexico's Indigenous past. Cahuantzi's broadcasting of his region's history—told by Indigenous peoples, on the global stage—is remarkable, considering how nation-builders like Chavero consulted few, if any, Indigenous voices when constructing national patrimony.

Another way that Cahuantzi shed light on Tlaxcalan history was to collect and donate local artifacts to world's fair commissions. In 1888 he called for "able" men to exhume a small hacienda believed to be a "cemetery for Tlaxcalan nobles." Initial excavations uncovered "bones, rock and clay tools, jewelry and adornments." The governor congregated a local committee to scope out other excavation sites to search for "still unknown antiquities, the study of which could prove very useful." As Cahuantzi explained, the committee was on a quest to reveal "our [Tlaxcala's] little known ancient history."[45]

Cahuantzi also sent requests to state and local officials to mine their archival and archaeological collections for artifacts to donate to the patrimonial cause. In his *Memoria de la administración pública del Estado de Tlaxcala*—a state of the state report Cahuantzi delivered to Tlaxcala's legislature—the governor itemized over one hundred historic documents and artifacts in the *Archivo General del Estado*.[46] The report began by outlining the titles and tributes that the Spanish bequeathed to the Tlaxcalans in the early 1500s. It also included a sampling of ancient hieroglyphs that represented pre-Hispanic towns still standing in Tlaxcala. Cahuantzi's organizing enabled him to showcase Tlaxcalan artifacts at expositions in Paris (1889), Madrid (1892), Chicago (1893), Mexico City (1895), San Antonio (1900), Buffalo (1901), and St. Louis (1904).[47] Cahuantzi was by no means the only regional official to answer commissions' calls for historical artifacts. Yet the hundreds of letters that the governor and his administrative staff wrote to local and national officials over the years seeking to obtain historical relics point to Cahuantzi's near obsession with measuring Tlaxcala's progress through the recovery of its antiquity.

Whereas, in their solicitations to state officials, national commissions parsed out the "Indigenous" past from the modern present, for Cahuantzi, the past and the present could not be separated so neatly. In 1903, the commission for the *Congreso de Artes y Ciencias de la Exposición Universal* (St. Louis, 1904) requested exemplars of "anthropology"—historical data about and representations of pre-Columbian cultures—as well as examples of "social economy," including information about electricity, transportation, mining and metallurgy, education, and agricultural production. The commission additionally asked for photographs "of isolated types of Indians of pure race that exist in the state" as well as photographs and artifacts that represented their lifestyles—where they lived, what they ate, how they cared for their children, and how they celebrated. For non-Indigenous peoples, the commission would have likely recorded some of this information under "social economy." Contrastingly, for people they judged to be "isolated types of Indians," the commission asked targeted, discriminatory questions. The commission's bifurcated appeal makes evident how those building national patrimony did not consider Indigenous peoples as actors in modern institutions such as public schools and industry.[48]

Nevertheless, when Cahuantzi answered commissions' entreaties, he sent things that justified the continued relevance of Indigenous practices for contemporary Tlaxcalans. To the St. Louis commission, for example, the governor sent clay statues representing a *tlachiquero* (a person who collects aguamiel, the juice from the maguey plant that is fermented into pulque), a priest, a rural soldier, a bullfighter, an Indigenous bride, and "a female Indian" with her family; a barrel of local aguardiente; various pre-Hispanic tableaux; different textiles and traditional clothing; and a bag each of agricultural products from the region—corn, fava beans, lentils, and various other beans and cereals.[49] Aside from the pre-Hispanic tableaux, these items still had significance for daily life in Tlaxcala. Cahuantzi also replied with a detailed response to the commission's four-page survey on "social economy."[50] He explained how Tlaxcala was handling and tracking its expenditures and debt; the number of schools in the region and teacher salaries; agricultural and mineral production; and the number of telegraph, telephone, and electricity lines that were in use and planned for installation. Notably, the governor did not include a separate section expressly on "Indians." Likewise, when he replied to the Chicago World's Fair commission, Cahuantzi sent cloths from local textile factories alongside cloth lithographs of pre-Hispanic scenarios.[51]

Cahuantzi conflated items that the world's fair commissions would have otherwise separated into representations of either Indigenous or modern life because he was using antiquity to engender excitement about the present day. As one state official who assisted the governor with amassing items to exhibit at the World's Fair in Paris in 1889 rejoiced, "The spirit of emulation and activity has awoken among the inhabitants of this state, [with an] understanding of the opportunities that exhibiting national products in Europe [may bring]." The state official believed it was the "duty" of contemporary Tlaxcalans to justify their continued relevance "so that the name of the state does not vanish, [especially] when its industrious and capable residents can raise it to the level that it deserves."[52] Cahuantzi did not want the observers of Tlaxcala's historical objects to think of Tlaxcala as a place where "isolated types of Indians" continued to live, and therefore as a place that was derogatively "Indian." The intent of those striving to create a national patrimony was to use the Indigenous past to demonstrate

Mexico's deep roots and forward-thinking ambitions. For Cahuantzi, to divide local artifacts into "Indian" and "non-Indian" would have been an inherently subjective endeavor that did not reflect most Tlaxcalans' day-to-day reality. It would also reinforce racist assumptions of Indigenous "backwardness" and undermine the raison d'être of the nation-building project: to prove that Tlaxcala was modern and worthy of international attention.

Another way in which Cahuantzi realized his goal of making Tlaxcala better known beyond Mexico was to encourage the publication of geographic studies. The governor oversaw the production of two publications: *Gran cuadro histórico, político, geográfico, industrial, y religioso de la ciudad de Tlaxcala y del Estado de su nombre* by regional geographer Pedro Larrea y Cordero (1886), and *Geografía y estadística del estado de Tlaxcala* by Alfonso Luis Velasco (1892).[53] The obvious function of these geographic works was to orient travelers and investors to the region, a purpose that became even more important after the Mexicano rail line through Tlaxcala was finished in the 1870s. They also offered another occasion for Cahuantzi to link Tlaxcala's present-day successes to its pre-Hispanic relevance. In the preface to the *Gran cuadro histórico*, Larrea y Cordero attributed Tlaxcala's "modern progress" to its "historical memories and traditions . . . its ancient monuments and grandiose ruins."[54] The *Gran cuadro histórico*—a work that was funded entirely by Cahuantzi's government—was also an opportunity for self-adulation. Its preface was dedicated to "Sr. Gobernador del Estado Coronel Próspero Cahuantzi" and listed many of Cahuantzi's accomplishments during his first two years in office, including that he had a "[good] management of public funds" and "honorable employees."[55] Geographic publications thus served the dual purpose of rendering Tlaxcala more recognizable to outsiders while also providing a public space where Cahuantzi's administration could praise itself and justify its continual rule.

Eleventh International Congress of Americanists (1895)

Cahuantzi's most public propagation of his region's patrimony occurred when he participated in the Eleventh International Congress of Americanists in Mexico City. Cahuantzi's active role in congressional proceedings makes clear how, by 1895, Díaz and his administration both acknowledged and rewarded Cahuantzi as a personified representative of Tlaxcalan antiquity. Other governors donated artifacts to and even attended the Eleventh Congress. But Cahuantzi was one of few regional officials whom the congressional commission selected to help prepare, organize, and execute this central event. The Congress was a critical chance for Mexico to show its pre-Columbian magnificence to "Americanists" from the United States, Canada, and Europe, whose opinions they revered.[56] Members of the congressional commission led tours and feasts in and around Mexico City. Various archaeological digs had been prompted by the coming congress, and attendees visited sites where excavations were underway. They also visited places, mainly museums, where historical objects were being stored and analyzed. The artifacts that had been featured and discussed at previous congresses were now being displayed in museums in Berlin, Boston, and Paris. Indubitably, Mexicans hoped that the Congress would help Mexico City to rise in fame like these cosmopolitan cities.[57]

Cahuantzi's main contribution to the Congress of Americanists was to head the Archaeological Commission. Díaz personally selected Cahuantzi for this position, a move that confirmed the president's trust in the governor, given the tremendous value that nation-builders placed on Indigenous artifacts. As director of the Congress's Archaeological Commission, Cahuantzi was charged with "enriching collections."[58] The governor received and organized all artifacts that state officials sent to Mexico City to be displayed for the Congress.[59] Officials were told to send artifacts directly to "*Delegado de la Federación, el Gobernador de Tlaxcala, Coronel D. Próspero M. Cahuantzi.*"[60] Cahuantzi additionally traveled to ongoing digs at Mitla, Teotihuacán, and sites in other states where the governor would take stock of the "most interesting artifacts that exist in state museums or in other private collections."[61] Once the conference was underway, Cahuantzi escorted congressional attendees on excursions to the archaeological sites that he had previously toured.[62]

Cahuantzi also played a key role in protecting artifacts once they arrived in Mexico City. Despite the commission's assurances to local residents that they would return relics to their original locations, historical items were known to disappear and were rarely returned to local collections.[63] The illustrious pyramids and elaborate ruins of Teotihuacán were of particular interest to the commission. Nation-builders prized and sought to "present [relics from Teotihuacán] as best as possible and in all of their grandeur to Americanist Congress members."[64] In response to concerns that Teotihuacán's artifacts would vanish, Díaz "specially" invited Governor Cahuantzi to join the team working on Teotihuacán to "take care of objects that had been taken [from the site]."⁶⁵ Díaz assured contributors that the governor would take instructions directly from Antonio García Cubas, the geographer mapping and studying the site, and that additional police, fire patrols, and soldiers would carefully guard objects day and night on site and in the National Museum.⁶⁶

Once proceedings began, Cahuantzi participated actively in the congress. In addition to accompanying congressional attendees on visits to ancient ruins, the governor dazzled attendees with a speech in Nahuatl at the Congress's opening banquet. He spoke in Nahuatl at other points during the Congress as well, engaging with attendees' discussions about the "Mexicano" language.⁶⁷ In one exchange, Cahuantzi dialogued with Agustín Hunt Cortés, a US priest, Nahuatl scholar, and longtime Mexico resident.⁶⁸ Cahuantzi responded to Hunt Cortés's speech on the "excellences of the Nahuatl or Mexicana language and on the Indigenous race's present condition" by underscoring Indigenous peoples' sophisticated spiritual knowledge, mentioning how "the ancient Mexican peoples had very advanced ideas about divinity, ideas that their descendants preserve with veneration and respect."⁶⁹ The published congressional record indicates how Cahuantzi moved fluidly between Nahuatl and Spanish; the governor spoke bilingually just as most Tlaxcalans did in their quotidian lives. By communicating in Nahuatl, and discussing contemporary Indigenous religion, Cahuantzi pushed congressional attendees to think beyond antiquity and to consider the modern vitality of Indigenous practices. If only for a moment within this specific space, participants lauded Cahuantzi for concurrently representing Indigenous past and present.

Cahuantzi's participation in the Eleventh International Congress of Americanists elucidates how Porfirian nation-builders saw the governor as acceptably Indigenous. Díaz and elite nation-builders allowed and even encouraged Cahuantzi to participate in the Congress as a recognizably Indigenous person, and to engage, albeit selectively, with Indigenous signifiers, such as speaking in Nahuatl. By insisting that Indigenous peoples could bring value to modern Mexico, the governor presented himself as a proto-*indigenista*: a person who valued Indigenous peoples and cultures.⁷⁰ While a form of *indigenismo* certainly existed during the Porfiriato, it was usually "confined to glorifying antiquity rather than promoting the wellbeing of Indians."⁷¹ Cahuantzi had not just proven himself a trustworthy custodian of Mexico's heritage. He had proven himself a trustworthy Indigenous person who was closely aligned with nation-builders' goals.

Notable as it was that congressional participants listened to Cahuantzi's viewpoint, attendees considered few other Indigenous peoples' perspectives. When congressional participants discussed the "Mexicano" language or even when they spoke in Nahuatl, these actions did not negate their firmly held belief that contemporary Indigenous peoples were, for the most part, uncivilized.[72] The congressional record stresses how attendees examined Nahuatl's "scientific" merits.[73] Speaking in Nahuatl was acceptable only within the context of celebrating American antiquity and only to examine the language from a scientific, and by inference, modern perspective. Nation-builders still held contradictory and exclusionary understandings of Indigenous identity.[74] This was also true of Cahuantzi. Throughout the congressional record, Cahuantzi is not labeled "Indio" or "Indigenous," nor does he use these terms to describe himself. Giving a speech in Nahuatl was permissible within the congress's bounds. Yet it was essential for Cahuantzi's political image that he distance himself from backward notions of Indianness, lest the governor risk being associated with Indians like the Maya and the Yaqui—groups who were actively protesting the Porfirian dictatorship's exploitative land and labor policies. The line between acceptable Indigenousness and barbarity was thin, and Cahuantzi had to walk it carefully.

The Congressional Grand Jury Case of 1896

Only a few months after the Congress of Americanists took place in Mexico City, Cahuantzi's image came under public scrutiny. In September 1896, Cahuantzi participated in the funeral procession and burial of Bishop Melitón Vargas. Although Melitón Vargas had been a bishop in Puebla, the funeral services took place at the Santuario de Ocotlán in Tlaxcala, an important Catholic pilgrimage site where a Tlaxcalan boy was supposed to have seen a Marian apparition in 1541. Given the closeness between Puebla and Tlaxcala, Cahuantzi may have had a relationship with the bishop, though the historic record does not disclose as much. Cahuantzi's involvement in the bishop's funeral passed without public remark, that is, until *El Imparcial* in Mexico City caught wind of the event. The newspaper reported that Cahuantzi, as a public official participating in a Catholic ritual, defied the separation between church and state outlined in the 1857 Constitution.⁷⁵ It was not uncommon for governors to come up for criticism in national publications. Such criticisms were even beneficial for Díaz, since they created spaces where the authoritarian government could claim that they allowed freedom of the press.⁷⁶ Hoping to circumvent "scandal," President Díaz penned a note to his "friend" Cahuantzi requesting that he lay low, because "there was no doubt [that Cahuantzi] had broken the law."⁷⁷ But it was too late. Other newspapers joined *El Imparcial* in denouncing Cahuantzi.⁷⁸ Worse, they asked that the case be brought before the Congressional Grand Jury (Gran Jurado de la Cámara de Diputados del Congreso), the judicial body in the legislature that tried crimes committed by officials.

Mexico City journalists successfully pressured the Congressional Grand Jury to try the case a few months later. Testimonies from the prosecution and the defense were given over the course of two months. Ultimately, Cahuantzi was acquitted, an outcome that was predictable, foremost, among other reasons, because of his closeness with Díaz, who influenced congressional decisions. Despite the likelihood of his exoneration, the governor and his defense team (three *diputados*, or congressional members) composed hundreds of pages of depositions to establish and explain his innocence. The Tlaxcalan state press published and disseminated four total depositions—three from the representatives who defended Cahuantzi as well as Cahuantzi's own rebuttal. Each deposition's length, thoroughness, and language indicates how the defense team used the case to solidify Cahuantzi's image as a deserving and rightful representative of Tlaxcala while, at the same time, distancing him from depreciatory impressions of Indianness. The depositions contained rhetorical strategies designed to absolve Cahuantzi and avow his ties to "pueblos civilizados."⁷⁹ Through the depositions, Cahuantzi and his defenders sought to convince congressional representatives, and the court of public opinion, that the governor's involvement in Bishop Vargas's funeral were the actions of a civilized rural leader rather than those of an antimodern Indian.⁸⁰ Just as Cahuantzi had claimed to represent Tlaxcalans during the Congress of Americanists, Cahuantzi used the trial as a space where he and his defenders could reinforce his image as acceptably Indigenous.

When the trial began, Cahuantzi stood accused of three crimes: "1. Allowing the burial of a body in a temple; 2. Participating in acts of Catholic worship in an official capacity; 3. Allowing a religious act of Catholic worship to take place in public, outside of a church."⁸¹ The prosecution recounted what they alleged to have happened: on the day of the bishop's funeral, Cahuantzi led a procession of six hundred women who carried various Catholic insignia, including a large cross. Immediately after the procession, Cahuantzi helped to bury the bishop in the Ocotlán chapel.[82] The accusers called out the governor for believing himself above the law, bemoaning that, "it seems that Mr. Cahuantzi has violated all divine and human laws; his actions endanger freedom and its institutions."[83] The prosecution laid bare Cahuantzi's hypocrisy: not only had the governor violated the Constitution, but his own administration had also imposed fines on residents for similar acts (and they continued to do so after the case was resolved).[84] The prosecution's reproach resonated well beyond the scope of the case: Cahuantzi, like so many other Porfirian officials, ignored or changed laws when it behooved him.

Cahuantzi and his defense team could not refute the argument that the governor had broken constitutional law. The separation between church and state was enshrined in the Constitution of 1857 and had been sacrosanct to liberal leaders like Benito Juárez who wanted to modernize, and therefore secularize, Mexico's political institutions. Most liberals, even those who were practicing Catholics, saw the Catholic Church as antithetical to national progress. And yet, while the Constitution had not changed since 1857, attitudes toward the church had. Liberals' once hardline anticlericalism softened considerably under Díaz, and Díaz's second wife, Carmen, who he married in 1881, was a devout Catholic.[85] Díaz walked in a public Catholic procession some ten years after he wedded Carmen, a crime for which he was not tried.[86] In the early 1880s, Cahuantzi's gubernatorial predecessor lost his chance at reelection in part because he participated in a public religious ceremony, opening the door for Cahuantzi's candidacy. Cahuantzi was exonerated for the same crime during this congressional case in 1896.[87]

Within this context—in which, as compared to previous years, the state was more amenable toward the church, and Díaz's and Cahuantzi's political positions were more secured—Cahuantzi and his defenders used the court case as an opportunity to affirm Cahuantzi's public image as a civilized rural leader. They built a defense that mocked Mexico City journalists for their ignorance of rural life, a mainstay of which, they argued, were Catholic rituals, including funeral processions. They began by addressing the first charge: that Cahuantzi had permitted Bishop Vargas to be laid to rest in a church. They noted that, had the journalists been familiar with Tlaxcala and Ocotlán, or at least taken the time to visit, they would have known that the bishop had not been buried in the chapel itself, but rather, in a sacred and separate space in the Ocotlán cemetery designated for people of note.[88]

Repudiating the second and third charges proved trickier. Cahuantzi and his defenders argued that being governor did not preclude a private life, one that was separate from gubernatorial duties. They cited the case in which President Díaz had similarly attended a Catholic burial, noting how the president's presence went undisputed because he bore no signs of his "official character."[89] Cahuantzi should be held to the standard of other officials, they insisted. Cahuantzi reasoned that, "It is perceptible, very clear, and very easy to distinguish the duality that makes up the Governor of Tlaxcala and the individual."[90] The governor emphasized how he had gone alone to the event, unaccompanied by other members of his administration, prompting him to ask the court: "Should a governor not attend other Catholic rituals such as wedding ceremonies or baptisms?"[91] After all, these rituals—baptisms, weddings, and funerals—though tied to the Catholic faith, were part of the fabric of provincial life.

In highlighting this final point, the defense described how public rituals were essential to the functioning of "pueblos civilizados."[92] The journalists, who were not judges—as one congressperson stressed—were not fit to pass judgment on their legality.[93] Cahuantzi's infractions should be arbitrated by "competent authorities, according to the laws common in every locality," one diputado averred.[94] Issues of "civil registry," such as church-related ceremonies, were not the federal government's domain, he insisted.[95] Most vitally, Cahuantzi and those defending him argued that a funeral procession in and of itself was not religious. This fact was lost on the urban journalists unjustly leveling the accusations. Even the great Athenians honored their dead, claimed one diputado, quoting a line in Greek historian Thucydides's *History of the Peloponnesian War* that explicated how the dead became immortal like the Gods.[96] The diputado insisted that such ceremonies were simply part of "dignified" town life.[97]

While explaining how rural Mexican towns valued rituals that honored the dead, one diputado disclosed their thinly veiled disdain toward the indicters' lack of rural acumen. He admonished that "In the capital of the Republic, it would be very difficult, if not impossible" for hundreds of "*mujeres de humilde clase*" (humble [poor] women) to assemble a procession.⁹⁸ Women in the capital would never endure the "harsh sun, the dirt on the street, or the subsequent fatigue" in order to undertake such a "very long journey on foot."⁹⁹ Cahuantzi's defenders indicated that the funeral procession had less to do with Christianity per se than local practice; it was simply what was done. Another diputado suggested that, by debating the validity of local customs, the court was imposing "judicial despotism."¹⁰⁰ A guilty verdict would endorse "bourgeois" journalists' allegations instead of defending "the noble efforts of the oppressed pueblos."¹⁰¹ To vindicate Cahuantzi, the defense advocated on behalf of an "oppressed pueblo" to continue with its deep-rooted cultural practices. They further stressed how Cahuantzi should lead their efforts, even if this was not a policy that the Porfirian administration arbitrated consistently, not even in Tlaxcala.¹⁰²

Cahuantzi and those defending him before congress built on ideas that the governor had already begun to publicly affirm about Tlaxcala before 1896: that Tlaxcalans were historically "good Indians."¹⁰³ Even in the twenty-first century, Tlaxcalans stage theater and dance performances that reinforce the idea that as early Christian converts and Spanish allies, Tlaxcalans "performed conquest while playing by the rules."¹⁰⁴ During the case before congress, the defense made the public claim that Tlaxcalans, with Cahuantzi as their leader, should be extolled for continuing to engage with practices, such as Christianity, that had historically distinguished them as honorable rural peoples.

Throughout their depositions, Cahuantzi and the diputados defending him were careful to never use the term "Indio" or "Indígena." Instead, they used terms such as "oppressed pueblo," "civilizado," and "humilde clase," terms that conveyed rurality without the derogatory sentiment that "Indio" implied during the late nineteenth century. The language Cahuantzi and others used to describe the governor in public forums makes clear how Cahuantzi constructed his image to conform to non-Indigenous persons' discriminatory criterion. National elites deemed it acceptable for Cahuantzi to speak in an Indigenous language in order to examine its "scientific" bearing during the Congress of Americanists. Cahuantzi would not dare to use Nahuatl during the congressional court proceedings only a few months later, however. Outside of a patrimonial context, national elites would have viewed speaking in Nahuatl as imprudent and antimodern. Cahuantzi sought to distinguish himself and his home state from Mexico's *indios bárbaros*, who Díaz's administration saw as hindering

Mexico's path toward progress. By distancing himself from "uncivilized" Indians, Cahuantzi helped his political reputation as well as the reputation of his state. But he also reinforced prejudice against peoples categorized by this characterization and the hypocrisy inherent to late nineteenth century indigenismo.

Conclusion: Public Image, Local Support

Cahuantzi and his defenders used the 1896 trial before the Congressional Grand Jury to affirm the governor's ties to "civilized" rural peoples. But it was also possible that Cahuantzi participated in the bishop's funeral to demonstrate to Tlaxcalans—who, like most rural Mexicans, were practicing Catholics—that he believed such ceremonies had value. While few Tlaxcalans were likely, or able, to read the published depositions, more would have witnessed Cahuantzi's actions. Had Cahuantzi been absent from such a major event, Tlaxcalans surely would have noticed. By 1896, the time of the funeral, there were various Tlaxcalans who were displeased with Cahuantzi's continuous leadership. Although the historic record does not indicate as much, the governor likely participated in the funerary procession to demonstrate his Catholic devotion to Tlaxcalans and attempt to assuage his naysayers.[105]

Yet Tlaxcalans appeared to care less about Cahuantzi's public image and more about how the governor's political decisions affected their everyday lives, whether they could access natural resources, for example, or negotiate down their property tax rates. The governor's ability to speak fluent Nahuatl presumably facilitated Cahuantzi's ability to communicate with residents, particularly with poorer constituents who were often bilingual. If Cahuantzi spoke in Nahuatl, however, it was not frequently noted in archival documents.[106] Unlike for attendees of the International Congress of Americanists, for most Tlaxcalans, speaking in Nahuatl was not remarkable enough to record. Most Mexico City elites had acculturated to whiteness and ceased to speak in an Indigenous language, if they ever had, especially in public. Still, just because Cahuantzi presented himself as a spokesperson for Tlaxcala's Indigenous heritage did not mean that he endorsed policies that aided Tlaxcala's rural majority. Cahuantzi was a Tlaxcalteco. But he was also a loyal Porfirian steward.

It is nevertheless extraordinary that Cahuantzi's identity as a person of Indigenous heritage became a political life preserver in a historical context that glorified an Indigenous past but disparaged the Indigenous present. Cahuantzi showed how regional and Indigenous representatives—not just metropolitan nation-builders—could claim and contest racialized differences as well as patrimonial meanings and spaces. The governor challenged Porfirians' Eurocentric ideals by inserting Tlaxcala into Mexico's patrimonial narrative, forcing these elite politicians to consider how the Tlaxcalans shaped Mexican history and had the capacity to be progressive and adaptable. Analyzing how Cahuantzi engaged with Indigenous signifiers, albeit selectively, illuminates one of the reasons why Díaz supported a recognizably Indigenous person in office in Tlaxcala but rarely in other states.

THREE

Building a State, Building a Regime

When Próspero Cahuantzi came to power, Tlaxcala was one of the youngest states in the Mexican federation. Statehood had been hard won. In the decades after independence, Tlaxcala was a territory of Mexico state, governed by a federally appointed jefe político. Puebla loomed large in Tlaxcala's political and economic affairs. Nearly three-fourths of Tlaxcala's perimeter was circumscribed by its larger, wealthier, and more populated neighbor. Together with merchants and clergymen, hacendados from Puebla and northern Tlaxcala campaigned to annex Tlaxcala to Puebla state, arguing that Tlaxcala was too underpopulated and economically feeble to deserve autonomy. Many from this cohort were also first- or second-generation Spaniards. Campaigns to annex Tlaxcala to Puebla were most fervent after the northern town of Huamantla—dominated by hacendados—helped to bridge communication between the port of Veracruz and Mexico City during the North American invasion in 1847. Finally, in 1857, after an assorted coalition of local politicians, intellectuals, and villagers aggressively lobbied the national congress, Tlaxcala became a state. But even then, hacendados who either came from or had strong ties to Puebla clamored for political sway in Tlaxcala. Two of the governors who immediately preceded Cahuantzi, Melquiades Carvajal (in office 1873–77) and Mariano Grajales (in office 1881–85) were both prominent hacendados in Tlaxcala-Puebla. The completion of the Mexicano and Interoceanico rail lines in the late 1860s and early 1870s made it even easier for landowners and industrialists from Puebla (and elsewhere, including

Mexico state, Spain, and France) to conduct business, own properties, and influence affairs in Tlaxcala.

This chapter explains how Cahuantzi secured and unified a rapidly transforming state over which he would preside and how he pacified Tlaxcala's socioeconomically diverse populations. The strategies that the governor used to establish and maintain his rule—centralization, patronage, electoral fraud—mirrored those used by Díaz and by caciques and caudillos throughout Latin America, as well as in any place where bosses subjugated democratic rule. However, Cahuantzi's ability to implement these strategies effectively hinged on his extensive local knowledge about the region's socioeconomic composition, its history, and its relationships with its neighbors, Puebla, especially.

The Railroad and the Socioeconomic Landscape of Tlaxcala

Because he lacked connections to erstwhile ruling circles, one of Cahuantzi's primary goals when he came to power was to temper the authority of those who had long dominated the state political landscape. The railroad helped him to do this. The railroad allowed Cahuantzi to make his socioeconomically diverse and geographically disparate state more cohesive, to attenuate the distance between northern and southern Tlaxcala, and to quell dissent when necessary.

Tlaxcala's northern and south-central regions were naturally divided by the Malintzin mountain (see map 3). Where Tlaxcala's pulque elites dominated in the north, villagers and small landowners lived mostly in the south. The maguey-rich *llanos de Apan* stretched from northwest Tlaxcala into the states of Hidalgo, Puebla, and Mexico. Along with grains, most northern haciendas produced pulque, an alcoholic beverage made from the fermented sap of the maguey plant that had been drunk in central Mexico since pre-Hispanic times.[1] Pulque was reliable. Maguey required little water to grow and was consistent relative to other crops.[2] Because pulque circulated domestically, it was less affected by the vagaries of international markets and currency depreciations.[3] Pulque therefore propped up Tlaxcala's economy, helping Tlaxcala to weather bad harvest and drought years. At the same time, because pulque and other products such as corn and wheat were limited to domestic consumption, they did not generate nearly as much income for Tlaxcala as compared to places with expansive export economies.[4]

Tlaxcala's hacendados were a heterogenous bunch. They differed in terms of their wealth, the size of their estates, the products they sold, their politics, and even their origins—many called Puebla or even Spain home, but not Tlaxcala.[5] Some owned additional properties in Puebla or Mexico state and were thus not exclusively reliant on their properties in Tlaxcala to supply their wealth.[6] As for the laborers who worked on haciendas, some lived on haciendas (*peones acasillados*). Others made seasonal trips to haciendas on demand and lived in their own communities and farmed their own plots (*peones no acasillados*) or were landless (*jornaleros*). Peasants, those with lands and without, resided throughout the state, especially in the south.[7]

Residents living in the folds of the Malintzin to the south were also a diverse lot. There were landowners of all sorts, from hacendados to small and middling farmers, to sharecroppers and tenant farmers.[8] Most were small landowners and villagers, some of whom still farmed land communally. Lands in the south-central region were fertile, if not abundant, and Tlaxcala's two main rivers, the Atoyac and the Zahuapan, were accessible.[9] As it was during pre-Hispanic times, the state's population was most dense in the *pueblos* (villages) and *barrios* (neighborhoods within towns or villages) that encircled the colonial *cabildo indio*, modern-day Tlaxcala City.[10]

Because of the south's proximity to rivers, the majority of Tlaxcala's textile and glass factories were built in this region. In 1881, Tlaxcala had five textile factories, two glass factories, five *de loza* (clay) plants, twenty aguardiente plants (a liquor similar to mezcal extracted from the maguey plant), one iron production plant, and approximately fifteen wheat mills. By 1910, the state had around sixty total factories and mills. Of these, Tlaxcala's thirteen textile factories were by far the most productive and profitable industrial entities in the state.[11] As was the case throughout central Mexico, factories benefited from generous tax exemptions granted to them by Díaz and his gubernatorial appointees.[12] Factory owners also had help from the government to put down strikes that arose among factory workers during the late Porfirian period. Most textile factory owners lived outside of Tlaxcala, in Puebla and Mexico state, as did many large landowners, some of whom owned properties in other states. Unlike factory owners who rarely participated directly in state politics, hacendados did, and always had. As for the few thousand Tlaxcalans who worked in factories, most were small landowners or villagers who took up factory work to supplement meager harvests and low agrarian wages. Tlaxcala's population density—second highest in all the Mexican federation—meant that residents particularly in the south-central region were constantly competing for resources.[13]

When the first rail line, the Mexicano, was completed in Tlaxcala in 1872, it was a boon for *pulqueros* and other landowning elites, as well as factory owners, but less so for the state's poorer residents. Backed by British investment, the introduction of the railroad in Mexico was nothing short of revolutionary.[14] Along with improved access to credit and commercial markets, regularized banking, and more mechanized technology, railroads propelled industrial growth and opened the fledgling nation to capitalist networks. Tlaxcala's closeness to the center of power, first to Tenochtitlán and later to Mexico City, meant that Tlaxcala was among the first regions in the nation to receive a railroad. The Mexicano, and a few years later the Interoceanic, rail lines connected Mexico City with the Atlantic world via the port of Veracruz. Both ran directly through different towns in Tlaxcala (see figure 6).[15]

The effects of the introduction of the railroad in Tlaxcala were palpable and multitudinous, but highly uneven across the population. Rail lines hastened and facilitated transport, transformed relatively small towns like Huamantla and Apizaco into railroad hubs, and brought all sorts of visitors to the region. The railroad helped Tlaxcala's products such as grains and pulque to circulate more broadly throughout the nation. Larger pulque producers secured contracts with British rail companies to build private lines directly to their properties.[16] The railroad also helped them to diversify production. As early as the 1860s, pulque haciendas such as "el Mazaquiahuac" and "el Rosario" sold timber and coal from their hillsides to railroad companies building in the vicinity.[17]

While hacendados and factory owners saw their profits increase because of the railroads, poorer residents confronted widening socioeconomic disparities.[18] Tlaxcala's small producers of pulque and aguardiente, most of whom relied on the local market, could not afford to build rail lines to their plants or properties.[19] The railroad accelerated deforestation around the Malintzin mountain as more trees were felled to build rail ties and other infrastructural apparatus. Although Tlaxcalans of all walks of life very much wanted some of the infrastructural improvements the railroad ushered in such as dams, bridges, and roads, these improvements exacerbated competition over natural resources. This was particularly true of timber.[20] Infrastructure was also expensive and contributed to public out-

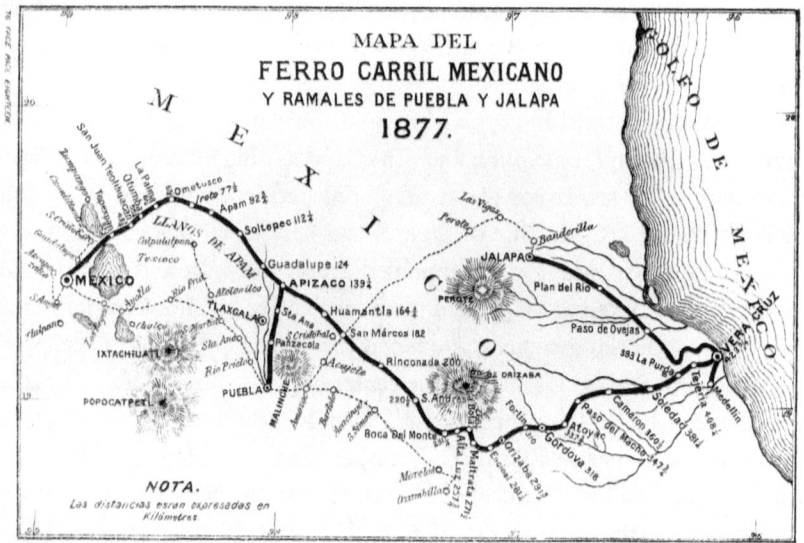

FIGURE 6. Mexicano rail line (1877). Source: H. C. R. Becher, *A Trip to Mexico*, Toronto: Willing and Williamson, 1880.

cries against state spending and taxation. Lastly, residents reported how railroads worsened crime—especially along the Tlaxcala-Puebla border—and that railroad accidents caused injuries and even death.[21] Overall, then, the railroad was more injurious to poorer Tlaxcalans while augmenting the wealth, status, and power of those who already enjoyed these privileges.

The railroad had important political ramifications as well. For Díaz and his underlings, the railroad was essential to monitor the countryside.[22] The people who did this monitoring were called *rurales*. Notorious for their ruthlessness, rurales were professional armed guards charged with patrolling Mexico's rail routes. Subordinate to Díaz, rather than to the army, Díaz used them to stamp out dissent throughout the countryside.[23] In Tlaxcala, rurales were constantly present along the rail lines.[24] Cahuantzi often praised their presence.[25] For most of Cahuantzi's rule, the head of the local rurales corp, who was appointed by the governor, was Agustín García. Listed as the commander of the armed forces on the state's administrative roll, colloquially, García was known as "*el colgador*," or the hangman.[26] Cahuantzi called on García to quell various uprisings in the area, especially as his opposition fomented during the second half of his rule. For those who opposed Cahuantzi's regime, García was a dreaded figure and a constant reminder of the governor's capacity for cruelty. Because of increased policing, Díaz's influence was most stringently felt, and eventually scorned the most, along the rail lines in the northern and central regions of the country, Tlaxcala included, but less so in the south, where fewer rail lines had been laid.

The railroad was politically useful to Cahuantzi in less obviously coercive ways, as well. Because of historical and environmental divisions between hacendados in the North, and villages in the South, residents within these spaces had conducted economic and political affairs with relative autonomy. However, in the 1870s, the northern regions became connected via rail with the towns of Huamantla, Apizaco, and Puebla City, as well as with the maguey regions of Calpulalpan, which Tlaxcala annexed from Mexico state in 1874. Railroad lines that intersected the state enabled Cahuantzi to undertake administrative restructuring that in turn helped to temper traditional power holders' authority there. Soon after Cahuantzi took office, he created Tlaxcala's sixth district, Cuauhtémoc, in the center of the state (see map 1).[27] He named the town of Apizaco, where the rail station now connected Puebla with the Mexicano rail line,

FIGURE 7. Mexicano rail line running over the Zahuapan River near the San Luis textile factory outside Apizaco, Tlaxcala. Source: CONAGUA-AHA, Aprovechamientos superficiales, Caja 141, Expediente 19590, Legajo 1, Foja 44 (1911).

as the new district's capital. Establishing this new central district meant that Huamantla and the northeast, the northwest maguey territory, and the populous southern communities were now more interconnected. The creation of this sixth district also allowed Cahuantzi to shift political authority away from the north and the northern hacendado elite, and toward the center-south regions instead.[28] Whereas Huamantla had functioned as a de facto state capital in the decades since Tlaxcala's statehood, Cahuantzi made clear how his government was going to operate administratively out of Tlaxcala City, not Huamantla or Puebla.

Cahuantzi's ability to undertake administrative reforms—and to impose his political will in general—was helped by Tlaxcala's central location as well as by its small size. After the railroad came, anyone with the means to do so in Tlaxcala could board a train to Puebla City or Mexico City and be there within the same day, as compared to more peripheral regions of the country where intra- and interstate travel was less possible.[29] Although his detractors maligned the governor's absence from the state as a sign of his poor governance, Cahuantzi made frequent trips to Mexico City.[30] The railroad facilitated Cahuantzi's many audiences with the president. The railroad also permitted more outsiders than ever before to visit and invest in Tlaxcala and to help Cahuantzi meet his goal of attracting investment to his state. But at the same time, the railroad made Tlaxcala vulnerable to interlopers who threatened state autonomy, as well as those who threatened Cahuantzi's political authority. As a native of Tlaxcala, Cahuantzi knew how hard-won Tlaxcala's sovereignty had been and how some people, especially Poblanos, still refused to respect it. Cahuantzi wielded this knowledge to defend Tlaxcala's borders from Puebla, which in turn allowed him to capture more wealth and stake his personal authority.

Asserting State Sovereignty

Tlaxcala and Puebla's relationship had been mutually inimical for decades, their poorly defined border a constant source of tension. The border between Tlaxcala and Puebla had been affirmed when Tlaxcala won statehood in 1857. But agrarian privatization and disentailment laws compounded border disputes in Tlaxcala-Puebla, as elsewhere in Mexico, during the second half of the nineteenth century. Officials in both states pointed to "the failure to mark the boundary between [Tlaxcala and Puebla]" as the cause of many quarrels. Tlaxcalans and Poblanos accused each other of

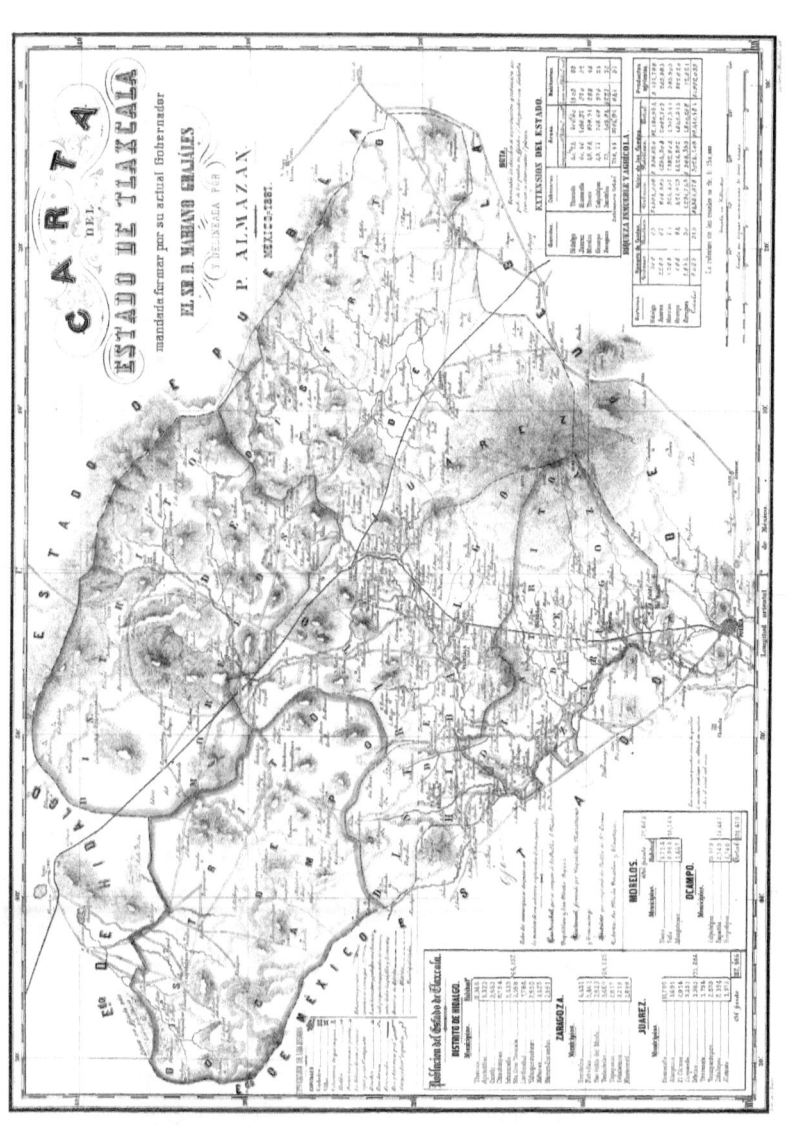

MAP 3. *Carta del Estada de Tlaxcala*, 1881. Source: CONAGUA-AHA, Aprovechamientos superficiales, Caja 4577, Expediente 6091, Foja 12.

robbery, trespassing, and natural resource "abuse."[31] Reports of damaged, moved, or absent boundary markers (*mojoneras*) abounded in the region and throughout Mexico as property users scrambled to corroborate their agrarian claims. Resolving these issues was more difficult along borders, where residents often had to submit documentation to administrators and judges in two or more states.

More so for Tlaxcala than Puebla, settling interstate border issues was a delicate dance. Tlaxcala needed to maintain amenable relations with Puebla, given its lopsided economic dependence on their neighbor's markets. Some Poblanos owned properties in Tlaxcala, including factory owners on whose revenues Tlaxcala increasingly depended in the 1890s and early 1900s. Yet some of these Poblanos were also first-generation descendants of those who had opposed Tlaxcala's statehood. If Cahuantzi outwardly allied with this group, he would undermine his authority as governor of his state. He would also incense the Tlaxcalans who had fought for statehood as a means of guarding some autonomy for their municipal governments (ayuntamientos) in the southern Nativitas Valley.

In more than one border dispute case, Tlaxcalans expressed how Poblano officials had "forced" them to abide by their terms. Take for example the years-long clash between officials in Puebla and villagers in Alzayanca and Xaltitla, Tlaxcala. Beginning in 1877, officials in Puebla accused villagers from Alzayanca and Xaltitla of destroying charcoal ovens, stealing axes, and felling trees on a forested property (*monte*) that the officials claimed to be Puebla's territory. The jefe político of the district of Juárez in Tlaxcala denied that the Tlaxcalan residents had committed the alleged crimes, insisting that the monte to which the Poblano officials laid claim was in fact shared territory owned by the municipality in Tlaxcala. Dozens of letters were exchanged between residents and officials on both sides of the border, and a bi-state commission was sent to survey the area and demarcate the state boundary. After the commission determined that the monte belonged to a private landowner in Puebla, the jefe político of Puebla informed Tlaxcala's then governor Miguel Lira y Otera that the Tlaxcalan vecinos had "ignored" the commission's "instructions" and that the Tlaxcalan residents should "be forced to" obey the commission's decision.[32] In another dispute, the owner of the hacienda San Diego Pinar in Huamantla, Tlaxcala, accused the townspeople in Tepeaca, Puebla, of trespassing. In 1886, Puebla and Tlaxcala composed a bi-state commission to evaluate the accusations.[33] Some months later, in April 1887, Cahuantzi expressed dismay that the "question of limits between Puebla and Tlaxcala had not been resolved" and that Puebla had "suspended" their "responsibilities" to the commission "without [providing a] reason."[34] In October of that year, Cahuantzi announced that he, along with Puebla's governor Rosendo Márquez, would conduct a *"visita de ojos"* (physical inspection) of the area to "bring the matter to a close."[35]

However, during his speech that opened the state congressional session in October 1890, Cahuantzi bemoaned that the "old and even irritating" question of territorial limits between Tepeaca, Puebla, and Huamantla, Tlaxcala, "continued" and that it had "caused communications full of acrimony to be exchanged between the government of Puebla and [Tlaxcala]."[36] Cahuantzi assured the congress that the border situation "had not disturbed the friendly relations that General Rosendo Márquez and [my] government have been cultivating for some years."[37] Yet members of the state legislature—which included prominent landowners from Huamantla—seemed dismayed.[38] The congressional president dictated how, "The Legislative Body hopes that you [Cahuantzi] . . . as a ruler [who is] watchful over the state's territorial interests, will not allow under any pretext for the pact between the governments of Puebla and Tlaxcala to be made illusory, even when[,] unfortunately[,] a hidden or bad-intentioned hand threatens to destroy [it]."[39]

As the border conflict between Tepeaca and the hacienda San Diego Pinar in Huamantla ramped up, a new governor came to power in Puebla. Díaz replaced Rosendo Márquez (in office 1885–92) with Mucio Martínez (in office 1892–1911) in 1892.[40] Despite his infamous grafting and corruption, Martínez remained in office for the rest of the Porfiriato and played a key role in rooting out sedition throughout central Mexico.[41] Where Cahuantzi's relationship with former governor Marquéz had been cordial, not so with Martínez. Martínez hated Cahuantzi. The governor of Puebla made his feelings known to Díaz when he declared his opposition to Cahuantzi's reelection in 1896, though Martínez did not specify reasons beyond Cahuantzi's alleged "incompetence."[42] The two governors became further entangled after Martínez purchased the hacienda La Compañía in the southern district of Hidalgo, Tlaxcala.[43] Martínez thus joined the ranks of Poblanos who owned properties in Tlaxcala and who, in theory, had to abide by Tlaxcala's state and municipal laws.

The border battle between the two states, along with Cahuantzi and Martínez's mutual dislike, came to a head as each governor battled to win the territorial rights to the textile factory La Covadonga. The Covadonga textile factory opened for business in 1897. The land on which the factory was built was purchased by José Díaz Rubín, a descendant of Reform-era Spanish émigrés.⁴⁴ Díaz Rubín chose the lands, a rancho formerly known as "Moratilla," because of its proximity to the Atoyac River and because the lands already contained water infrastructure, including a dam and canal.⁴⁵ Yet because the land lay along an ill-defined stretch of the Tlaxcala-Puebla border, and because the Covadonga had the potential to beget tremendous tax revenue, Cahuantzi and Martínez each claimed jurisdiction over it. They did so fiercely.

According to Cahuantzi, Puebla's claim to the territory was based on a lie. In 1898, the government of Puebla informed Tlaxcalan officials that they, officials in Puebla, had received a letter from the Tlaxcalans about how they had "uncovered an error . . . in the archives . . . that shows that the rancho Moratilla, where the factory is located . . . had belonged for some years to Puebla." To contest what he insisted was a falsehood, Cahuantzi prepared to send Tlaxcala's territorial titles to Puebla. But before he had the chance to do so, Martínez sent "armed forces" to "guard" the Covadonga factory. The governor bewailed, "Why even ask . . . for the titles . . . if they [officials in Puebla] were not going to wait for my reply and [instead] proceed in such an unacceptable way [as to send armed forces]?" Cahuantzi's exasperation and anger at the situation, and at Governor Martínez, were evident.⁴⁶

Cahuantzi conceded how some owners of the lands that surrounded "Moratilla" had paid property taxes to Puebla state. But he also asserted that Tlaxcala had much older, and therefore more legitimate, claims to the territory. Cahuantzi outlined these claims in a public address in the official state newspaper. Cahuantzi's dictation could only have been made by a person with deep knowledge of, and who cared deeply about, Tlaxcala. It spanned twenty columns instead of the usual six or eight, referenced specific locales in Tlaxcala, and cited extensive archival and taxation records. Cahuantzi emphasized Tlaxcala's antiquity as compared to Puebla. The governor explained why and how the rancho Moratilla, known previously as "Tenexac," was part of Tlaxcala, and not Puebla. He began in the 1500s, explaining how Tenexac "was property of Indians from Cuauhtotoatlan," where various "*tribus tlaxcaltecas*" resided.⁴⁷ The "*pueblo* of Cuauhtotoatlan . . . never belonged to Cholula" (part of modern-day Puebla state). Cahuantzi underscored, "I do not say Puebla [instead of Cholula] because

Puebla did not exist."⁴⁸ Cahuantzi brought his personal experiences to bear on the conflict, citing his own memory of a granary that was burned during the French assault on Puebla in 1863 where the Covadonga was now located.⁴⁹ The Tlaxcalteco also slyly maligned Governor Martínez, juxtaposing him to the "unforgettable" Juan N. Méndez, the governor of Puebla from 1880 to 1885. Unlike Martínez, who was from Nuevo León, Méndez had been from Puebla. By comparing the two governors of Puebla, one a native, the other an outsider, Cahuantzi highlighted how Martínez's lack of local knowingness made him ill-suited to make judgments about border conflicts. Cahuantzi explained, "[Méndez's] conduct was, as it should have been, that of a governor who understood the jurisdictional limits of the state that he administered . . . [and who] abstained from arousing controversies."⁵⁰ He further insisted how, by collecting taxes on properties along the Tlaxcala-Puebla border, Puebla had "violate[d] the ancient rights [of Tlaxcala]" and that it was "extremely dangerous" to have done so.⁵¹

Martínez ridiculed Cahuantzi for evoking "ancient rights" to make territorial claims in the present day. He countered:

> these documents [proving Tlaxcala's jurisdiction over the rancho Moratilla, previously Tenexac] . . . do not have any current value, since our laws [today] should not be informed by colonial rulings, but rather [by] those [laws] that have been made after our glorious Independence. So, the point that you [Cahuantzi] made, that in our case [the dispute over the rancho Moratilla] should be decided by arrangements made three hundred and fifty-four years ago, is in my judgment invalid.⁵²

Much to Cahuantzi's chagrin, a federal commission determined that Martínez was right. The Covadonga textile factory remained in Puebla's jurisdiction. By the 1910s, the Covadonga had approximately doubled in value and was one of the largest textile factories in the region.⁵³

Because the conflict over the Covadonga became so heated, it prompted the national congress to compose a commission to reevaluate and reaffirm Tlaxcala and Puebla's entire border and to settle various ongoing territorial disputes.⁵⁴ During the case before congress, the lawyer representing Tlaxcala, José N. Macías, submitted a twenty-nine-page brief that expanded on the arguments Cahuantzi had used in his statement published in the *Periódico Oficial* the year before. Like Cahuantzi, Macías drew on hundreds of years of history to justify Tlaxcala's territorial claims. In his concluding plea the lawyer bemoaned the "serious attacks that Tlaxcala has suffered on its sovereignty [as a state] . . . all of which have been provoked by Puebla, who has used the armed forces to usurp [Tlaxcalan territories], as if we lived in Central Africa . . . as if we did not live in a *civilized* nation."55 The commission's results were published in a congressional decree titled *Convenio de límites, Decreto aprobando los que celebraron entre los Estados de Puebla y Tlaxcala* on December 15, 1899, along with a new topographical map of Tlaxcala.56 Tlaxcalans successfully beat back Puebla's claims to other lands along the border, some of which were sold off to residents in Tlaxcalan villages nearby as part of the commission's effort to curb future conflicts and continue land divisions and privatization.57 In his biannual congressional address in April 1900, Cahuantzi declared that he found the terms of the agreement "satisfactory."58 In addition to publishing excerpts in the *Periódico Oficial,* Cahuantzi sent a copy of Macías's lengthy deposition—in which he justified Tlaxcala's historical relevance vis-à-vis Puebla—to every *agente municipal* (local representative) in the state—eighty-two in total.59

The national congress found that the rights and privileges that Tlaxcalans had fought for during the centuries prior were indeed bygone. It is nevertheless noteworthy how Cahuantzi used his region's antiquity to defend Tlaxcala's sovereignty and attempt to capture revenue. Had Cahuantzi not been from Tlaxcala, had he not been so intimately familiar with the state's history of struggles for sovereignty, he would not have been as compelled or prepared to defend Tlaxcala's rights. Macías, the lawyer defending Tlaxcala before national congress, likened Puebla's land grabs along the border with Tlaxcala to actions taken in less "civilized nations" such as "Central Africa." Both Cahuantzi and Macías emphasized the civilized status of Tlaxcalans, past and present, by invoking discourses about civilization and antiquity, as well as the racism that underpinned these discourses, evidenced by Macías's denigration of a nonexistent African nation. When they defended Tlaxcala's state sovereignty, Cahuantzi and Macías drew on national discourses to fulfill regional purposes, demonstrating how the rhetoric of late nineteenth-century nation-building was not limited to national actors and spaces. Materially, when Puebla claimed the Covadonga factory, Tlaxcala lost out on valuable tax revenue. But politically, by publishing the record of himself defending state sovereignty, and disseminating that record to every locality in Tlaxcala, the governor reminded Tlaxcalans of his local ties.

Cahuantzi's willingness to defend Tlaxcala's state sovereignty begs the question of whether he allowed districts and localities within Tlaxcala to do the same. Various localities in the south-central region—including the town of Ixtulco where Cahuantzi was from—had pursued statehood to protect their political autonomy and thwart Puebla's attempt to subsume them.[60] The administrative changes Cahuantzi made—creating a new central district and locating his power in Tlaxcala City—reflected how Cahuantzi acknowledged the long-standing authority of these towns, some of which traced their lineage to the pre-Hispanic era. Cahuantzi also recognized the threat that municipalities and localities posed to his own authority as governor. By evaluating the political dialogue that emerged during state and local elections, Cahuantzi made decisions about how he would manage these threats.

Elections and Patronage

Elections—both state and municipal—were opportunities for Díaz and Cahuantzi to gauge political dissent and make decisions about how to handle that dissent, whether through conciliation or patronage, or through more oppressive means. State elections, though rigged, opened important discursive spaces wherein residents voiced criticisms of the administration.[61] Municipal and town elections served the same purpose, though the degree to which Cahuantzi and his district prefects meddled in local political affairs depended on place, time, and political expediency.

The first election of Próspero Cahuantzi in 1885 garnered the usual pomposity of a Porfirian election, with officials expressing their "agreement and excitement" with the new leader.[62] Cahuantzi was "unanimously reelected" in 1888 after the Tlaxcala state legislature passed a constitutional amendment allowing governors to serve consecutive terms.[63] Subsequent state elections told a different story. President Díaz received dozens of letters in 1892 and again in 1896 calling for Cahuantzi's ouster. By the early 1890s, Díaz had abandoned his policy of "no reelection" of governors and had converted governorships throughout central Mexico into permanent appointments.[64] Since 1893 would mark Cahuantzi's third term in office, residents no doubt feared that Cahuantzi would become Tlaxcala's perpetual head of state. Like anyone who criticized the national patriarch's decisions, Cahuantzi's naysayers had to prostrate to Díaz while also communicating their grievances.[65] Some chose to remain anonymous, like one group of "various Tlaxcalans" who wrote to Díaz how "anyone but Mr. Don Próspero would work for the well-being and improvement of this state, where General Díaz has a friend in every resident and a supporter in every citizen."[66] Other critics alluded to Cahuantzi's background. Members of the "Club Central Tlaxcalteca," composed of Tlaxcalans living in Mexico City, used coded language to cast Cahuantzi as antiprogress. They contrasted the "imminently unpopular" Cahuantzi with the "peace" and "progress [under Díaz] . . . [that] had brought admiration [to Mexico] from the civilized world."[67] "[Under Cahuantzi]" they insisted "the state of Tlaxcala . . . has gone back in time."[68] While making clear how they "obey [Díaz's] authority," Juan González y González wrote briefly but urgently to Díaz: "We beg you sir to send someone whom you trust to travel through this state, and you will be convinced that there is not a single *pueblo* that accepts [Governor Próspero] Cahuantzi. For only one man should an entire *pueblo* be sacrificed?"[69]

Of all of the complaints Díaz received about Cahuantzi during the electoral period of 1892, the letter that contained the most signatures was sent from eighty-some hacendados in Huamantla and Puebla. Among the signatories were some of the region's most prominent landowning families, including members of the Bretón, Carbajal (or Carvajal), and Petricioli clans. Their main objection was that the governor had "imposed" Plutarco Montiel as prefect, one of Cahuantzi's "tiresome friends" (*pesados amigos*).[70] As the eyes and ears in the provinces, the jefe político, or district prefect, position was a vital one in Porfirian Mexico.[71] By the time Cahuantzi took office, Díaz had converted the jefe político position to one that was appointed rather than elected.[72] Montiel was precisely the sort of jefe político Díaz and Cahuantzi wanted in Huamantla. At eighty-some years old, Montiel had fought alongside Cahuantzi and Díaz against the French from 1864 to 1867. Because of his military background, Montiel was someone who both Díaz and Cahuantzi presumably trusted to watch over Huamantla, where it was clear that hacendados were not happy with Cahuantzi. Instead of the outsider Montiel, hacendados proposed Colonel Gregorio Nava as their district prefect, a military general and politician from Huamantla whose name had been previously batted around as a potential gubernatorial candidate.[73] The petitioners depicted Nava as "liberal, dignified, appropriate, desired and a friend [to Díaz]."[74] Díaz does not appear to have responded to most of the complaints he received about Cahuantzi, at least in written form. When a group of opponents tried to meet with Díaz in 1892, the president dismissed them after an ally of Cahuantzi convinced Díaz that they were merely "a group of troublemakers."[75]

The administrative changes made in Tlaxcala after residents complained about Cahuantzi during the electoral period of 1892 suggest that, while Díaz may not have responded to complainants directly, he read and heeded their letters. By 1893, Plutarco Montiel was out as district prefect in Huamantla.[76] Cahuantzi first replaced Montiel with Eduardo Audirac, a local school director in Huamantla. But he quickly dismissed Aurdirac after observing "irregularities" in his "conduct."[77] Díaz gave "thanks" to Cahuantzi for dismissing Aurdirac, indicating that he "hoped" [Audirac's replacement is] well-chosen by you [Cahuantzi], and that [Audirac's] substitute reflects the confidence I have placed in you [Cahuantzi] . . . [my] comrade and friend."[78] It was often the case that Díaz appointed jefes políticos directly. But the exchange between Díaz and Cahuantzi indicates how the president gave Cahuantzi latitude to make this district appointment himself, in a region in which many well-to-do residents opposed Cahuantzi, no less. In the end, Cahuantzi appointed Amado Balcázar, a merchant from Apizaco, as district prefect.[79] So, while the hacendados of Huamantla saw Montiel pushed out, they were nevertheless denied their chosen appointee.

In addition to jefe políticos, other political appointments that the governor controlled included that of secretary of state (*secretaría de gobierno*), state treasurer, and tax collectors (*recaudores de renta*). Within the judicial and legislative branches, Cahuantzi appointed district judges (*juez de primera estancia*). Governors were also allowed to nominate substitute candidates for the federal judiciary and congress.[80] Cahuantzi changed most of these positions when he took office.[81] In Huamantla, where Tlaxcala's most prominent hacendados lived—many of whom had made their dislike of Cahuantzi known to Díaz during the 1892 state elections—appointees included many hacendados, particularly to judgeships.[82] Cahuantzi installed more members of the influential landowning Bretón family in his administration, including in posts as assistant (*auxiliar*) to the district prefect and as district tax collector.[83] These appointments were clearly designed to quell dissent among landowning elites.

Tlaxcala's relative insignificance within the international export economy, as well as political turnover in Puebla, likely influenced Díaz's decision to keep Cahuantzi in office despite his naysayers. It was less economically vital, and therefore more possible, to use patronage to placate Tlaxcala's hacendados than the henequen barons of the Yucatán or cotton producers in the north. In 1892, Puebla was experiencing political tumult: Governor Rosendo Marquéz had fallen out of favor among elites in Puebla City, prompting Díaz to replace Márquez with Mucio Martínez.[84] Because Tlaxcala and Puebla were linked in many ways, it did not behoove Díaz to replace both governors simultaneously. Díaz may have also kept Cahuantzi in office because he had Cahuantzi play spy on Martínez, though these rumors were not substantiated by evidence.[85]

Cahuantzi countered his objectors by encouraging the formation of reelection clubs, some seventeen of which were created across the state. Reelection clubs published their enthusiastic approval for the governor along with their membership rolls in newspapers and broadsides.[86] Published membership rolls included Tlaxcalans from all walks of life, including the "*pueblos and fincas rústicas*" of the southern municipality of Nativitas and another club composed entirely of textile workers.[87] Since reelection clubs were used as political propaganda throughout Mexico during the Porfiriato, it is difficult to know whether a person's "membership" in a reelection club reflected genuine support for the governor. The mere existence of these reelection clubs nevertheless demonstrates how Cahuantzi acknowledged dissent against his regime and the need to counter this dissent publicly.

When patronage, negotiations, and other political mechanisms failed, Cahuantzi used violence against those who opposed his reelection. Librado López, a lawyer and landowner in southeastern Tlaxcala, was among those who wrote to Díaz to object to Cahuantzi's reelection in 1892 and again in 1896.[88] Díaz had personally recommended López for the position of official attorney (*procurador*) of the state supreme court in 1885, and Díaz and López remained in contact over the years.[89] López's varied business ventures in Tlaxcala—he attempted to open a factory in Tlaxcala City and requested to drain a large lake—were rebuffed by Cahuantzi for reasons that the historic record does not make clear.[90] Then in 1891, per Cahuantzi's request, Díaz refused a meeting with López in Mexico City.[91]

Cahuantzi and López's quarrel came to a head in 1898 when López was killed by then state treasurer Trinidad Vela Farfán.[92] In the months following López's death, an anonymous publication circulated throughout the state that honored López and blamed Cahuantzi for López's "assassination."[93] The publication lambasted Cahuantzi for his "absolute despotism," among other disparaging remarks.[94] Although there was no evidence that tied Cahuantzi directly to López's death, many locals, especially those from López's hometown of Ixtacuixtla, presumed that Cahuantzi had ordered his state treasurer to carry out the deed. The following November, residents of Ixtacuixtla protested the governor publicly. Cahuantzi requested arms to squash these and other protests that manifested during the state electoral period of 1899, most of which centered on the property tax increase that Cahuantzi implemented in 1897.[95] When protests got unruly, as one did in December 1899, Cahuantzi summoned the head of the rurales, Agustín García, to put it down.[96] As with Díaz, Cahuantzi's rule became more barefacedly undemocratic over time.[97]

This pattern is also glimpsed in how Cahuantzi handled local elections and electoral conflicts. The governor encroached on local level sovereignty and used violence to quell local electoral conflicts more in later years. Complaints from residents about corrupt and abusive officials, whether officially appointed or "elected," abound in the Tlaxcala state archive. Take for example the elections for agente municipal and *juez merino* (local judge) during the years 1885 and 1886 in the Ayuntamiento of Tlaxcala, the capital municipality. In this election, ten new agentes municipales were elected, one by each town, to the ayuntamiento.[98] Typically, three men—they were always men—were up for the position. Each member of the town's "electoral college" voted for their candidate, then their votes were tallied—literally by a vertical dash next to each of the candidate's names—and the results were sent to the ayuntamiento. In this election, no candidate ran uncontested, and a few of the races were close calls, with each town's candidate receiving a portion of the votes.

In this local election as in others, disagreements over results ensued. The townspeople of Metepec wrote to ayuntamiento officials pleading that the elected agente municipal Manuel Romero be "removed" from office because of the "abuses" that he imposed on their "once peaceful" town and his inability to "offer them protection."[99] Ayuntamiento officials responded in kind that they would overrule the electoral outcome and that another representative, suggested by the townspeople, would serve in Romero's place.[100] In Ayecac in 1885, townspeople complained directly to Cahuantzi that their neighbor Tepetitlán, a more populated town, manipulated municipal elections to make it so that all representatives to ayuntamiento leadership came from Tepetitlán and none from Ayecac. Ayecac residents, most illiterate, "begged" Cahuantzi to "order" the municipal president to name a resident of Ayecac as *alcalde* (local mayor) during the next term.[101] Later, in 1895, the governor overruled a different municipal president who imprisoned a townsperson after the townsperson was accused of falsifying his town's primary election results for ayuntamiento.[102]

These are only a few of numerous examples in the historic record that show how higher-level officials affected local electoral outcomes during this period. Even in cases where there was no documented conflict, it is almost assured that Cahuantzi pressed his appointed prefects to generate favorable local election results. This was standard practice throughout Mexico during the Porfiriato and later under the one-party rule of the Partido Revolucionario Institucional.[103] The existence of electoral competition, or even just the appearance of it, distinguished local elections from most presidential and gubernatorial races in which Díaz always, and gubernatorial appointees usually, ran unopposed. Most municipalities in Tlaxcala had functional *colegios electorales*, and localities vied for membership in these. In the conflict in Ayecac outlined above, when townspeople there were displeased with electoral results, they accused the neighboring town of Tepetitlán of hijacking the municipal election by manipulating the number of representatives they had serving in the colegio electoral. Their ire toward Tepetitlán indicates how the townspeople of Ayecac believed that they could exert real influence through representation in the colegio electoral.

Cahuantzi appears to have granted towns some electoral autonomy—but not always and not everywhere. The prolific correspondence between Cahuantzi and ayuntamiento officials in the municipality of Tlaxcala—especially between the governor and the municipal president—shows how Cahuantzi was keenly interested in managing politics there. The municipality of Tlaxcala contained the capital, which Cahuantzi aimed to revitalize in order to attract investment to the state.[104] By locating his power in Tlaxcala City, Cahuantzi also sought to dampen regional power brokers' autonomy in the populous towns surrounding the city, as well as force northern hacendados to travel south on occasion to have an audience with the governor. It was thus essential that Cahuantzi had a municipal president in Tlaxcala who would carry out his and Díaz's agenda. Rafael Anzures held the post of municipal president of Tlaxcala from 1901 through the end of Cahuantzi's rule.[105] Prior to this post, Anzures was prefect for the central area of Calpulalpan also under Cahuantzi.[106] The length of his tenure coupled with his previous appointment strongly implies that the governor had a hand in appointing Anzures as municipal president in Tlaxcala City.

Because local electoral records were not organized in any standardized fashion during the nineteenth century, and incidents of electoral corruption were not consistently recorded in the written record, it is difficult to know the extent to which Cahuantzi influenced local electoral outcomes. Cahuantzi's unique familiarity with the local political landscape—specifically how ayuntamientos prized their sovereignty and had fought for statehood to protect it—probably made Cahuantzi reluctant to flout municipalities' political autonomy. But the preponderance of local electoral conflicts coupled with increased public protests and violence in the early 1900s point to municipalities losing more political autonomy as Cahuantzi's and Díaz's rule became more entrenched. In the municipality of Tzompantepec, in front of an audience of district and local officials and municipal residents, Cahuantzi declared the 1902 elections there "null."[107] In the early twentieth century, antigovernment protests, particularly over the issue of taxation, broke out in Tzompantepec and in other southern, village-dominated municipalities.[108] News of protests reached Díaz's desk, as well.[109] Although nothing in the historic record indicates as much, nullifying Tzompantepec's elections was undoubtedly a way for Cahuantzi to counter antigovernment protests there. Overall, though, Cahuantzi used patronage and other back-door channels to build the local roots of his authoritarian regime, and it was rare for Cahuantzi to brazenly overturn municipal election results as he did in Tzompantepec. That he did was a clear sign that he was losing his grip on his state.

Conclusion

Cahuantzi was the rare locally born Porfirian governor who was unwaveringly loyal to Díaz and remained in power for consecutive terms. Cahuantzi's extensive familiarity with local circumstances past and present allowed him to face down challenges to his rule, defend his state's sovereignty from Puebla, and engage patronage effectively. And yet, complaints sent to Díaz about the governor, often during electoral periods, make clear how Cahuantzi was viewed by many in and around Tlaxcala as an inappropriate, even a terrible choice to lead. For the Poblanos who desired to control their neighbor's affairs, Cahuantzi was too Tlaxcalan. For large landowners, Cahuantzi was not educated, wealthy, or "civilized" enough. For the small landowners and villagers of the south-central Nativitas Valley, Cahuantzi was a threat to municipal political autonomy. However, it was precisely Cahuantzi's ability to harness his local knowledge, while remaining unaligned with any one political group, that anchored his long-term rule.

FOUR

Litigating Water

Just before midnight on a Saturday evening in September, the people of central Tlaxcala were awoken by the sounds of police alarms and shouts as waters from the Zahuapan River were "invading" the city. The *Periódico Oficial de Tlaxcala* described that a "panic had gripped families" as they fled their homes "looking for safety in the higher elevations and hills that encircled the capital." According to the newspaper's report, the cause of the flood had been the "torrential rain that had not ceased since the early morning hours." Over the course of the day, water levels had "risen prodigiously," eventually "breaking the sides [of the river], furiously plunging into cemeteries, destroying and carrying away everything it found in its path." Eventually, the water encountered a bridge that "served as a dike" repressing the floods, but not before widespread inundations caused serious damage.[1] The most severe destruction was done to the towns and neighborhoods that lay directly along the riverbanks. These spaces contained smaller, individually owned properties (*terrenos rústicos* or *pequeñas propiedades*), as well as some municipal-owned lands used for communal purposes (described often as *de la corporación*).[2] In other towns, crops had been destroyed, sheep drowned, and trees—a vital source of timber—pulled from the roots by the violent winds that accompanied the torrential rains. The *Periódico Oficial de Tlaxcala* depicted a particularly horrific incident in which the "current overtook a man, a woman, a young boy, and the 332 sheep that they cared for."[3] The ranchos and haciendas adjacent to smaller towns were also ravaged by floodwaters.[4] Water broke through myriad dams, levies, and dikes that landowners had constructed to irrigate crops and help control water levels during the tumultuous hydrological seasons. On the Hacienda Rosario, water wrecked river embankments and took out a bridge. Residents' travel on and between El Rosario and other properties was impeded as a result. The few factories in the area also incurred damages. At the textile factories La Josefina and La Tlaxcalteca, "water rose more than a meter from the surface, destroying [the factories'] dams . . . the repairs [for which] will be long and costly."[5] An aqueduct located on the factory El Valor was destroyed, as was all of the work that "owners had undertaken to construct a railroad to connect with the Panzacola [rail] station."[6]

Floods like the one that occurred in 1888 throw into relief how water—whether too little, or more often, too much—had always been a problem in Tlaxcala.[7] This chapter lays out the water-related laws and practices, and problems and conflicts, that existed in Tlaxcala in the late nineteenth century. The next chapter then explains how Cahuantzi managed natural resource reforms to placate residents—most of whom were small and middling landowners—while advancing the authoritarian modernization project. Neither colonial customs nor nineteenth-century federal law legitimated state authority in water-related matters. Yet Cahuantzi understood that his political viability was in some part shaped by his ability to control how residents used the waterscape, which had been precarious for centuries. Together, the chapters reveal the role that water politics played in buttressing Cahuantzi and Díaz's long-term rule.[8]

State Water Management

During his twenty-six years as governor, Cahuantzi significantly increased the state's role in water management in Tlaxcala. He did this by reinforcing centuries-old water mores, known as the communal order of water, to mitigate larger land and factory owners' water access and to prevent flooding. Cahuantzi could have let large land and factory owners steal as much water as they cared to. Instead, he expected water users, especially those with financial capability, to acknowledge and help sustain water as a shared good.

Beginning with and because of colonialism, Tlaxcalans lived in a hydrologically perilous environment. Unlike their Nahua brethren in the Teotihuacán Valley, Tlaxcalans made few attempts to control their waterscape prior to the arrival of Hernán Cortés in their *altepetl* (city-state) in 1519.[9] It was only after the Spanish invasion of Tenochtitlán that Tlaxcalans began their interminable fight against the "fluvial beast," the Zahuapan River.[10] Unlike pre-Hispanic Tlaxcalans who built their neighborhoods atop the hills surrounding the Nativitas Valley, the colonial administration built the region's new capital, Tlaxcala City, squarely in the floodplain of the Zahuapan River valley.[11] Erosion and the expansion of wetlands during the colonial era worsened flood events.[12] Despite using innovative engineering techniques such as reservoirs and dikes to control the riverbed, as well as ample Indigenous manpower, floods worsened in the eighteenth and into the nineteenth centuries. The Spanish governor of provincial Tlaxcala lamented how Tlaxcala City's "greatest enemy . . . [was] the voluminous river that passes nearby called the Zahuapan."[13]

Population recovery, high population density, and socioeconomic diversity, coupled with increased demands on waterways for irrigation projects and power, exacerbated the region's water problems in the late nineteenth century.[14] Across Mexico, the Porfirians built dams, created larger irrigation channels and networks, and drained lakes to improve hygiene and create more productive lands.[15] The administration's crowning achievement was the completion of the colonial-era Desagüe General del Valle de México (General Drainage of the Valley of Mexico, or the draining of the central Mexican lake basin) in Mexico City.[16] To Porfiristas, the desagüe epitomized man's ability to dominate the environment, and therefore, to be a modern nation-state.[17] Other regions were targeted for development, as well. In the Laguna region, or region of lakes surrounding the Nazas River in Chihuahua, Coahuila, and Durango, the Porfirian administration collaborated with hacendados to build dams that facilitated cotton production.[18] Cotton, along with sugar, coffee, and henequen, fueled Mexico's burgeoning export economy.[19]

Although Tlaxcala was not heralded for its contributions to national development during the Porfiriato, competition over water resources was fierce there, and the conflicts that resulted were often intense. Water users in Tlaxcala's populous southeastern region, known as the Nativitas or Zahuapan River valley, relied on Tlaxcala's two rivers, the Zahuapan and the Atoyac. These rivers and their streams formed the beginning of the larger Balsas Watercourse at the base of the Malintzin mountain (see map 2).[20] The vast majority of Tlaxcalans lived in the Nativitas Valley, where small and middling farmers shared water with haciendas, mills, and increasingly, factories. Like most rural Mexicans, most Tlaxcalans did not have access to potable, piped water.[21] Peoples' everyday activities—bathing, cooking, and laundry—usually required naturally occurring water, which they obtained from wells and springs, some naturally occurring, others man-made. Owners of smaller properties constructed *canales* (embanked lots) and other water infrastructure such as dams and dikes to irrigate lands and to power dozens of small mills and aguardiente factories.[22]

As compared to smaller outlets such as mills, larger-scale irrigation projects and factories used much more river water and caused more damage to the waterscape. Between 1876 and 1901, ten textile and glass factories were built in Tlaxcala (see table 2). Larger land and factory owners constructed river deviations, dams, and other infrastructural apparatuses to siphon off large quantities of water, which in turn fueled steam engines, hydraulic motors, and eventually hydroelectric dams.[23] As a result, during the rainy season, levees broke, and riverbeds and reservoirs overflowed. During the dry season, new water infrastructure exacerbated water scarcity. Factory owners insisted that their water use did not affect natural water levels. Many farmers disagreed.

TABLE 2. Textile factories in Tlaxcala (1905–1906). Source: Data from Memoria de la Administración Pública del Estado, 1893; La Antigua República (Tlaxcala), Semanario de política, variedades y anuncios, 29 July 1906, 48; Diana López Martínez, "La construcción de una nueva territorialidad a través de los usos del agua: El caso de la región del Rio Zahuapan (1888–1919)," Master's thesis, Instituto de Investigaciones Dr. José María Luis Mora, 2013, 64, 74.

Factory	Year Inaugurated	River	Owners
San Manuel	1876	Zahuapan	Compañía Mexicana Manufacturera "Sociedad Anónima" (Mier family)
El Valor (& La Alsacia)	1877	Atoyac	Gavito family
La Josefina	1881	Atoyac	Letona family
La Tlaxcalteca	1883	Atoyac	Gavito family
La Trinidad	1884	Zahuapan	Ignacio Morales Benítez
Santa Elena	1888	Zahuapan	Quintín Gómez & Conde family
La Xicoténcatl	1894	Zahuapan	Concha family
San Luis Apizaquito	1899	Zahuapan	Ángel Solana
La Estrella	1900	Zahuapan	Agustín del Pozo
La Providencia	1901	Zahuapan	Concha family

Throughout the Porfirian period, Tlaxcalans complained interminably and constantly about their neighbors' water use. Neighbors often accused each other of using more than their fair share of water. Poblanos also protested, factory owners especially, who insisted that their neighbors upstream in Tlaxcala lowered the natural water levels thereby causing their power sources to fail. Complaints about water in the Nativitas Valley did not really diminish until the 1930s and 1940s when motorized groundwater pumping and larger dams lessened the extent to which individuals depended on nearby rivers or lakes.[24] But even then, Tlaxcala City and its environs faced, and continue to face, problems with floods.

Increased water usage during the Porfiriato disrupted what was known as the communal order of water, a usufruct water management system that had existed since colonial times.[25] The communal order of water functioned as a moral economy whereby administrators imposed "mutual obligations and expectations" on water users in exchange for their usage rights.[26] During the colonial and early national periods, municipal governments managed, and collected fees on, residents' water usage.[27] Before independence, the crown technically "owned" the colony's waters and leased out their access, granting *mercedes de agua* (grants of water shares) and *repartimientos de agua* (distributions of water shares).[28] For the purposes of daily usage, water was considered a shared good, in contrast to land, which could be owned privately and exclusively.[29] Although naturally occurring water was inherently shared, municipal officials were able to grant exclusive rights to a water access site (*toma de agua*). These sites were usually located along a river or a lake, or sometimes a well. Determinations over who could access a toma de agua were negotiated between private parties and arbitrated by municipal officials. Under the communal order of water, when a person's toma de agua was located on private property, the municipality had the right to require the landowner to share the toma with surrounding residents, by constructing a channel or dike to increase the public water supply or to prevent flooding, for example.[30] When a toma de agua was positioned on public lands owned by the ayuntamiento, and a landowner wanted to access it, residents were required to petition the ayuntamiento.

For Cahuantzi, as state governor, disruptions to the communal order of water were problematic because they aggravated residents, caused expensive infrastructural damage, and stunted modernization. Hundreds of letters exchanged between state and local officials and residents during the Porfirian period make clear how municipalities had been struggling to handle water problems on their own. Water infrastructure was failing throughout the region and municipalities were often unable to cover costly repairs. During the rainy season of 1888 alone, municipal and district officials sent dozens of letters to the governor expressing their fears about high water levels on the Atoyac and the Zahuapan.[31] Problems with water management were so bad in the southern town of Zacatelco that water users, including hacendados from both Puebla and Tlaxcala, as well as neighborhood and municipal representatives, came together to write to the governor about the Zahuapan River's shoddy levees.[32] Zacatelco area residents relayed how "each year [we] run great risks with the volume of water" in the Atoyac, and they feared that during the next rainy season "the Zahuapan River levee [would not be able to contain] the water's rise."[33] A few years later, that very region would be racked by the flood of 1888 that opened this chapter.

Soon after taking office, Cahuantzi took what had previously been usufruct practices under municipal domain and codified them into state law. Although municipalities, not the state, granted water access rights, the governor could nevertheless impose requirements on those who had been granted those rights. Cahuantzi's gubernatorial predecessor, Mariano Grajales, did this to some extent in 1881 when he issued two state ordinances pertaining to water.[34] One ordinance informed residents that they needed to take care of water infrastructure to prevent flooding. The other required residents to share outside wells with surrounding neighbors. Cahuantzi clarified and extended these provisions in a decree he announced in 1885. The purpose of the decree was to "avoid the losses and other damages that for many years [have caused] farmers' suffering . . . along the margins of the Zahuapan, Atoyac, and Atl-xextla Rivers." The governor called for extensive repairs to water infrastructure along the Zahuapan and Atoyac Rivers, as well as the construction of new walls and other reinforcements that would deter flooding. Cahuantzi established "committees" headed by district prefects who would "monitor the projects" and in turn appoint three people from each locality to report to them.[35]

A central purpose of the decree was to involve individual property owners, especially those with economic means, in the construction and maintenance of water infrastructure. Article 4 of the decree stated that individual landowners had a "strict obligation . . . if necessary . . . to plant trees along the walls [of the river] to reinforce them." Article 5 instructed property owners to "clean out . . . rocks and dead sticks" from the rivers "that impede the free flow of waters" during the dry months. Article 6 "expressly prohibited, under the penalty of a 10 or 20 peso fine, cutting down trees that upheld river walls or allowing cattle [to pasture in these areas] . . . which destroy the walls." Likewise, if a crack appeared in a wall that girded a river along an individual owner's property, Article 7 "required [the landowner or landowners to repair it] . . . or pay for a replacement." The decree also restricted the size of irrigation trenches. In cases where water trenches crossed through a public road, owners were obligated to build a "solid bridge, five yards in width" and "maintain it in perfect service . . . to allow for free passage for all." Lastly, any dam built to facilitate irrigation could only exist during a "permitted time" and "had to be built in such a way that it could be easily destroyed [when not in use] and did not alter the riverbed." After the decree went into effect in December 1885, Cahuantzi embarked on several tours to survey regions that had been damaged by floods.[36] A few years later, in June 1888, the governor sent out a circular to municipal presidents, calling on them to take the "necessary measures" to secure river embankments during periods of heavy rainfall.[37] Municipalities, in turn, passed this information on to agentes municipales.[38]

Usufruct water laws had always provided that, in exchange for municipalities granting them private water rights access, water users had to contribute to the maintenance of the general water supply in some way.[39] Yet it was rare for states to involve themselves in water arbitration, given how they did not collect money on water usage rights.[40] The stipulations that Cahuantzi imposed on water users make clear how he understood that water was a high-stakes political and environmental issue in Tlaxcala. He also understood that free-flowing water was shared and limited, and he was willing to use the state apparatus to hold water users accountable to long-standing usufruct practices. In addition to enhancing state authority vis-à-vis water, through the 1885 decree, Cahuantzi created a new state revenue stream by endowing the state with the capacity to levy fines on those who did not adhere to water use regulations.

Of the many Tlaxcalans who wrote to Cahuantzi after the 1885 decree went into effect, hacendados were the most aggrieved. Since they used large quantities of water, hacendados were expected to build and fund water-related infrastructure projects in accordance with the 1885 decree and the communal order of water. The years-long disagreement between two landowners, Francisco Sela and Plinio Petricioli, exemplifies one of these grievances. Both Sela and Petricioli vehemently denied that their use of the Atoyac River was what caused surrounding lands—which included various small and communal holdings—to flood. Sela insisted that he did "not oppose" Cahuantzi's 1885 declaration.[41] Yet he also alleged that it was Petricioli's mill that was "producing the floods . . . that attract attention from the press and make [flooding problems] known to the public."[42] Sela accused Petricioli of moving the properties' boundary markers and indicted him for lacking "*el carácter de la servidumbre*" because he refused "to fix damages [that] he . . . or another person . . . caused."[43] Petricioli fired back that Sela "was not familiar with the situation at hand" and that he had already moved the dam Sela believed was causing the problem.[44] Higher water levels present in the Atoyac were "natural" as "sand" accumulated in the river, Petricioli explained.[45] Petricioli also insisted that Sela let his "cattle drink water from the river . . . which provoke more and more floods."[46] By way of conclusion, Petricioli appealed to the governor that "I [Petricioli] accept the [decree of December 16, 1885], but I respectfully request that you [Cahuantzi] make Sr. Sela comply with the law, [as] he has always tried to disobey it."[47]

Cahuantzi framed water infrastructure as a public benefit driven by private initiative. By imposing regulations on water use, the governor hoped to develop and modernize Tlaxcala and capture revenue while also preventing floods. But water users did not always assent to the burden the 1885 decree imposed on them to repair and replace water infrastructure using personal, rather than government, resources. In the end, Petricioli ended up paying $280 MXN to repair infrastructure along the Atoyac a few months after his exchange with Sela.[48] In July 1887, Petricioli's lawyer wrote to the state asking for an "indemnity payment" to cover the costs incurred.[49] While the state acknowledged that it received Petricioli's request, the historic record does not make clear whether the state remunerated Petricioli. Neither of these landowners opposed the 1885 decree outright in their correspondence. Yet, as will be explained, both men were among the dozens of landowners who petitioned the federal government for exclusive water access rights after some of Mexico's waterways were federalized by the Ley sobre vías generales de comunicación in 1888.[50] Both Sela and Petricioli likely hoped that they could evade the state's stipulations once the waterways they used transferred from municipal to federal domain. However, members of the Petricioli-Kennedy family, Francisco Sela, and many others continued to deal with the governor and other regional parties who obstructed their water access even after the federal government affirmed their water rights.[51]

Federalizing Water

Water laws changed drastically in June 1888 when the federal government passed the Ley sobre vías generales de comunicación (hereafter referred to as the Waters Law of 1888), the first federal law to regulate water in Mexico. The Waters Law of 1888 gave the federal government, represented by the Porfirian Development Ministry (Secretaría de Fomento), the power to grant private water concessions along navigable waterways or waterways that constituted borders between states or countries.[52] All other waterways remained under erstwhile usufruct laws (*servidumbre de aguas*). Through the law, Porfirian nation-builders aimed to facilitate dam construction and other modernization projects.[53] The law was also designed to bring in more tax revenue to federal, rather than municipal, coffers, as had been the custom under usufruct laws.[54] In Tlaxcala, however, the Waters Law produced a legal and environmental quagmire. Large land and factory owners such as Sela and Petricioli wrote to the Secretaría de Fomento, asking for the federal government to grant them private water access, hoping that the law would allow them to shirk water-related requirements imposed on them by Cahuantzi and other regional and local officials. Yet the law's unclear stipulations caused innumerable conflicts. Through these conflicts, Cahuantzi found ways to interfere with, and sometimes stymy, residents' water access requests.

When applied in Tlaxcala, many aspects of the Waters Law of 1888 were befuddling. To begin, the Waters Law separated the jurisdictions of Tlaxcala's two main rivers, the Atoyac and the Zahuapan. Since the Atoyac River divided Tlaxcala and Puebla states, the law federalized it. Henceforth the Secretaría de Fomento arbitrated conflicts and made decisions about private access rights on the Atoyac. The Zahuapan, in contrast, remained under local jurisdiction. The definition of navigable was also nebulous. It often confused Tlaxcalans how a waterway's navigability, which varied based on season and location, determined a waterway's jurisdiction. When the Waters Law federalized the Atoyac, the law inferred the Atoyac to be navigable. The Zahuapan, in contrast, according to the Waters Law, was not considered navigable, and its jurisdiction remained municipal as it always had been.

Yet the separation of the two rivers based on their navigability did not reflect Tlaxcalans' lived reality, since some Tlaxcalans considered the Zahuapan to be more navigable than the Atoyac. Many factories and haciendas drew water from the Zahuapan, rather than from the Atoyac, during the dry season.[55] After the Secretaría de Fomento denied Gerardo Emilio Herrerias access rights to the locally managed Zahuapan for his textile mill, Herrerias indicated to the Secretaría de Fomento that he "did not agree" with the federal decision and insisted that "a more thorough study" would no doubt reveal how the Zahuapan "is navigable."[56] The Waters Law similarly failed to mention whether streams or tributaries were navigable. This made it difficult to determine who was responsible for their management. Those who owned multiple properties and used waters from both rivers—such as Alfredo and Bernardo Caso, who had three farms that drew water from the Atoyac and one from the Zahuapan—were frustrated by having to manage separate bureaucratic processes.[57] That the Atoyac and the Zahuapan ran so close together and eventually formed part of the same watercourse made it even more vexing (see map 2).

The Waters Law also imposed new provisions on federal water users that encouraged the involvement of regional parties in water management. Article 2 of the law specified that "Riverside residents will have free use of the waters that they need for their domestic purposes." Moreover, petitioners asking for private water access rights had to provide "legitimate titles" or, failing these, they had to prove that they had been using the water source for ten years. The Secretaría de Fomento would only grant exclusive rights to a water access point—even on a federalized river such as the Atoyac—when the request did not "threaten or alter the course of the rivers or canals" or affect residents' water usage downstream. The law concluded by stating that any complication that violated the "communal order" of water, or any conflict "between private parties" would be handled by the "appropriate local jurisdiction" rather than the federal Secretaría de Fomento.[58]

The federal government may have passed the 1888 Waters Law to centralize Mexico's waterways and grant water concessions to export producers as occurred in la Laguna. But, in places like Tlaxcala, where international export production barely existed, and less was at stake for Mexico's national finances and its international reputation, the federal government did not care as much about the law's consequences. The people who enforced the laws in Tlaxcala were those who were apprised of local geography, conditions, and relationships on the ground. Determining whether a petitioner met the law's requirements nearly always necessitated local parties' input. Because of its ambiguities, the Federal Waters Law in some instances enhanced the ability of state and local officials and private parties to interfere in water disputes.

Petitions from water users in Tlaxcala to the Secretaría de Fomento between 1888 and 1910—the twenty-two years in which some of Mexico's waterways were federalized while others remained under local jurisdiction—affirm these arguments. Approximately fifty files can be found in the Archivo Histórico del Agua in which a petitioner, most often a hacendado or textile factory owner—residents who relied on large quantities of water—wrote to the Secretaría de Fomento asking for private waterway access in Tlaxcala. Petitioners usually requested to build a dam, canal, or pipeline, or to expand one of these. The summation of petitions presented in table 3 makes clear why an owner of a larger property or factory wanted the federal government to confirm their water access rights: doing so, they likely hoped, would streamline their requests and get regional administrators and their stipulations off their backs.

Yet few petitions passed federal muster, regardless of whether petitioners requested access to the federally managed Atoyac or the municipally managed Zahuapan. Much to their chagrin, dozens of water users along the Zahuapan received the notice that "I [the Secretaría de Fomento] have the honor of informing you [the petitioner] that the river about which you inquire is not of federal jurisdiction."[59] Even along the federalized Atoyac, regional parties often worked to obstruct petitions after the Secretaría de Fomento granted a petitioner exclusive water access. Petitioners' neighbors usually complained that opening another toma de agua would alter the natural water level, resulting in one of two problems, depending on the season: the toma would either flood nearby lands, or it would diminish the communal water supply.

When complainants had the latter concern—diminishing the communal water supply—they charged that neighbors were using more than their fair share of water. In Tlaxcala, attempting to determine one's fair share of water was a challenging and inherently subjective endeavor. Most Tlaxcalans did not have the same kind of financial backing, either from the federal government or foreign investors, as those building hydraulic infrastructure in the Valley of Mexico or the Laguna region.[60] Water users in Tlaxcala often paid for infrastructural projects out of their own pockets. It was not until 1910 that the Secretaría de Fomento comprehensively assessed and mapped the Tlaxcala-Puebla water basin, published as *Carta de las cuencas hidrográficas del Estado de Tlaxcala* (see map 4). Only when a waterway was federalized, and the federal government began to levy a tax on water users based on the liters of water they used, did the Secretaría de Fomento begin to record reliable statistics about individuals' water use. So, water use along the locally managed Zahuapan River would not be systematically tracked and recorded until after the river was federalized in 1919.[61]

As compared to export-oriented regions during this period, attempts to regulate Tlaxcala's water were done on a case-by-case basis. Federal and local case files contain myriad exemplars of these attempts. Petitions to the Secretaría de Fomento, housed today in the Archivo Histórico del Agua, include elaborate mathematical calculations, blueprints, and maps that petitioners and engineers used to puzzle out users' fair share of water. Hacendados and factory owners hired notaries, lawyers, and engineers to compose these documents. Local documentation, housed today in the Archivo Histórico del Estado de Tlaxcala, contains schema and maps, as well. In contrast to federal petitions, locally produced documentation was usually composed by petitioners themselves. A sketch of a riverway and its dams and dikes appeared rudimentary by comparison to an elaborate blueprint drawn to scale by a federal engineer. Yet locally produced maps were often quite exact, drawn as they were by the people who inhabited and used the waterscape every day. Because of their accuracy, copies of local schema and maps can also be found in the federal petitions.

The federal government did not target Tlaxcala for national development. At the same time, though, Tlaxcala was no backwater. After all, Mexico's first railroad ran right through the region. Puebla City lay just to the south, Mexico City to the west. Plenty of people saw Tlaxcala as a desirable place to invest. Businessman Sebastian Mier wrote to the Secretaría de Fomento in 1899 to draw attention to the "increased number of requests coming into the Ejecutivo de la Unión to use [Atoyac and Zahuapan River] waters as irrigation or motor power."[62] Mier exalted the "Atoyac and Zahuapan Rivers" as "present[ing] important services to the textile and agricultural industries in the states of Puebla and Tlaxcala."[63] He emphasized that "[use of the Atoyac and Zahuapan Rivers] constitutes one of the primary sources of wealth of the federation. The considerable progress that [the textile and agricultural industries] have recently achieved, has

TABLE 3. Petitions from water users in Tlaxcala state to the Secretaría de Fomento (1888–1910). Source: Data from Archivo Histórico del Agua, Aprovechamientos Superficiales.

Petitioner	Factory/Property	Waterway/Year	Jurisdiction	Federal Response	State Response Summary
Commission of Water Users from Puebla	La Josefina & Tlaxcalteca (Textile factories)	Atoyac/1907	Federal	Use granted	Various complaints from surrounding water users; ordered to fix river embankments; ordered to build new dam
Bernardo & Alfredo Caso	Haciendas (hac.) Santa Clara, San Antonio, Santa Barbara	Atoyac/1900	Federal	Use for irrigation granted	Various complaints; under investigation through 1910–
Bernardo & Alfredo Caso	Hac. Santo Tomas	Zahuapan/1902	State	Contact state	Complaints of taking too much water; engineers to inspect; under investigation through 1919–
Trinidad Vela Farfán	Rancho San Isidro	Zahuapan/1917 (previous petitions sent to state only)	State	Contact state	Ordered to stop expanding river causeway, damaging community lands; under investigation through 1918–
Concepción Petricioli/Kennedy family	Hacienda San Juan del Molino; San Juan Atoyac	Atoyac/1902	Federal	Use granted	Complaints of taking too much water; engineers to inspect; under investigation through 1919–
Baldonero Rejón	Various agrarian properties	Atoyac/1902	Federal	Use for irrigation granted	Complaints of taking too much water; engineers to inspect
Ignacio Morales Benítez, Manuel M. Conde	Hac. Santiago Michac; La Trinidad (textile factory)	Atoyac/1905	Federal	Use granted	Complaints of taking too much water; engineers to inspect
José Díaz Rubin	Covadonga (Textile factory; located in Puebla but Tlaxcala disputes Puebla's jurisdiction)	Atoyac/1891	Federal	Use granted	Complaints of taking too much water; engineers to inspect; under investigation through 1960s
José Cuesta Mendizabal	Santo Domingo factory (Puebla); toma de agua "San Lorenzo"	Atoyac & Zahuapan/1898	Federal & State	Federal use granted	Use blocked by state, other water users; complaints of flooding nearby villages, taking too much water

Francisco Fernández Ibarra	Hac. Atotonilco	Atoyac/1895	Federal	Use granted	Complaints from water users, taking too much water; engineers to inspect; case archived in 1901
C. Librado López	Various properties	Lake Acuitlapilco/1897	Undeclared	None	López not permitted to drain the lake
Blas Reguero y Caso	Hac. Los Santos Reyes & San Joaquín	Zahuapan/1898	State	Contact state	Not found
Mariano Muñoz	Hac. De la Compañía	Atoyac/1902; 1905	Federal	First request granted; subsequent request to open another toma blocked, per advice of state	Complaints that Muñoz destroying village lands; ordered to make repairs; under investigation through 1908
Gerardo Emilio Herrerias	New textile factory in San Pablo Apetatitlán town	Zahuapan/1896; 1905	State	Contact state	Not found
Pablo Escandón	Hac./Mill San Diego Apetlahuaya	Zahuapan/1901	State	Contact state	Access denied

elevate[d] the value of these waters."[64] As both a land and factory owner in Tlaxcala, as well as a diplomat under Díaz, Mier likely had the finances and influence to hire the cadre of professionals necessary to calculate, map, and construct water infrastructure.[65] Díaz had even visited the irrigation channels Mier had built by deviating water from the Atoyac.[66]

But laws, codes, regulations, and maps did not necessarily make water arbitration easier. Moreover, knowledge and experts, as helpful as some felt they were, could not radically transform Tlaxcala's waterscape, which had endured centuries of human abuse. The first attempt to survey the Zahuapan-Atoyac watercourse in Tlaxcala by a federal engineer—at least since the advent of new factories there—exemplifies this argument. The survey, which took place in 1904, was sparked by complaints from factory owners in Puebla who alleged that Tlaxcalans "upstream" were "repress[ing]" their water and were thus in violation of the 1888 Federal Waters Law.[67] The industrialists shot fiery claims at their neighbors. They insisted that for "years" Tlaxcalans had been increasing the height of their dams and raising "provisional infrastructure" such as water holding tanks.[68] Recently, though, the "abuses" their neighbors were committing were becoming "truly alarming . . . [with] lamentable consequences." Lower water levels meant that factory machines in Puebla could not run. Production had stagnated as a result, and unpaid workers threatened to "resist."[69] The factory owners insisted that the situation posed "a danger for the state [of Puebla]."[70]

In 1904, the Secretaría de Obras Públicas (Ministry of Public Works) sent civil engineer Ramón de Ibarrola to inspect the Atoyac-Zahuapan watercourse. Ibarrola had previously inspected the Atoyac River in the Atlixco region of Puebla, as well as the Laguna.[71] Ibarrola's review of the Zahuapan-Atoyac region lay bare the paradoxes of the 1888 Waters Law as it was applied in Tlaxcala-Puebla. The engineer surmised that agriculturalists were taking too much water for irrigation. He also observed that farmers' water usage was going unregulated.[72] Ibarrola wrote that "water used to power industrial establishments . . . returns to the riverbed [so] the water level does not diminish, but, the same does not occur with water that [is used] for agriculture, the majority of which is absorbed by irrigation."[73] The engineer emphasized how "each individual should exercise their right [to water] in such a way that does not impede or hinder the right of others."[74] He concurrently stressed that "it is not possible for [Atoyac River users] to enjoy the same advantages [during the dry season] as during the

FIGURE 8. Deviation dam "San Diego" over the Zahuapan River. Source: CONAGUA-AHA, Aprovechamientos superficiales, Caja 141, Expediente 19590, Legajo 1, Foja 45 (1911).

rainy season," and that "textile factories" should expect "lower production rates . . . from the moment in which the river goes down . . . during the dry season."[75] In a subsequent report, Ibarrola noted how residents "further northwards" extracted water from the Zahuapan River during the times when the Atoyac "does not have a drop of water" during the difficult dry season.[76] Ibarrola concluded his reports in 1904 by recommending a "punishment" for those who abused water, including suspension of their water access.[77] The Secretaría de Fomento mandated that river users present land titles. They further "prohibit[ed] the damming of waters for reasons [discussed in the report]," specifying that "damming should not interrupt factories' work."[78]

In response to Ibarrola's reports, textile manufacturers, landowners of all kinds, and municipal representatives sent their land titles to corroborate ownership and defend their water use.[79] One water user located upstream from the complainants indicated that his factory in Amatlán did not use the Atoyac, but rather one of its *afluentes*, a stream that ran from it, which he called by its own name, the San Francisco River.[80] The owner expressed that, if the Secretaría de Fomento were to rule that the San Francisco

River was part of the federal Atoyac, he would "comply with Ibarrola's orders."[81] However, determining whether a stream met the Waters Law's criteria often required vigorous scrutiny and analysis.[82] The Secretaría de Fomento does not appear to have sent a reply to this defendant. The owner of the factory in Amatlán likely went on to use water as he always had.

The inconclusiveness of Ibarrola's report speaks to the ongoing hydrological challenges in Tlaxcala. In August 1907, the Secretaría de Fomento closed the complainants' file after it appeared that they had not pursued the case further. In a concluding document, an engineer summarized that "all of the factories dam the water and as a result[,] any infrastructural project that diverts [the river water] will have to introduce appropriate modifications."[83] But the pages-long case file does not specify what those modifications ought to be.

In Tlaxcala during the Porfiriato, more technically advanced ways of augmenting the water supply, such as motorized ground pumping and potable water and sewer systems, had yet to be deployed, at least effectively. Most people relied on free-flowing, naturally occurring waterways. Modern engineering during the late nineteenth century could not conjure up more water. Meanwhile, water infrastructure could not effectively prevent floods while residents like Mier were extracting more water than ever before. Factories' water consumption peaked during the Porfiriato, as over time, factories came to rely more on electricity.[84]

After federal engineers like Ibarrola left town, the people left to manage Tlaxcala's capricious water supply were those who governed, lived, and worked there. When mill owner Gerardo Emilio Herrerias petitioned the federal government for access rights along the Zahuapan River, the Secretaría de Fomento denied his request, given that the Waters Law had not changed the Zahuapan River from municipal to federal domain. Yet, in their reply to Herrerias, the Secretaría de Fomento advised him to consult with his state government instead of the appropriate municipality.[85] Legally, states had no jurisdiction over waterways. Cahuantzi came to press his influence in water-related matters, nonetheless. In part, Cahuantzi was able to leverage his will in water-related disputes because he was the appointee of the national dictator. However, Cahuantzi's ties to Díaz do not fully explain how and why the state came to press its authority in water-related disputes. The actions the governor took during his first years in office demonstrate how Cahuantzi was aware of his state's water problems. He also understood how fixing these problems, or at least tempering them,

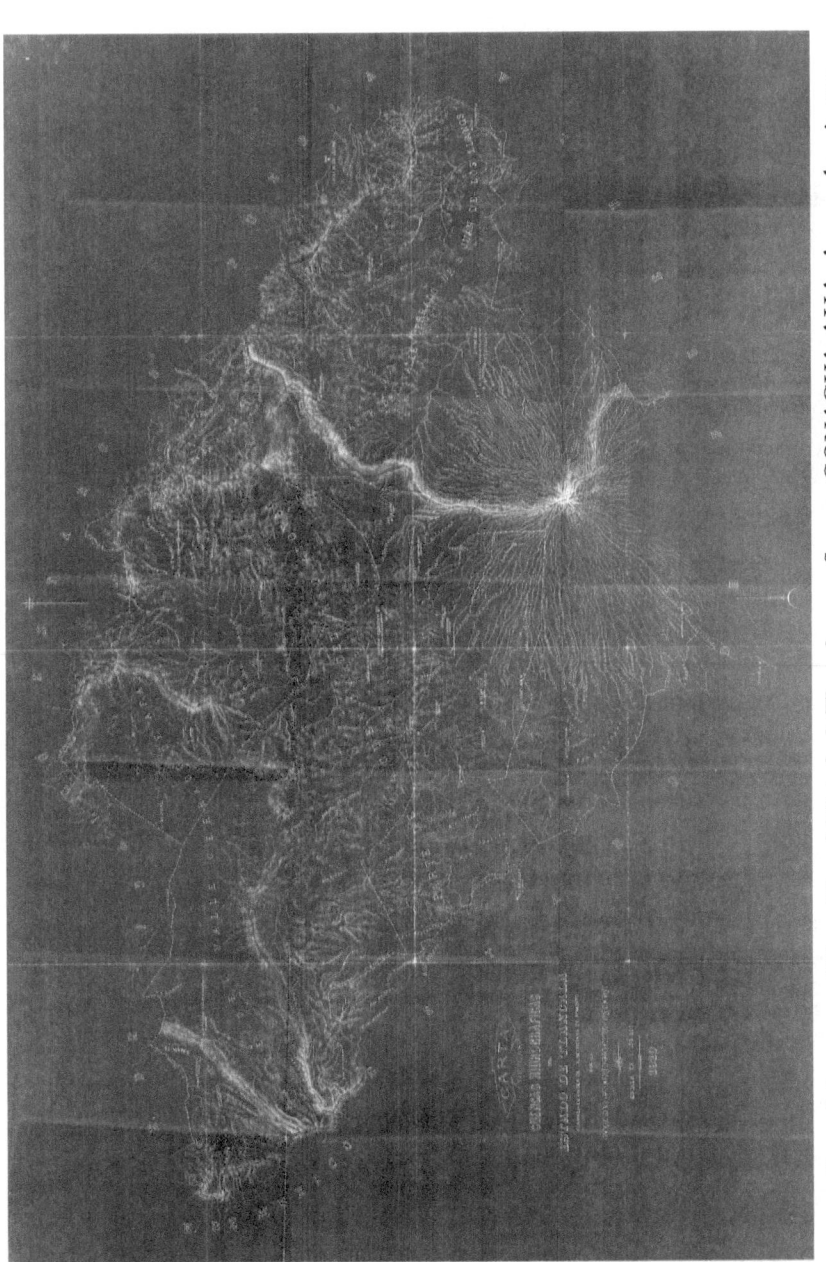

MAP 4. *Carta de las cuencas hidrográficas del Estado de Tlaxcala*, 1910. Source: CONAGUA-AHA, Aprovechamientos superficiales, Caja 3487, Expediente 47891, Legajo 1, Foja 2.

FIGURE 9. Iron water pipeline leading to textile factory San Luis. Source: CONAGUA-AHA, Aprovechamientos superficiales, Caja 141, Expediente 19590, Legajo 1, Foja 42 (1911).

would be crucial for him to maintain political control, even if this meant angering the factory owners and larger landowners who were helping to modernize his state.

Conclusion

The Waters Law of 1888 was designed by the federal government to assure those who needed large quantities of water in Mexico—usually large land and factory owners—that they would have enough of the resource to fulfill their developmental aims. However, instead of expediting and facilitating water-related development in Tlaxcala, the 1888 Waters Law often exacerbated the very challenges that the federal government hoped to overcome through new water legislation. Because of the law's unclear terms, conflicts involving water often became messier and more protracted. Moreover, the engineers who the federal government sent to scientifically map Tlaxcala's waterscape did not necessarily beget definitive or even helpful solutions to the state's water problems. Calculations and blueprints did not create more water, nor did they stop residents from causing floods when they disrupted the communal order of water. Through ordinances he passed in 1885, Governor Cahuantzi had already begun to use water as a tool of political mediation in Tlaxcala. The Waters Law of 1888, coupled with long-term authoritarian rule, enabled Cahuantzi to make himself into the foremost arbiter of natural resources in Tlaxcala during the Porfiriato. The ways in which he used this position are expounded in the next chapter.

FIVE

The Political Currency of Water

Although the 1888 Waters Law was the first federal law to regulate water in Mexico, the federal government had begun to regulate another natural resource, land, decades earlier. In 1856, Mexico passed the Ley de Desamortización de Bienes de la Iglesia Ley Lerdo de Tejada, colloquially known as the Ley Lerdo.[1] The Ley Lerdo ordered the disentailment and sale of lands held by civil and ecclesiastical "corporations," mainly Indigenous villages (*pueblos de indios*) and the Catholic Church. Both pueblos de indios and the church accorded rights based on individuals' belonging to these institutions, rather than on the liberal model that accorded rights based on individual citizenship. Liberals' goals in enacting the legislation were to code inalienable, individually based property rights into the 1857 Constitution and to increase private landholding in Mexico. Yet neither the Ley Lerdo nor the 1888 Waters Law addressed land and water as symbiotic parts of a holistic ecological system. The Ley Lerdo made no mention of how agrarian privatization affected water use. And as with the Waters Law of 1888, the terms of the Ley Lerdo were deeply ambiguous.

This chapter unearths connections between water and land and how these connections simultaneously buoyed and challenged authoritarianism in Tlaxcala. The lack of clarity in the Ley Lerdo and the Waters Law, coupled with their contradictory terms, enabled Governor Cahuantzi to determine how the federal laws would be applied locally. Unclear and contradictory federal resource laws also enabled Tlaxcalans—particularly the small proprietor and village majority—to contest industrialization and privatization of natural resources and to demand that officials and neighbors uphold customary natural resource rights (*usos y costumbres*). Tlaxcalans of all stripes insisted that the governor, as well as other officials and neighbors, acknowledge water as a shared resource and that they take steps to protect and control it as such, regardless of who owned the property. Thus, in Tlaxcala, water became a cheap but valuable form of state- and local-level political currency during the Porfiriato.

This chapter begins by outlining how agrarian privatization in the second half of the nineteenth century affected Tlaxcalans and how they accessed water. The chapter then explains how Cahuantzi brokered between unclear federal resource laws and local customary resource practices to adjudicate residents' water disputes. By no means did Governor Cahuantzi solve Tlaxcala's water problems, which continued well after Mexicans pushed Díaz out of office. But even though Cahuantzi saw development as essential for his region to progress, he did not always side with the hacendados and factory owners who had the power and finances to make development happen. The governor grasped the potential political and to some extent environmental ramifications of unregulated water use for his state's residents.

Agrarian Reform in Tlaxcala

Historians of Mexico had long contended that liberal land policies during the second half of the nineteenth century led to mass expropriation of peasants' lands, and that peasants, especially Indigenous peasants, opposed agrarian privatization and the Ley Lerdo. In the past few decades, however, historians have uncovered documentation—particularly in regional archives—that has led them to question this narrative. They have found that on the ground, experiences of agrarian reform during this period were diverse and often involved contestations between and among communities. They have also shown how mixed race and Indigenous peasants did not always oppose private landownership as historians heretofore assumed. In Tlaxcala, documentation regarding landholding and use reveals a starkly different picture than the one proposed decades ago by historian George McBride, who found that, like most regions, 99.3 percent of heads of households in rural Tlaxcala owned no individual property.[2] Although the Ley Lerdo affected landholding patterns in Tlaxcala significantly, federal disentailment did not completely dismantle customary agrarian usage rights (*usos y costumbres*). Landholding patterns in Tlaxcala were much more diverse than what historians once believed, and official property designations often belied how lands were used in practice. Lastly, land management, like water management, remained primarily in state and local officials' hands.[3]

Whereas political upheavals of the 1860s and 1870s slowed the Ley Lerdo's implementation in Tlaxcala and elsewhere, disentailment accelerated during the relative peace and stability of the Porfiriato. Some forty properties or portions of properties, mostly ranchos and haciendas, were purchased by and divided up among individual owners in Tlaxcala over the course of the Porfiriato. Most of these transactions took place in the south-central region in the districts of Zaragoza and Hidalgo, where properties and labor practices of all kinds had long coexisted (in contrast to northern parts of the state, where pulque haciendas worked by residential workers [peones acasillados] dominated the agrarian landscape). Although most had transferred ownership, many of the haciendas in the Tlaxcala-Puebla region had been established under colonial rule, well before the Porfiriato. To facilitate privatization in the nineteenth century, inhabitants (*vecinos*), usually from one or two villages (*pueblos*), but sometimes more, formed agrarian societies (*sociedades agrícolas*).[4] In the cases for which data was recorded, the number of purchasers varied widely, ranging from fifteen at the lowest and over three hundred at the highest. Properties' stated "values" also varied. The amount that a property owner contributed to the land sale typically determined the owner's lot size. These conditions meant that for smaller properties with multiple owners, an individual's lot could be paltry. Indeed, disputes over lot size and boundaries often erupted between and among vecinos, and sometimes official contracts were not drawn up until years after properties were divided. As such, state property records did not always reflect how property divisions had taken place. Some lands continued to be farmed or otherwise used collectively, most often as cattle pastures or in the case of forests (*montes*) to extract timber and broom root (*zacatón*), as they had been for decades or in some cases centuries.[5] To be sure, agrarian removals (*despojos* or despoilments) occurred in Tlaxcala throughout the Porfiriato.[6] But land privatization did not instigate interclass conflicts in Tlaxcala to the extent that it did in nearby states like Morelos, where sugar production created intense agrarian struggles.[7]

Agrarian privatization was also less contentious in Tlaxcala as compared to other regions, especially the northern and southern frontier

FIGURE 10. Pipeline down La Malintzin mountain to the San Luis textile factory. Source: CONAGUA-AHA, Aprovechamientos superficiales, Caja 141, Expediente 19590, Legajo 1, Foja 47 (1911).

states, because *terrenos baldíos* were declared nonexistent there. Expropriating terrenos baldíos—fallow and presumably untitled lands—was a primary means through which liberal administrations amassed more territory for development. Terrenos baldíos were often properties that residents had been farming for ages, with or without legal title. To do this work, the federal government hired out private survey companies, which in turn conducted land surveys and received a portion of land sale profits.[8] Tlaxcala was one of eleven, out of a total of thirty-one states, most in central Mexico, where private survey companies rarely came, if at all.[9]

The determination that Tlaxcala contained no terrenos baldíos was made in 1891 after a group of hacendados sent notice to Cahuantzi to oppose a surveyor's contract, approved by the Secretaría de Fomento in 1890, to begin surveying lands in the state. To corroborate their objections, the hacendados tendered documentation from the seventeenth and eighteenth centuries of "arrangements and agreements" Tlaxcalans had made "with appropriate authorities" of the *"Metrópoli* (mother country) . . . through which it was declared that in Tlaxcala there were no *terrenos baldíos.*"[10] The hacendados also submitted proof of payment to the colonial treasury.[11] When Cahuantzi called a meeting to discuss the hacendados' objections to the land surveys, representatives from haciendas and ranchos, as well as one sociedad agrícola and three pueblos, showed, adding their voices to the opposition. Subsequently, in April 1891, standing in front of the old Xicoténcatl theater in Tlaxcala City, Cahuantzi endorsed the colonial ruling to a mixed audience of officials and residents. By all accounts, the governor's declaration was well-received.[12] The uniqueness of Cahuantzi's declaration should not be overstated; similar determinations about terrenos baldíos were made in other nearby states. Communities in these regions had lands expropriated through separate but simultaneous processes of disentailment, nonetheless.[13]

In addition to appeasing residents, the declaration strengthened the state's administrative capacity and generated more property tax revenue for state (and federal) coffers. In Tlaxcala, the state, rather than private survey companies, conducted new property surveys.[14] Through these surveys, the state often increased property values and therefore collected more property taxes. For Tlaxcala's small and middling holders, state-driven property surveys meant that they could sometimes keep their lands, even their communal lands (*terrenos de adjudicación*), with the caveat that someone paid the property's taxes to the state. For example, in the pueblo of Huilopan in 1901, a resident denounced and attempted to adjudicate lands that his fellow vecinos had "farmed communally" since 1826. After the farmers paid the required *8 al millar* in taxes to the state, in addition to a "one hundred peso donation" toward state public education, the government allowed the farmers of Huilopan to continue farming lands collectively.[15] Sometimes the governor was willing to negotiate residents' tax contributions down. Other times, he was not. Either way, provincial authorities retained and even expanded their negotiating power vis-à-vis this declaration.

Compared to Maya farmers of the Yucatán or mixed-race peasants of Morelos, who tried valiantly but vainly to contest commercial developers' encroachment, villagers and small landowners in Tlaxcala were better positioned to press their agrarian claims because the federal government did not explicitly target their state for development. In one remarkable instance, villagers were even able to stop the governor from usurping their lands. In 1892, Cahuantzi attempted to seize ejido lands from the south-central village of Contla to expand his personal estate. The governor, who owned no lands before coming to office, insisted that residents in Contla had illegally occupied the ejidos for years.[16] Led by Juan de la

Rosa Cuamatzi, the villagers responded to the governor's actions by lodging a federal *amparo* (lawsuit) and submitting land titles to prove village domain.[17] Although these land records do not appear in the Tlaxcalan state archives, the federal court ledger states how Contla litigants indeed possessed and presented their legal land titles. Given how the colonial ancestors of Contla had close ties to the Spanish crown, it was quite possible that they had been able to pursue the administrative and legal processes through which they sanctioned their communities as official "pueblos" and thus drew up official land titles. In Morelos, by contrast, hacendados were able to contest the de facto water rights of pueblos by arguing that a pueblo had never had its legal status affirmed by the court.[18] Having official titles likely helped Contla to eventually win their case against Cahuantzi.[19] The Federal Supreme Court upheld Contla's rights to use village ejidos over Cahuantzi's claim to privatize and expropriate the lands. The dispute's resolution was unusual for the Porfiriato: Contla was one of few rural communities that were able to leverage a federal amparo to protect their communal properties during the Porfiriato.[20] The outcome was even more unusual given Cahuantzi's close allyship with the national regime.

Although unique in comparison to cases in other Mexican regions, the lawsuit's outcome is less so in light of the economic and political circumstances in Tlaxcala at the time. The economic stakes in this case were low: because Cahuantzi was proposing to expand his own personal estate, expropriating Contla's ejidos was not financially beneficial to anyone but Cahuantzi. The governor accused the people of Contla of "confus[ing]" his "private life . . . with my role as a ruler."[21] Yet both Díaz and Cahuantzi were aware that people in Contla, including Juan Cuamatzi, objected to Cahuantzi's reelection that year.[22] The Federal Supreme Court's decision may have been a way for Díaz to quietly allay Contla protesters.[23] Ongoing animosity between Contla villagers and Cahuantzi adds credence to this argument.[24] In their statement to the court, the Contla litigants complained of "arbitrary imprisonments . . . *golpes* and threats" under the governor.[25] The official who wrote the case's resolution further noted how Cahuantzi "abused the armed forces that [Cahuantzi] has at his disposal as governor of the state."[26] The Contla complainants also snidely disparaged the governor's recent financial gains, writing that, "It is also true that these properties—however acquired—should be enough [for Cahuantzi] to call himself rich, and should satisfy him, because given as poor and humble as he was six years ago, his ambition and thirst for riches have already been fulfilled."[27] The same year that Contla and Cahuantzi butted heads over land, Díaz pushed Rosendo Márquez out of the governor's seat in Puebla after Márquez failed to broker peace between political factions there. Díaz may have intervened in the 1892 dispute between Contla and Cahuantzi to keep the peace in Puebla's neighbor and prevent turnover in both Tlaxcala and Puebla during the same year.

Regardless of why Contla was able to beat back Cahuantzi's claim, the case highlights the fortitude of the villagers and small landowners who fought to keep their lands in the face of disentailment and an authoritarian political system. The case also underscores the variance in natural resource dispute outcomes in Tlaxcala. Barely a year later, Cahuantzi blocked a hacendado from expelling hundreds of renters off a portion of hacienda lands that their families had been farming for generations.[28] In general, patterns of land tenure and usage, as well as agrarian dispute outcomes, were diverse in Tlaxcala. Many Tlaxcalans in the Nativitas Valley owned, leased, or worked individual lots. Cahuantzi sometimes allowed usufruct agrarian practices—which entailed both individual and collective farming—to continue.[29] With the notable exception of Contla, the governor, more so than the federal government or private surveyors, oversaw the implementation of agrarian reform and mediated the conflicts that resulted.

Some scholars have argued that Cahuantzi, like Díaz, occasionally respected village land rights because he felt paternalistic toward his state's poor majority.[30] The variance in natural resource dispute outcomes, coupled with the greed and barefaced despotism Cahuantzi exhibited in Contla and in other instances, casts doubt on these arguments. More than paternalism, Cahuantzi approached natural resource disputes pragmatically. He allowed some customary agrarian practices to continue because he likely understood that if he were to completely upend usos y costumbres, Tlaxcala's small landowning and village majority would never tolerate his long-term rule. So, too, with water.

Private Land, Shared Water

Cahuantzi held on to power in part because land privatization engendered less interclass discord than other more export-oriented regions. However, increased rates of natural resource privatization, and its frequent companion, industrialization, generated conflicts over natural resources, between

FIGURE 11. Waterfall from the Zahuapan River. Source: CONAGUA-AHA Aprovechamientos superficiales, Caja 141, Expediente 19590, Legajo 1, Foja 57 (1911).

FIGURE 12. Hydroelectric pipeline located on the Hacienda San Diego Apatlahuaya. Source: CONAGUA-AHA, Aprovechamientos superficiales, Caja 141, Expediente 19590, Legajo 1, Foja 54 (1911).

and among Tlaxcala's diverse socioeconomic contingents, nonetheless.³¹ A foremost cause of these disputes was the failure of two federal resource laws—the Ley Lerdo and the 1888 Waters Law—to address land and water symbiotically. The Ley Lerdo of 1856—which disentailed and privatized "corporate" lands—and the 1888 Waters Law—which federalized Mexico's navigable rivers—were drafted by separate but similarly liberal administrations. Their authors had the same goal in mind: to modernize the countryside by increasing federal oversight over and private access to natural resources. Yet, when residents and officials in Tlaxcala attempted to mitigate the disputes that arose over alleged water misuse or abuse, the laws laid out by the federal government to expedite and facilitate the privatization of natural resources confounded them. The Ley Lerdo made no mention of how agrarian disentailment and privatization ought to affect customary water mores.³² As explored in the previous chapter, the Waters Law, which was enacted thirty-two years after the Ley Lerdo, affirmed that water users, even those who owned an immovable land parcel and who were legally granted exclusive water access rights, were obligated to respect the communal order of water and to undertake certain measures to protect water as a shared good.³³

Ongoing clashes between villagers from Ayecac and Concepción Petricioli (née Kennedy), the widowed owner of the hacienda San Juan Molino, illustrate how, when applied on the ground, the terms of the Ley Lerdo and the Federal Waters Law often conflicted, making it all but impossible to know whether private landowners could wield the Ley Lerdo to control and augment their water supply. In 1903, the agente municipal (town representative) of Ayecac wrote to the prefecto politico (district representative) of Tlaxcala to complain that Petricioli had abrogated an oral agreement she had made with the villagers. According to the agente municipal, Petricioli had permitted villagers from Ayecac and Villa Alta to build a canal to drain excess waters from the aqueduct that ran behind her property—which drew water from the Atoyac River—so that they could irrigate village lands. The file containing the dispute does not specify whether Ayecac villagers were allowed to continue with their plan to construct the canal after Petricioli went back on her word. However, documents from later

FIGURE 13. Canal and reservoir from the Zahuapan River and location of the hydroelectric plant on the Hacienda San Diego Apatlahuaya. Source: CONAGUA-AHA, Aprovechamientos superficiales, Caja 141, Expediente 19590, Legajo 1, Foja 52 (1911).

years indicate how neighboring villagers continued to have problems with Petricioli, who refused to sell them quality lands, specifically those that contained irrigation infrastructure.[34]

It was unclear which law ought to dictate this dispute's outcome. According to the Ley Lerdo and Petricioli, her property and presumably the water on it were hers alone. This was indeed a presumption, however, since the Ley Lerdo did not specify whether or how water could be accessed on privatized lands. Petricioli's hacienda San Juan Molina drew water from the Atoyac River. Under the 1888 Waters Law, the Atoyac had been federalized. Thus, after Petricioli petitioned the Secretaría de Fomento for exclusive water access rights in 1902, her request was granted, pending an engineer's inspection.[35]

Yet this inspection did not prove to be the simple formality that Petricioli likely hoped it would be. According to a federal engineer's report, villagers and small landowners complained that Petricioli was using too much water and that she had violated the communal order of water, despite that this was expressly forbidden by the 1888 Waters Law. Vecinos also complained that Petricioli's water use was exacerbating floods that had long plagued the area. During his inspection of Petricioli's property in late October, the engineer explained how Petricoli's *"tomas de agua* are not in the shape or condition that they should be" and that "because of the considerable height of the river" he could not even complete his inspection "until the course of the river is returned to where it is supposed to be."[36] Further complicating this matter was that the area straddled the Puebla-Tlaxcala border, and owners of larger properties like Petricioli often resided elsewhere. These circumstances meant that officials from both states were involved, and bureaucratic processes were prolonged. Petricioli and her son and legal representative, Diego Kennedy, were frequently traveling in Europe; inspections were delayed further still.[37] In December 1908, another federal engineer attempted to calculate the amount of water needed for Petricioli and her vecinos to irrigate their properties. The sixteen-page-long report concludes with the engineer encouraging all parties to "come to a friendly agreement that would best take advantage of their natural resources."[38] However, no such agreement appears in the historic record, and records do not indicate whether the case reached a resolution.[39]

It is significant that Ayecac residents held on to their lands in the face of disentailment and development during the late Porfiriato. But villagers' properties were only useful insofar as they could access and control water to make their lands productive and keep them from flooding. Hence, Ayecac water users insisted that Petricioli comply with the water mores delineated by federal and state mandates. Petricioli's socioeconomic privilege relative to her neighbors, and laws like the Ley Lerdo that buttressed that privilege, enabled her to renege on oral arrangements she had made with her neighbors to uphold centuries-old water mores—in this case, agreeing to let her neighbors draw water from the stretch of the Atoyac River that abutted her property. Until the advent of ground pumping, owners of larger properties like Petricioli would likely never enjoy the unfettered water access they believed was necessary to irrigate their lands or power their mills and machinery. Hacendados and industrialists continued to exploit natural waterways and ignore the water mores reaffirmed in the Waters Law. Meanwhile, poorer water users pressed their neighbors to conform to water mores and encouraged officials to make them do so.

Like Ayecac and Contla, villagers from San Hipolito successfully contested a local rancho owner's attempt to adjudicate their lands. In 1888, Trinidad Vela Farfán, the owner of rancho San Isidro, attempted to usurp ejidos in San Hipolito. San Hipolitanos brought their dispute to their ayuntamiento and successfully battled Vela Farfán's claims, arguing that they had "possessed" the territory "peacefully . . . since time immemorial" as cattle pastures, to dispose waste, and other *"usos convenientes y necesarios."*[40] Vela Farfán demurred. In his defense he invoked the Ley Lerdo and portrayed himself as a "victim" of a "corporate entity."[41] He insisted that according to the "Ley Lerdo . . . this [ejido] title would be null and of no value."[42] The Ayuntamiento of Tlaxcala shot him down and San Hipolito held on to their lands—a testament to the municipality's enduring authority.[43]

Years later, in 1902, Vela Farfán came together with some of his village and townsfolk neighbors to alert the governor of "rising waters" along the Zahuapan River.[44] They called on Cahuantzi to send out an engineer to inspect the region. In September 1903, engineer Pedro Lira carried out the inspection and composed a map of the area (see figure 14). But accusations that the neighbors lobbed at one another in subsequent years suggest that Lira's work did little to solve water problems there. From 1903 onward, small landowners and villagers in Tepeihtec and Panotla accused each other, their respective officials, and Vela Farfán of opening unauthorized causeways, aggravating floods, and committing "abuse" of both water and power.[45]

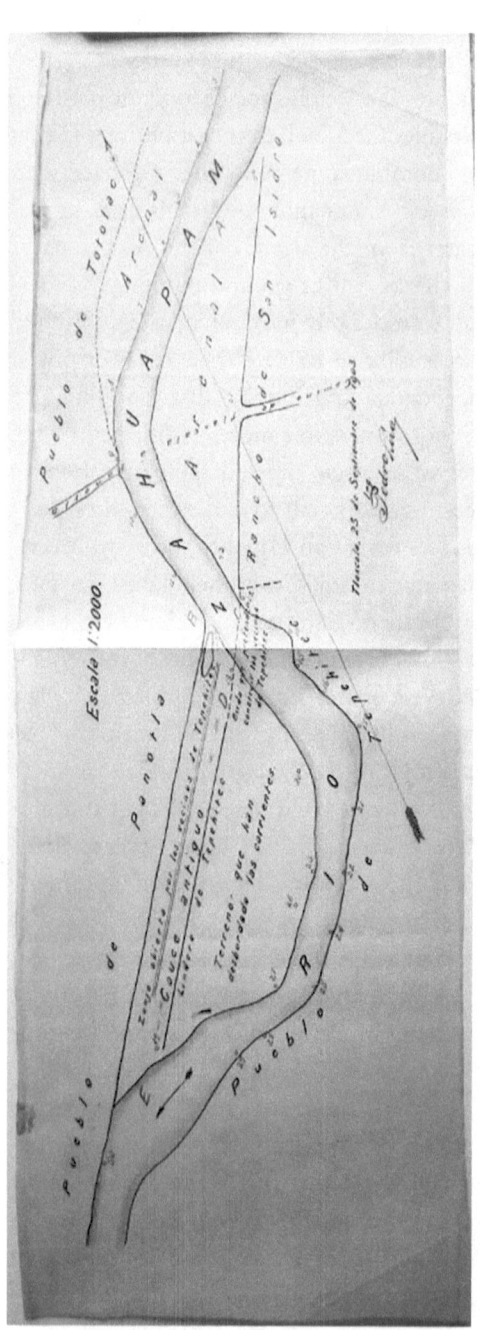

FIGURE 14. Sketch of the Zahuapan River near the rancho San Isidro and towns of Panotla, Tepehitec, and Totolac, September 23, 1903. Source: Archivo Histórico del Estado de Tlaxcala, Fondo Sin clasificar siglo XIX, 1903, Caja 1, Expediente 12, foja 70.

Water users' complaints like the ones from Ayecac, San Hipolito, Tepeihtec, and Panotla typify the environmental, economic, and human devastation that resulted when the Ley Lerdo was applied while the Waters Law was ignored.[46] The complaints are almost entirely from the flood-prone and densely populated Nativitas Valley. They came from Tlaxcalans of all socioeconomic backgrounds and did not always cut across class lines, albeit poorer communities were hit hardest. At least two riverside communities were forced to relocate because of floods.[47] In one of these cases, Ignacio Morales Benítez, the factory owner who adjudicated the now unoccupied territories, presumably did so because unlike the previous occupants he could afford to build flood-control infrastructure there.[48] Local governments' inability to curb flooding in the wake of development occasioned municipalities to sell off lands they leased. When the Ayuntamiento of Tlaxcala sold a *terreno* (plot of land) that lay along the Zahuapan River to eleven individual owners, they forsook the territory's leasing fees with the hopes that, "given how threatened [Tlaxcala City] is by the river, [the new landowners] could make some very important infrastructural improvements there."[49] Even when villagers and small landowners faced down disentailment threats as in the instances already explained, they still had problems controlling and accessing water.

To solve natural resource disputes in Tlaxcala, the federal government occasionally sent an engineer to make maps and recommendations, but little else. For the federal government, land privatization and water lease contracts had many benefits: they facilitated development, generated federal income, and curtailed local governments' authority, thereby strengthening its own. Yet the residents whose livelihoods and businesses were at stake cared deeply about the outcomes of water disputes. They were concerned about flooding in the rainy season and water conservation—ensuring that there would be a sufficient supply of water—during the dry season.[50] Governor Cahuantzi also cared about water-related issues because it was his job to prevent conflicts from breaking out in his state. Thus, when the contradictory terms in the Ley Lerdo and the Federal Waters Law clashed, and conflicts between residents erupted, they compelled state intervention. Mitigating water-related conflicts permitted the governor to control how federal laws were applied on the ground in Tlaxcala. Water therefore became an important means through which Cahuantzi placated residents and asserted his authority.

Water Conservation and State Mediation

Governor Cahuantzi was an indisputable defender of the national modernization project and very much desired to develop his state. At the same time, though, he understood how Tlaxcala's hydrological environment was strained, and that development strained it further still. He also grasped how his political viability was tied to residents' ability to access water. The governor did more than tolerate some residents' usufruct natural resource practices. Cahuantzi sometimes defended small landowners and villagers' water access over the demands of hacendados and industrialists.

One way that Cahuantzi proposed to conserve water for all residents was by repairing and creating water infrastructure. The governor's 1885 state decree, which he made soon after he took office, fined water users when they did not adhere to myriad and sometimes centuries-old water use obligations. These obligations mandated that water users keep canals and dams free of debris, obtain permission from the state to open a new diversion dam, and many other similar specifications.[51] The governor also leaned on private residents to construct water infrastructure that was difficult for the state to afford. In 1894, two major developers in the region, the Caso brothers Alfredo and Bernardo, approached the governor proposing to build new dams along their haciendas that used both the Zahuapan and the Atoyac Rivers. The Nativitas Valley had experienced another "extreme" year of flooding in 1893, with water cascading over river embankments into towns, roads, and fields.[52] Cahuantzi threw his support behind the Caso brothers' project, explaining how in "building the dams on their farms" the Casos were doing "important work that would prevent the dangers brought upon by the rainy season in the Valley [of Nativitas]."[53] The governor hoped the Caso brothers' project would serve as an "echo" to "other farmers in the region."[54] Inasmuch as dams and river embankments deterred flooding in a socioeconomically diverse and highly populous region, building them had a clear public benefit. The other benefit for Cahuantzi, of course, was that the Caso brothers would fund this project, not the state.

Water infrastructure projects also created jobs for local workers. Emergency repairs were especially lucrative. When a dike broke along one of the Caso brothers' properties, the brothers ended up paying workers $2 MXN a day—four times the average agricultural laborer's salary in Tlaxcala.[55] Whereas the engineer reporting these statistics indicated how workers were committing "abuses" by demanding "exorbitant and unjustifiable salary increases," the workers who performed the labor likely did not agree.⁵⁶ Cahuantzi offered various incentives to ensure a sufficient labor force to work on infrastructural projects related to water. He exempted public works laborers in flood-prone areas from paying the head tax (*impuesto personal*) and shortened prisoners' sentences for those who agreed to work on these projects.⁵⁷ At the same time, Cahuantzi made it clear to larger landowners and lower-level officials that compulsory labor on public works projects (*faenas*) was outlawed and that workers were to be compensated for their labor. The governor even sometimes fined project overseers for not doing so.⁵⁸ The governor believed, or at least he espoused to believe, that water development projects could and should benefit the larger community in different ways.

But it was easy for the governor to support private enterprise projects that had public benefits. More compelling are cases in which Cahuantzi denied water access to larger land and factory owners so that small landowners and villagers could conserve their water and protect their lands from floods. When José Mendizabal lobbied the federal government in December 1898 to open another toma de agua along the San Lorenzo River, a tributary of the Atoyac, his neighbors—who included landowners of all sorts as well as townspeople—were concerned that floods would result.⁵⁹ Mendizabal, a Spaniard and owner of the Santo Domingo factory in Puebla, proposed to build a new canal to funnel water to a factory he planned to build in Tlaxcala. Two weeks after Mendizabal sent his proposal to the Secretaría de Fomento, the department granted his request. Despite Mendizabal's assurances that the project "would not harm a single person" and that, instead, the Tlaxcalteca and Josefina factories nearby "would actually gain waterpower," his vecinos wrote to the federal government to oppose its decision to grant Mendizabal's request.⁶⁰ Some months later, Mendizabal's opponents planned a meeting with the head of the Secretaría de Fomento in Mexico City to persuade him to reverse his decision.⁶¹

In anticipation of this meeting, Cahuantzi added his voice to those challenging Mendizabal. Using personal letterhead and forgoing the minister's formal title, Cahuantzi wrote directly to the Secretaría de Fomento, Señor Lic. Don Francisco Martínez López. In a letter to "his most devoted friend," the governor explained how, "according to state reports, the residents of [the town of Santo Toribio Xicotzinco] fear, with reason, that the work [to open a new deviation from the river] that Mendizabal is proposing would cause floods, since the riverbed would now be higher than their lands." Cahuantzi continued: "in light of the justice [I seek] for my constituents, I have interest in resolving this matter . . . I wish to convey my agreement [with those who oppose Mendizabal] . . . and explain how[,] with regards to the opposition's motivations, it is not egotism that guides them, but rather the urgent necessity of avoiding [floods] that would bring terrible consequences."[62] Mendizabal's opponents appeared to have successfully blocked his request. When Mendizabal continued to "insist" on his request years later, he was similarly rebuffed.[63]

In his letter to the Secretaría de Fomento, the governor called for "justice" for his "constituents," naming the townspeople of Santo Toribio Xicotzinco specifically. But some of Mendizabal's opponents were also prominent land, factory, and mill owners. Cahuantzi's interdiction against Mendizabal would have appeased all of these parties. Considering the long-standing tensions between Tlaxcala and Puebla, perhaps Cahuantzi did not wish to support another descendant of Spanish émigrés who conducted business in his state, but who resided in Puebla. Cahuantzi's support of other developers, and his desire to meet Porfirian standards of progress, casts doubt on this explanation, however. His motives notwithstanding, Cahuantzi's actions in this case reveal how he understood that free-flowing water had to be conserved for other water users to some extent. While the governor did not give any indication that he was concerned about development's long-term impact on the environment, he did seem to understand how unfettered development affected the environmental conditions in which Tlaxcalans lived and worked.[64]

Outcomes like that in the case above were not aberrant in Tlaxcala during this period. As glimpsed in table 3 (see chapter four), Cahuantzi and other state administrators often intervened in water-related disputes, even those that legally should have been arbitrated by the federal government after the 1888 Waters Law went into effect. Take for example the case in which a local hacendado and lawyer, Librado López, petitioned the federal government to adjudicate Lake Acuitlapilco in 1896. Citing the Waters Law, which federalized navigable waterways, López insisted that the lake was navigable because people canoed on it. Because of its navigability, he argued, the federal government should have been able to grant López exclusive access rights to the entire lake. The hacendado proposed to drain the lake and cultivate the territory, or, failing this, use the lake for commercial fishing. In response to López's request, the Secretaría de Fomento solicited an engineer's inspection as well as the governor's opinion.[65]

When Cahuantzi responded to the Secretaría de Fomento to oppose López's petition, he explained how the "land where the lake is located . . . belongs to the *pueblos* [that surround it]," and furthermore that these pueblos use "[lake waters] for domestic uses and for their cattle."[66] He clarified how San Francisco Tepeyanco, a town to the lake's south, also "makes use of [water from Lake Acuitlapilco] to irrigate their lands during the dry season."[67] Indeed, in 1897, the people of Tepeyanco complained of having insufficient water to irrigate their lands and were subsequently granted access to Lake Acuitlapilco by their ayuntamiento.[68] A similar determination was made when hacendado Ricardo Carvajal opened up a diversion dam along the Zahuapan River in 1895. Villagers from Tepeihtec and Panotla alleged that Carvajal's unauthorized dam forced too much water into other local causeways, prompting the diversion dam that they used to rupture.[69] After touring the region, a coalition of municipal-, district-, and state-level officials ordered Carvajal to shutter the dam and imposed a 25 peso fine if Carvajal "abuse[d]" this agreement.[70]

Water dispute outcomes, just like land dispute outcomes, were inconsistent in Tlaxcala. Not a decade before the governor denied Librado López's request to adjudicate Lake Acuitlapilco, Cahuantzi approved hacendado Carlos Lennox Kennedy's petition to partially drain another lake, Lake Rosario.[71] The governor had supported Kennedy's proposal in spite of neighbors' concerns that partially desiccating the lake would alter the Atoyac River's course, which fed the lake, and would cause "inevitable floods," since the lake served as a water repository during the rainy season.[72] State officials countered these claims, arguing that the lake had caused "infinite damages" that stemmed from "infected water" that they believed to be spreading disease.[73] They further averred that the project was "generally approved by residents from around the region."[74] By the spring of 1887, Kennedy's project was complete and the hacendado adjudicated the drained territory.[75]

Juxtaposing the disputes over Lake Rosario and Lake Acuitlapilco underlines once more the variation in water dispute outcomes under Cahuantzi. With Lake Rosario, the governor granted one hacendado's request to drain and adjudicate a portion of the lake because of its supposed links to disease. When Cahuantzi made this decision, he spurned residents who disagreed with his assessment. These residents may have also been none too pleased that Kennedy was expanding his territory. Ten years later, with Lake Acuitlapilco, Cahuantzi denied another hacendado's request to drain and adjudicate that lake because too many residents relied on its waters. Most Tlaxcalans did not have access to sufficient capital, nor did the state draw enough interest from developers, to pay engineers to make assessments the likes of which were seen in the Laguna region. A professional survey of Lake Rosario and surrounding territories was completed in 1901, fourteen years after Kennedy partially drained it. But Lake Rosario was believed to have caused hygienic problems and floods up until it was fully drained in 1966.[76]

Limits of State Mediation in Water Disputes

The measures Cahuantzi pursued to conserve water for all residents and to prevent floods are significant given how Porfirian officials usually flouted natural resource equity in favor of profits. Yet various factors limited these measures' impact. Inequality among agrarian holders and workers, and an economic, legal, and political environment that favored capitalistic producers, meant that reprimands and fines levied by government officials on larger producers who violated mores only went so far. Five years after landowner Ricardo Carvajal was ordered to close one deviation dam, his village neighbors reported how Carvajal had deviated a canal along the Atoyac River that was supposed to feed into Lake Rosario. Locals clamored for the federal government to intervene, insisting that "the governor has supported [Carvajal's dam] despite [our] complaints." Defending himself, the governor wrote to the Secretaría de Fomento alleging that "if their [villagers'] lands are flooding" it is because Carvajal "is determined to oppose this government's decisions" that Carvajal "destroy his section of the dam." Accusing private landowners of failing to conform to water mores, as Cahuantzi did with Carvajal, was also a way for the governor to shirk blame for water equity problems that, according to the governor, were beyond his control.[77]

Cahuantzi gave a similar response to villagers of Tepetitla, Ayecac, and Villa Alta in 1909. For years these communities had been writing to anyone who would listen about how the Atoyac River overflowed onto their lands and how their hacienda and rancho-owning neighbors—who resided in Puebla—exacerbated flooding.[78] Townspeople lamented how local authorities in Tepetitla were ordering them to "construct defensive infrastructure" using their own "unpaid labor" along the Atoyac "where . . . there is [much] inequality, and little fairness."[79] Cahuantzi agreed with the villagers. Writing to the Secretaría de Fomento, the governor indicated how the complainants "are correct" and that "the work that the vecinos do along the Atoyac to avoid the damages floods do to their farmlands annually, are useless in part, because the owners of the farms [Matienzo and Sela] do little to reinforce the riverbanks."[80] Cahuantzi also explained how "[the complainants should] only be obliged to lend their cooperation to those [projects] that interest them, for the security of their own lands, as well as for the common lands in their town of residence."[81] In other words, Cahuantzi expected water users to uphold the water mores outlined in his 1885 decree and the 1888 Waters Law. But he also stressed how their labor should not be required beyond these "communal" obligations. Notably, he also affirmed the right of these villagers to keep their common lands, with the caveat that they uphold water mores—and, although he did not say so explicitly here, pay taxes—on the lands.

Residents sometimes ignored the governor's dictates. Cahuantzi indicated how he had "written to the Governor of Puebla recommending that he require that landowners [Andrés Matienzo and Eduardo Sela] . . . do their part to repair the riverbanks."[82] But Matienzo and Sela scoffed at these recommendations. Hacienda owner Matienzo professed that "I have no need to construct infrastructure nor [incur] any expense, since I am not at all affected by the floods . . . and when I have suffered any significant damage, I have not bothered anyone nor have I asked anyone for personal or financial help to repair it."[83] In his report summarizing the case one year later, federal engineer Rafael Serrano explained how water users throughout the region would undertake "appropriate infrastructure projects under my guidance and direction."[84] He further explained how "it did not seem right for the Tepetitla authorities [to be] directing these projects" but that, instead, "every one of the [interested parties involved] should contribute to the [projects'] execution."[85] Documentation from subsequent years suggests, however, that hacendados continued to ignore Serrano's recommendations and that residents continued to protest water inequity in the area.[86]

Disputes like the one above that went unresolved years, even decades later, make clear how the inconsistency with which Cahuantzi handled local natural resource conflicts was not a sustainable resource management strategy in the long term. This was true from an environmental and a political standpoint. Water users with more finances and access to labor like Andrés Matienzo were better positioned to reject water mores. Factory owner Ignacio Morales Benítez simply "deposit[ed] waters in the middle of the night" after the federal government explained that he had "no legal authorization" to use more water because his deviation dam was diminishing his neighbors' well water supply.[87] Meanwhile, poorer residents whose ability to access water was dependent on others to uphold water mores were frustrated by those who failed to fulfill their obligations. In Santa Ana Nopalucan, vecinos reported how they "had cleaned 960 meters of the canal [they use] and that [they] were the only [vecinos] who had complied with this order."[88] Nopalucan villagers' complaint was by no means unique.

Many of these disputes continued well after 1910. Their lack of resolution suggests that later administrations likewise failed to address Tlaxcala's water issues even after resource equity was enshrined as a central goal in the Constitution of 1917. During the Porfiriato, Cahuantzi's interventions in natural resource disputes, and measures such as regulations and fines on water users, proved effective, albeit temporary, means of allaying widespread political dissent. Inevitably, though, provisional measures were insufficient to overcome Porfirian cronies' overwhelming desire to demonstrate progress and stimulate capitalistic growth. But the fact that one of Díaz's cronies chose to enforce centuries-old usufruct water mores, and that he mandated that all water users acknowledge and proactively safeguard water as a shared good, probably helped Cahuantzi to endure in office longer than any other governor. Cahuantzi was compelled to uphold these mores in large part because Tlaxcalans, especially villagers and small landowners, insisted that he do so.

Conclusion: Hydrological Despotism

Through natural resource management—whether preventing landowners from acquiring more property or accessing more water—Cahuantzi also obstructed would-be challengers' authority and wealth. This was true of Ricardo Carvajal, a landowner who was denied private water access rights along the Zahuapan River and later wrote to Díaz to complain about Cahuantzi's personal abuse of water resources in the Nativitas Valley.[89] This was true for Librado López, a one-time Cahuantzista ally, local landowner, and generally law-bucking figure who was denied access rights to Lake Acuitlapilco (and was similarly denied when he asked for property tax exemptions).[90] Residents later accused Cahuantzi of having López assassinated.[91] And it was also true of another local landowner and one-time state treasurer Trinidad Vela Farfán.

For years the small farmers and villagers who lived around Vela Farfán's rancho San Isidro accused Vela Farfán of flooding their lands. Yet Vela Farfán continually ignored local and state officials' demands to cease construction of new deviation dams and to fix river embankments along his properties.[92] Meanwhile, sometime around 1900, Vela Farfán and the governor went from being *compañeros* to enemies. Their quarrel escalated quickly. Cahuantzi accused his treasurer of embezzling state funds and cooking expenditure books.[93] Writing to federal finance minister (*Ministro de Hacienda*) José Yves Limantour, Vela Farfán explained how Cahuantzi sent some "friends" to tour the drainage he had built along the Zahuapan River.[94] Accusing Vela Farfán of failing to keep his canals clean—in other words, of failing to uphold the communal order of water—Cahuantzi expelled Vela Farfán from his property.[95] "Because of threats ... directed to me ... by my powerful rival [Cahuantzi]," Vela Farfán "felt obligated to leave Tlaxcala."[96] Vela Farfán pleaded with Limantour and Díaz to help him find a property in Mixcoac in Mexico City. He subsequently sold rancho San Isidro and left Tlaxcala for good.

Without Vela Farfán's money and connections, the villagers and small landowners who lived around San Isidro were left to manage water problems on their own. In 1917, seven years after the Zahuapan River was federalized, vecinos from Panotla wrote to the Secretaría de Fomento to explain how they had endured decades of water-related hardships. Because Vela Farfán "had the support of then governor [Cahuantzi]," the villagers explained how their constant opposition to Vela Farfán's deviation dams were in vain.[97] State and local governments tried to stop Vela Farfán from usurping lands and abusing waters. But no doubt Vela Farfán ignored government directives. "Now that *con beneplácito* constitutional order has been established [in 1917]," and the Zahuapan was in federal hands, the people of Panotla turned to the federal government, hoping to receive the help they so desperately needed to manage their water.[98]

In October 1917, federal engineers came to inspect the region. They determined how, because of erosion and landslides, and because "Vela Farfán had ignored government orders," the "pueblos [had been] left in horrible misery."⁹⁹ Early in 1918, engineers made the recommendation that the river needed to be returned to "its original causeway."¹⁰⁰ However, the engineer also articulated how the question of "who should do this work" was unclear.¹⁰¹ In the end, the engineers indicated that the people of Panotla and Totolac, the new and current owner of San Isidro, and the state of Tlaxcala should work to ensure the "happy" conclusion of this project.¹⁰² Thus, even after the Zahuapan was federalized, and a new constitution and revolutionary government were installed, water users in the Nativitas Valley continued to face tremendous hydrological challenges. Tlaxcala's water management problems derived from centuries of interactions between humans and their hydrological environment. Fixing them would require much more than a democratic revolution.

Tlaxcalans of all sorts—from Governor Cahuantzi to the villagers of Panotla—took advantage of ambiguous and confusing resource laws in order to turn water into an accessible political tool in late nineteenth- and early twentieth-century Mexico, one that could be used both to assert and contest despotic power. More than pitied patrons in need of protection, small landowners and villagers like those of Panotla and Totolac played key roles in upholding usufruct water mores. Small landowners and villagers pressed their officials to make other water users conform to these mores. They also pushed against the attempts of landowners and government officials to privatize what was an inherently shared resource. This story is as much about the agency of Tlaxcala's small landowners and villagers as it is about the political strategies of a state-level autocrat under the national authoritarian regime.

Turning back to the book's central query—how did this regional dictatorship endure—examining how Cahuantzi managed local land and water disputes helps to explain why the governor of Tlaxcala remained in power while so many other governors did not. The ambiguous terms outlined in federal natural resource laws and their failure to address water and land as part of an ecological whole, coupled with Tlaxcala's environmental precarity, turned water into a tool of state-level mediation. Though inconsistent and provisional, Cahuantzi's interventions in natural resource disputes helped to stave off interclass struggles that beset other regions during the Porfiriato. While the state government increased their power vis-à-vis water management in Tlaxcala during the Porfiriato, ayuntamientos saw their control diminish. After the Federal Waters Law of 1888 was implemented, municipalities lost the usage fees they previously collected along the now federalized Atoyac River. Legally, ayuntamientos could still grant private usage rights along the Zahuapan River and collect fees on these rights. But Cahuantzi interfered in municipal decisions where he saw fit, sometimes abrogating municipal authority. The governor increasingly meddled in municipal affairs—in water conflicts, local-level elections, and fiscal autonomy. Over time, Cahuantzi's intrusion on municipal sovereignty soured residents on his enduring rule.

SIX

The Price of Progress

In 1908 Tlaxcala City installed electric lights in the *centro* of their small capital town. The ceremony to inaugurate the lights took place in front of the Xicohténcatl theater, which the state had purchased two years earlier. State-sponsored newspaper *La Antigua República* reported how the event celebrated "the progressive work" undertaken by Cahuantzi in "Tlaxcala's capital." The editorial further relayed how residents, "through whose veins flow the glorious blood of the illustrious Xicohténcatl," had just "wrapped up their *fiestas patrias*."[1] The conflation of a glorious Indigenous past and an electrified future was precisely the image Cahuantzi wanted to project of Tlaxcala. It was an image designed to counter pathetic impressions of the state that appeared in national publications such as *La Voz de México*, which described Tlaxcala in 1871 as "ruins and memories ... their commerce is limited and their industry even more so."[2] Under Cahuantzi, displays of quantifiable "progress"—new bridges, schools, and public works—along with ceremonies and celebrations to inaugurate these projects, took place throughout the state. The infrastructural improvements Cahuantzi's administration made in part represented their efforts to meet local needs and prevent conflict among residents who shared the same spaces. But many of these projects were also designed to showcase Tlaxcala's modernity and Cahuantzi's capacity to imprint Porfirian "urban planning" ideals onto the physical landscape of Tlaxcala.[3] This was especially true of the state's small capital, Tlaxcala City.

Although Porfirian elites focused much of their attention on transforming the nation's capital, modernization (*mejores materiales*) projects could be seen throughout many Mexican regions at the turn of the century, including in more peripheral cities and provinces. Tlaxcala state may have been provincial, lacking a true city the likes of nearby Puebla or Veracruz, but it was far from peripheral. Tlaxcala abutted economic and cultural centers such as Mexico and Puebla states and as of the late 1870s, it was connected to these places via rail. Tlaxcala's geographic and ecological conditions—especially its forests and water—were favorable for the sorts of modernization plans Porfiristas pursued. As Cahuantzi communicated in his biannual address to the state congress in 1891:

> This is what real progress looks like . . . [Tlaxcala] has a good climate, water in abundance, fertile lands . . . and important railroads like the Mexicano and the Interoceánico that cross all over the state, [that] transport our products to distant markets where not so long ago they had never heard of us . . . industries are now being established in [Tlaxcala City] and in other important localities [here]. . . . Who could possibly deny the indisputable progress that [Tlaxcala] is achieving?"[4]

Cahuantzi's determination to measure Tlaxcala's progress echoed Porfirian elites' positivistic and westernized ideals of modernity. According to these ideals, towns were orderly, clean, safe, and mechanized.[5] Dams, bridges, lighting, plumbing, and the like were physical examples of Tlaxcala's capacity to develop and exist on its own, apart from its much more formidable neighbor, Puebla. Infrastructure and public works projects were also ways for Cahuantzi to mark his authority over the young state and over its disparate towns, villages, and factions, some of which had not wanted Tlaxcala to become a state at all. Moreover, physical manifestations of "progress" complemented Cahuantzi's efforts to shape and promote Tlaxcala's ancient past by conveying how Tlaxcala's proud Indigenous history did not detract from its enlightened, westernized present. State governors were often involved in modernization projects. But conditions in Tlaxcala—its small size, relatively low national economic output, and Cahuantzi's longevity in office—meant that, more so than national engineers or policy makers, the state's primary urban planner was Cahuantzi. Modernization projects in Tlaxcala fell into three interrelated categories: transportation networks and infrastructure; public spaces and buildings; and public services including those pertaining to urban development, hygiene, and crime. Improvements to infrastructure and public spaces were oftentimes wanted and even demanded by residents of all walks of life.[6]

However, as this chapter explains, Tlaxcala lacked the fiscal and bureaucratic capacity to carry out modernization plans, regardless of who demanded them. Díaz and his fellow oligarchs were most concerned with modernizing Mexico City and expanding the railroads, which provided critical support for the export economy.[7] They were also more focused on collecting tariffs than developing a sound system of internal taxation.[8] Aside from the railroads, few modernization projects in Tlaxcala were supported by federal funds. Some, such as water-related infrastructure, were funded by private residents. But, for the most part, state and local governments shouldered the financial burden to maintain and build infrastructure and public works. Modernization drove Cahuantzi to squeeze ever-increasing amounts of revenue from residents and local governments, precipitating and solidifying dissent against his regime and—along with other factors—against the Porfiriato in Tlaxcala.

Local Transport

Examinations of local transport—railroads, bridges, and roads—illustrate the acute differences between projects that received federal or private funds versus state or municipal funds.[9] By 1891, 267 kilometers of rail lines had been laid in Tlaxcala. Two of these lines, the Interoceánico and the Mexicano lines, were public. They were supported by federal funds, patrolled by federal rurales, and regulated by federal laws. All other rail lines in Tlaxcala were private, funded and accessed by the hacendados who built them.[10] In addition to rail lines, the nation also had thirty-four federal highways that were maintained by the federal government. But because none of these ran through Tlaxcala, the state received no federal money for road maintenance. Instead, Tlaxcala's roads—like most roadways throughout the country—were sustained solely by state and local finances and labor.[11] According to federal law, only landowners who lived along federal highways were required to share and contribute to the maintenance of roads that ran through or along their properties. Compelling private landowners to take part in road maintenance fell to local governments, and occasionally the state.[12]

As railroads brought more foot and mule traffic to the region, the conditions of Tlaxcala's pathways worsened. The innumerable letters Tlaxcalans wrote to regional and local officials, complaining about the "mortifying" conditions of roads and bridges and pleading with officials to attend to them, make this clear.[13] Residents reported how roads needed to be widened or repaired after flood waters or general neglect had rendered them impassable for mules or horse carts. Other roads were blocked completely by private landowners who inhibited travel through stretches of roadways that traversed or bordered their properties. This issue—privatization of usufruct public roads—was particularly problematic in the southern Nativitas Valley where haciendas, ranchos, and villages often coexisted in the same diversely and highly populated space. Obstructing one expanse of a road meant that residents were forced to take more circuitous or dangerous routes, or no route at all. Tlaxcalans also complained about roadside banditry, especially along the Tlaxcala-Puebla border. The old *camino real* that connected Tlaxcala and Puebla, a crucial roadway for Tlaxcalans to be able to sell their products in Puebla City, had become notorious for crime, since thieves could easily abscond into the folds of La Malintzin to escape local authorities.[14]

Although roads became busier and less safe, municipal coffers did not increase commensurately to maintain and patrol them. Municipalities in Tlaxcala derived revenue primarily from rents collected on leased properties, stores, market stalls, and waterways. For the most part, municipal revenue forms did not change during this period. In some cases, they shrunk. After the 1888 Waters Law federalized the Atoyac River, municipalities no longer collected water leasing fees along the Atoyac River. Ayuntamientos also lost out on income from *alcabalas*. Alcabalas were a colonial-era interstate sales tax that liberals outlawed in the Constitution of 1857, believing that they hindered "a unified national market."[15] Some places continued to collect alcabalas for decades after 1857 nonetheless, including in Tlaxcala, until at least 1895.[16] Most municipalities in Tlaxcala did not have access to fiscal mechanisms such as loans that federal and state governments often used to pay for development projects, although occasionally municipalities, mainly the municipality of Tlaxcala, borrowed from the state.[17] Lower-level officials often had to resort to begging. Writing to his district prefect, the municipal president of Tlaxco asked, "because this Ayuntamiento's funds . . . [are] really just enough to cover the most basic expenses . . . [could you send] . . . dozens of pickaxes and hatchets" in order to finish repairs "of great importance" along the stretch of the camino real that connected Tlaxco and Zacatelco.[18] The municipal president asked to pass the message on to the governor and "if possible" the Secretaría de Fomento, as well.[19]

Cahuantzi addressed Tlaxcala's shoddy transport system in much the same way he managed waterways. As with water users, Cahuantzi affirmed laws and ordinances that upheld shared usage rights and imposed regulations and conditions on private landowners to keep open and maintain roads in and around their properties. In a circular to prefects from May 1885, Cahuantzi dictated how landowners were not permitted to "close or make more narrow public roads" and "in the case that they do so [landowners] will be forced to open them."[20] Examples of Cahuantzi and other officials forcing landowners to make good on these dictates are abundant in state and municipal holdings.[21] In another 1885 ordinance the governor called on private property owners and towns to attend to their roads.[22] He and his jefes políticos followed through with the ordinance by writing private missives directly to hacienda owners.[23]

As with waterways, Cahuantzi made infrastructural improvements conditional of landowners' natural resource access. In 1907, Agustín del Pozo, a hacendado, requested private access rights to a point along the Zahuapan River. Yet the people of the pueblo of Belém contested the state's decision, since the canal that del Pozo proposed to build would run directly through pueblo lands. Inevitably, state officials permitted del Pozo to construct his canal while also "oblig[ing] [del Pozo] to construct out of his own pocket four bridges to facilitate traffic" from four surrounding communities. Del Pozo was also ordered to "employ" vecinos from the nearby pueblo of Belém "on public works projects" and to provide $100 MXN annually to public education in Belém. Lastly, del Pozo was ordered to construct a drainage line that would irrigate pueblo lands nearby during the dry season.[24] The state's handling of del Pozo's petition exemplifies how Cahuantzi's administration used residents' petitions for private water and land rights as opportunities to broker compromises between disputing parties and to hold private property owners accountable for improving infrastructure in and around their properties. This strategy—imposing conditions on those petitioning for water and land—permitted the governor to push road, bridge, and irrigation costs onto private landowners instead of onto local governments that struggled to keep up with infrastructural maintenance.

Lack of funds was not the only problem municipalities faced when trying to repair and build infrastructure. Local officials also faced labor shortages since the coercive system of *faenas* was—in theory—abolished. Initiated during the colonial period, faenas required residents to perform compulsory labor on public works projects.[25] Faenas had been particularly useful to municipalities in Tlaxcala-Puebla during the rainy season when residents were obliged to repair flooded riverbanks, roads, and bridges.[26] Faenas were resoundingly unpopular throughout the region, and although they were officially outlawed in Puebla and Tlaxcala in the 1860s, they continued in many places well into the twentieth century.[27] In the town of Contla, for example, the municipal president relayed how villagers ignored municipal ordinances that outlined their "duty" to fix roads and that roads there had been "reduce[d] to [mere] pathways" because of villagers' neglect.[28] In Calpulalpan, where passable roads were necessary to reach the rail station that was located there, authorities decided to "ask . . . anyone" with a wagon to come help "pave" the roads by shuttling and placing stones.[29] Calpulalpan officials belittled local residents for failing to "comply with the urgent necessity . . . to improve and beautify the places [where they lived] and . . . to live up to the standards . . . of a civilization."[30] In making these accusations, however, officials were trying to compel local labor. There are various instances in the historic record in which Cahuantzi overrode lower officials when they tried to use faenas and fined them if they did so again; this was atypical of most governors and jefes políticos during the Porfiriato.[31] But without more money coming in to pay for labor, Cahuantzi's disavowal of faenas did little to solve municipalities' labor problems.

Residents' and local authorities' complaints about roadways in Tlaxcala typify the fiscal crises towns in Mexico and throughout Latin America faced during this period.[32] As nation-states expanded market-based capitalism and eliminated colonial economic mechanisms such as alcabalas, they simultaneously eroded the capacity of localities to capture enough revenue to take care of their residents' basic infrastructural needs. Cahuantzi called on district and local officials to do a better job of maintaining local roadways, particularly during the rainy season.[33] Along with his state treasurer, the governor pressured localities to be more fiscally solvent by requesting regular, detailed municipal budget reports. Because of the constraints municipal budgets faced, Cahuantzi often foisted road maintenance onto larger land and factory owners who had more resources to fix the roads near their properties. This approach also freed the state to set its sights on more grandiose public works projects like plumbing and electricity. While sometimes effective, this strategy was not without political consequences. After businessman Mariano Fortuño of the central town of Chiautempan was told by the governor to "pave" the principal road that surrounded his property in 1887, Fortuño smarted back how "neither now nor ever have any of the roads been paved in Santa Ana Chiautempan."[34] The businessman further explained how "the local authorities here [in Chiautempan] are imposing new obligations on this business every day."[35] Residents in Tepeyanco had similar complaints. Writing to Díaz in 1900, they lamented how Cahuantzi had "burden[ed]" them with the costs of new bridges and a new Palacio de Tlaxco.[36] As "governor in perpetuity," they wrote, "[Cahuantzi's] power has extended throughout the municipalities."[37] Nearby villagers agreed.[38] Residents of all socioeconomic backgrounds understood the value of structurally sound and passable roads and bridges. But while residents welcomed and even insisted on these improvements, they often resented the state incursions, fiscal and otherwise, that accompanied them.

Marking Modernity

Modernization projects were ongoing throughout the region. But the governor's priority was to develop Tlaxcala City. Revitalizing Tlaxcala City was part of Cahuantzi's broader goals to diminish the autonomy of municipalities and regional factions, consolidate state authority, and encourage investment in his state. Cahuantzi's plans for the city included building bridges, canals, and flood control measures; renovating public buildings and spaces; and installing public services such as potable water and electric lights. For a state capital, Tlaxcala City was meager. Hovering just below 3,000 during the Porfiriato, the population of Tlaxcala City was smaller than other cities in Tlaxcala, including Apizaco, Huamantla, and Chiautempan.[39] Yet its environs, which included the Nativitas Valley, were among the most densely populated in the nation. Despite that residents often wanted the improvements that Cahuantzi's administration proposed to make in and around Tlaxcala City, state and especially municipal governments lacked sufficient money to create functional spaces and effective services for their residents.

The first major project that Cahuantzi completed was to build a large bridge over the Zahuapan River along the northern ramparts of the city.

The purpose of the bridge was to allow those who lived in the numerous communities and towns above the river to access the city more readily and reliably. Juan Arellano, the federal engineer who oversaw the project, promised that the bridge would "unite . . . the city . . . with the *pueblos* on the other side of the river," and that it "would be the first bridge [of its kind] in the country."[40] Arellano's words must have been music to Cahuantzi's ears: the bridge would physically embody Tlaxcala's progress under his watch. Arellano proposed for the bridge to have a wooden walkway that spanned 17.6 meters, suspended by cables and iron spires that allowed the bridge to hold the weight of fifty men and fourteen mules.[41] By making the bridge's spires out of iron, state and municipal administrators hoped to avoid the annual cycle of repairs that had to be made to all-wooden bridges after they were pelted by floodwaters during the rainy season. The iron spires would also help to prevent the loans that the ayuntamiento, or less often the state, took out to make these repairs. Construction on the bridge was completed in 1889, and it opened to foot and mule passage in 1890.[42]

Arellano calculated that the bridge would cost Tlaxcala state $8,290 MXN.[43] Of this, approximately one-third was the responsibility of the Ayuntamiento of Tlaxcala. The state purchased the iron for the bridge from Bowes Scott, Read, and Campbell LLC, a British company with an outpost in Mexico City.[44] However, state and municipal fiscal records (*cortes de caja*) do not clearly convey how the state and the municipality obtained the funds to cover the bridge's costs. For its part, the state likely drained months' worth of funds that it had allocated for public works. According to annual state budget reports, the state spent $11,446 and $16,216 MXN on public works in 1889 and 1890, respectively.[45]

More mysterious still is how the municipality came up with their share. For the municipality, $3,000 MXN—one-third of the bridge's cost—was no small sum. In 1889, 12 percent ($1500 MXN) of the annual municipal budget had been allocated for public works, $1000 MXN of which, the municipal treasurer announced, would go toward the bridge.[46] It is unclear where the municipality got the rest of the money. The municipality had managed to collect some of the necessary funds by pursuing backlogged debts from residents who owed land and water rents as well as other miscellaneous fines.[47] But the sum of these taxes, fees, and fines was not enough to cover the bridge's costs. In October 1890, the municipal treasurer announced that the $1500 surplus from the year 1890 would cover

FIGURE 15. Iron bridge over the Zahuapan River in Tlaxcala City. Source: Cahuantzi, *Memoria de la administración pública del Estado de Tlaxcala*, Tlaxcala: Imprenta del Gobierno, 1894.

the municipality's remaining outlay.⁴⁸ Curiously, the municipal surplus equaled the precise amount needed to cover the bridge project.

Municipal officials in Tlaxcala City supported Cahuantzi's plans for the bridge and for the improvement of the city in general. In 1888, the municipal president relayed how

> [the municipality of Tlaxcala] cannot stand to lose any amount, small as it may be, since that sum might just be enough [to cover the costs of] certain urgent projects, such as those related to public health and the beautification of the city and the comfort of its residents[;]those related to constructing and cleaning drain pipes and streets . . . and other projects that must be carried out in important towns like this one. [Tlaxcala City], because of its historical memories, [and] because it is the state capital, is visited constantly by national residents and foreigners alike.⁴⁹

The municipal president's claim that Tlaxcala City was "visited constantly" may have been aspirational, but his statement nevertheless makes clear how Cahuantzi was not alone in his desire to improve the capital. Collaboration between state and municipal officials was essential to accomplish modernization goals, especially since municipalities rarely had the funds to meet these goals on their own, as with the Zahuapan bridge.[50] Cahuantzi's determination to modernize Tlaxcala City also helps to explain why he wanted to influence electoral outcomes there, since it was important to have ayuntamiento officials who supported his plans.

Many residents in and around Tlaxcala City supported modernization projects as well, though modernization did not benefit all residents equally. Infrastructure such as dikes, roads, and bridges was used and demanded by residents of all socioeconomic standings. But public services such as potable water and electricity, at least during the Porfiriato, were only available to residents in more urbanized areas, and only for those who had the means to pay for them. As compared to other regional population centers such as Veracruz or Puebla City, Tlaxcala City was hardly urban. Even for those who could afford to build potable water pipelines to their private homes and businesses, state and municipal governments were unable to implement these services effectively. Residents who paid for public services became irritated when these services did not work as promised.

Potable water, for example, had all sorts of benefits. It was a way to alleviate residents' perennial problems accessing water, if only for those who lived in and around Tlaxcala City. Plumbing was a boon for public health since putrid water in open air pipes was often linked to disease.[51] Public services such as plumbing and electricity generated additional state and municipal revenues since governments collected fees to use these services.[52] And as with the Zahuapan bridge, plumbing and electric lighting were ways for Cahuantzi and municipal officials to stamp Porfirian ideals of modernity onto Tlaxcala's physical space. In the late 1880s, the Ayuntamiento of Tlaxcala proposed to expand and improve the current potable water system by replacing many of the city's adobe pipes with iron ones.[53] The state and the municipality ordered wells, springs, and other *abastos de agua* (water sources) to be repaired and cleaned to supply the system's water.[54]

Dozens of claims came into the ayuntamiento from residents who requested that potable water taps be installed in their homes and businesses. Most of these residents had already laid the pipes to deliver the water. In addition to private taps, public potable water taps were installed throughout the city for residents to use for a fee. Residents paid water fees (*mercedes de agua*) directly to their municipality. These fees usually generated between $250 and 350 MXN in municipal revenue per month.[55] To support plumbing infrastructure, the governor created a water commission in Tlaxcala City as well as a *vigilancia de agua*—essentially, an official state plumber.[56] The foremost job of the vigilancia de agua was to go door to door to trace the source of water when it became polluted. Tlaxcala was in no way unique or innovative in establishing a water bureaucracy; other localities in Mexico had hired a water commissioner (*aguador*) as early as the late eighteenth century.[57] Regions larger than Tlaxcala such as Puebla City had already outsourced plumbing inspections to private companies.[58] By finally hiring water inspectors, Tlaxcala City was attempting to catch up to other more well-developed, better funded, cities.

Despite investments made by the state, municipality, and residents to implement a potable water system in Tlaxcala City, water often did not arrive as promised. One water user who lived along the *portales* of the main square grumbled that he had not received "a single drop of this liquid."[59] Others complained that if potable water did come through, it arrived "foul" and "unusable."[60] Many potable water users refused to pay their fees as a result. In 1901, the municipal treasurer lamented how some residents had opted to close their taps, even after paying out of pocket to lay plumbing pipes.[61] He further indicated how he was "unable to apply the [water tax] law" if water never arrived at homes and businesses.[62] Municipal revenues diminished after the treasurer was forced to close a number of accounts, though the municipality continued to track water users' "debts" nevertheless.[63]

At the turn of the twentieth century, Cahuantzi and the Ayuntamiento of Tlaxcala set out to resolve the city's chronic water problems once and for all. Together they initiated a massive project to construct water-related infrastructure—dams, canals, and dikes—that would harness water from the Zahuapan River for two purposes: first, to generate more water for residents in and around the city who complained that it was lacking both in public and private sources; and second, to create hydraulic current to replace turpentine lights with electric ones in the capital as well as in the neighboring municipalities of Chiautempan and Apetatitlán. Tlaxcala lagged well behind dozens of other urban centers that had already installed electric lights.[64] In addition to representing dated forms of lighting, turpentine lights often failed to work, leading to complaints from residents that roads were "impassable" and dark."[65] Turpentine extraction also contributed to the erosion of Tlaxcala's precious forestlands.[66] When the price of gas increased at the turn of the twentieth century, Cahuantzi and other lower level officials attempted to purchase electric light bulbs from different electric companies such as La Compañia de Luz Blanca, the Mexico City outpost of "Peerless Lamp" in St. Louis, Missouri.[67] This deal fell through, however, because officials could not pay.[68]

In 1902, under the guidance of federal engineer Pedro Lira, the *canalización* project began. It was still ongoing in 1910. As with the Zahuapan bridge, financing for the project was split between the state and the Ayuntamiento of Tlaxcala.[69] However, as months and then years went on, it became clear that the state would have to shoulder most of the project's labor and material costs. Official state records from 1904 estimated the project's costs to be $25,400 MXN. By 1906 this number had increased to $66,000 MXN.[70] To put these numbers in perspective, the municipal budget for Tlaxcala in the year 1905 was $13,618 MXN as compared to the state, which was reported as $294,112 MXN.[71] Of this, the state indicated that it spent $22,222 MXN on public works.[72] The municipality of Tlaxcala's budget exceeded all other municipalities by a significant margin (except for Huamantla). Yet because regular municipal revenues fell well short of what was needed for the project, ayuntamiento officials pursued additional forms of revenue. For one, they sold a terreno that they still owned at the base of La Malintzin.[73] They also took out loans, mostly from the state, and a few from other lenders.[74] In 1906, the ayuntamiento borrowed $54,000 MXN from the Banco Central Mexicano to pay for the machinery for the new hydroelectric plant that would power electricity in and around the capital.[75] The machinery was purchased from Schöndube & Neugebauer, a European investment firm that had supported similar public works projects in other states.[76] In order to cover their $2,400 MXN interest payment to the Banco Central in 1907, the ayuntamiento borrowed yet again from the state.[77] The ayuntamiento also used this loan to find a new land plot on which to build the hydroelectric plant, since inspectors had found that the original site was insufficiently "solid."[78] As was the case for many properties in the Nativitas Valley, the lands flooded too often.

In state and municipal budget reports, expenditures almost always matched revenues down to the cent. That state and municipal expenditures and revenues corresponded so exactly calls these records' reliability into question—the state, and especially the municipality of Tlaxcala, likely spent much more than the amounts relayed in official records. The state and the municipality were likely accumulating a lot of debt, although neither state nor municipal fiscal records reveal how much. One source indicates that when Cahuantzi left office, the Tlaxcalan state treasury owed some MXN $184,000, to say nothing about the ayuntamiento.[79] Over the course of Cahuantzi's regime, official records show that approximate spending on public education doubled; social services increased fivefold; public works increased by four and a half times its original percentage; military spending doubled; and lastly, bureaucratic costs increased by two and a half times its original percentage.[80] Of the five spending categories listed above, the total percentage of state income allocated toward social services and public works increased more than other categories and outpaced total state expenditures.[81]

Although the state and the municipality of Tlaxcala were spending more on infrastructure and public works than ever before, residents' gripes were the same during the final years of Cahuantzi's rule as they were almost three decades before: there was not enough water. Electricity in and around Tlaxcala City malfunctioned because nearby factories were siphoning off too much water. Thus, Cahuantzi proposed yet another dam in 1909. He paid for the dam using a $10,000 MXN credit supplied by the banking house Descuento Español. Labor, the governor announced, would be supplied by residents in Tlaxcala and four other neighboring towns. Workers would be exempted from the head tax, but they would otherwise not be paid. Cahuantzi had previously forbid lower officials to coerce labor on infrastructure and public works projects such as road repairs. But such was not the case when Cahuantzi desperately wanted to electrify the state capital while continuing to power factories.[82]

A similar pattern—in which Cahuantzi's modernizing ambitions exceeded the state's ability to implement modernization effectively—could be glimpsed in the public education sector. Public education was a quintessential liberal goal, and there was a great deal of grandstanding in state-sponsored papers about advancements in primary school education for boys and girls under Cahuantzi. *La Antigua República* featured regular reports on school openings, exams and exam results, and commemorations and celebrations taking place in local schools. Unlike larger states, which had professional education bureaucracies, in Tlaxcala, local officials, jefes políticos, and often Cahuantzi himself presided over school-related events, including administrative affairs such as exams.[83] Public schools were funded through myriad means outlined in state laws. Municipalities were required to give 15 percent of their monthly revenues to the state. The state then redistributed these funds among local schools.

Revenues that municipalities collected when they sold communal properties were also designated for public education.[84] Tlaxcala had a high number of schools per capita, though this number waned during the last decade of the Porfiriato.[85] Historian Elsie Rockwell indicates how "this system achieved a relatively equitable fiscal distribution among Tlaxcala's municipalities, a situation not always found in other parts of Mexico."[86] Approximately one-fourth of primary-school-aged children attended school in Tlaxcala—children of farmers often joined their families in the fields—and more children attended school as the Porfiriato went on. The agente municipal of the village of Tepeihtec, who wrote to his ayuntamiento in 1897 to indicate that the number of boys and girls who attended school there had increased, took higher school attendance as a sign of his village's "advancement and progress."[87] Two teacher-training institutes, El Instituto de Estudios Científicos y Literarios de Tlaxcala and its equivalent for women, La Escuela Superior de Niñas 'Eduación y Patria,' both founded in the late nineteenth century, also garnered local and national attention.[88]

Yet it was not possible for the state and municipalities to develop and sustain an effective public education system when governments prioritized electric lights over teacher pay. Haciendas were required to provide teachers for their workers' children.[89] But especially in the Nativitas Valley, where few families lived permanently on haciendas, municipalities were unable to cover the costs of basic infrastructural repairs, let alone remunerate teachers or buy school supplies and books.[90] When municipalities failed to comply with the state mandate that 15 percent of all municipal revenues be sent to the state to distribute to schools, Cahuantzi pressed municipal officials and threatened to fine them, as with the town of Terrenate where he accused officials of being "frozen from indifference . . . [toward their] sacred duty [to support public education]."[91] Officials in Terrenate replied that they simply did not have the money to send.[92] Families throughout the Nativitas Valley indicated how they had no way to get their children to school, let alone attend regularly.[93] It was clear that Cahuantzi valued public education. But the governor also wanted to build and hold elaborate celebrations to inaugurate schools to mark Tlaxcala's liberal progress, even though local governments often lacked the means to staff and supply these schools.

There were plenty of residents in and around the capital who demanded improvements to the spaces and services where they lived and worked.

They wanted dikes and other flood control measures, well-lit and passable roads and bridges, access to water, and schools. Some residents in population centers such as Tlaxcala City were willing to pay for services like electricity and potable water. It was because of residents' demands—not only because Cahuantzi wanted to exhibit Tlaxcala's modernity and please elite Porfiristas—that the governor pursued different fiscal mechanisms to make these improvements possible. The inability of the state and localities to effectively implement modernization goals, even if residents supported these goals, cannot be blamed on national- and state-level despotism alone. However, over time, Cahuantzi's administration became more concerned with imprinting modernity on the state landscape than meeting residents' needs. As a result, the state and many municipalities incurred large debts to try to reach Porfirian standards of modernity that were utterly unreasonable for a state as small as Tlaxcala to meet.

Cooperation, or perhaps better stated, collusion, between state and local officials was essential to implement modernization projects. If the Ayuntamiento of Tlaxcala had once enjoyed a certain level of autonomy from the nation and the state, this autonomy was long since gone by the early twentieth century. As time went on, Cahuantzi made more demands of local officials, and local officials did the same to residents. In 1906 and 1907, the same years that Tlaxcala City residents complained about the potable water system failing, the municipal president bade city residents to fix or build storm drainage along the roads that passed by their properties and to repaint the facades of their homes and businesses.[94] He threatened residents with fines if they failed to comply. As state and local governments took on more modernization projects, local governments had less autonomy, and residents endured more coercion.

Fiscal Coercion and Revolutionary Dissent

In 1910, Mexico's national minister of finance, José Yves Limantour, published a hundred-page-long report that provided economic data for each state in the Mexican federation. Tlaxcala's contribution was among the most comprehensive, even as compared to larger states. It included economic data for all six districts and thirty-six municipalities. It also spelled out an eighteen-point taxation plan ranging from property taxes to taxes on specific goods to taxes on professional titles and burial plots in cemeteries. Tlaxcala's state budget paid for public education, public good (*beneficencia pública*), public works and modernization projects, military costs, and the state bureaucracy, among other expenditures. Spending in all these categories increased significantly from 1885 to 1910. Overall, under Cahuantzi, state income more than tripled, from $125,041 to MXN to $422,948 MXN, a total real increase of about 40 percent when accounting for inflation. Cahuantzi's attempts to create a more efficient fiscal system in Tlaxcala worked. Revenue from property taxes alone more than doubled. The report encapsulated Governor Cahuantzi's efforts to make his state more fiscally solvent over the course of nearly three decades of continuous rule.[95]

Increased state revenues came at a high political cost, however. In 1899, one thousand villagers led by Andrés García gathered in the center of Tlaxcala to protest the new tax law (Ley de Hacienda). The law, which Cahuantzi had announced some months before, increased most Tlaxcalans' property taxes significantly.[96] Many Tlaxcalans were dismayed by the tax hike. But smaller property owners—those whose properties were valued between $50 and $100 MXN and who had never previously paid a property tax—protested it most vociferously and publicly. Accompanied by rurales, Cahuantzi put García's protest down swiftly and imprisoned García briefly for sedition.[97] Meanwhile, *El Hijo del Ahuizote* out of Mexico City reported that Cahuantzi's property tax increase was "killing small proprietorship in Tlaxcala."[98] In the early 1900s, small landowners from the Nativitas Valley joined Andrés García in protesting Cahuantzi's property tax hikes.[99] National economic crises and poor harvests of the early 1900s exacerbated Tlaxcalans' financial problems, especially among the poorest residents. In 1905, protests renewed. This time, Cahuantzi had García assassinated, and multiple national news outlets reported the incident.[100]

Objections to Cahuantzi's rule, usually written in private missives to or in conversations with Díaz, were nothing new. But the 1905 assassination of García, coupled with other public protests that continued on and off until Cahuantzi was ousted in 1911, signaled how dissent against the governor was coalescing. Moreover, the increased violence that the administration was using to quell dissent indicated how the usual political mechanisms—patronage, selective appeasement of demands, and the like—were failing. After 1905, when Cahuantzi had Andrés García murdered, leaders like Isidro Ortiz, Juan Cuamatzi, and later Domingo Arenas followed in García's footsteps.[101] As with García in 1905, Cahuantzi used rurales and other local police to put their protests down, jailing many for sedition.[102]

Although protests by more elite residents were less public than those of small proprietors and factory workers, Cahuantzi's taxation policies irked them as well. Pulque producers were not at all pleased when Cahuantzi began to tax pulque based on the number of barrels of pulque produced, rather than the previous measure, which taxed the number of pulque plants cultivated. Whereas pulqueros had always lied about the quantity of drink their plants yielded, Cahuantzi's policy change—taxing barrels rather than plants—made this much more difficult to do. Some smaller producers were forced to close up shop as a result of the new tax policy, with one pulquero fearing these new policies would result in a "monopoly."[103] Cahuantzi also targeted pulque vendors (*casillas*), accusing them of "defrauding the state treasury" and "never tell[ing] the truth" about how much pulque they sold.[104] In 1905, the governor began to regulate casilla pulque sales by imposing a fixed monthly fee that the casillas would have to pay based on the amount of pulque that the casilla had at the beginning of the day. When smaller casillas protested this new regulation, Cahuantzi agreed to allow them to pay their fees daily, rather than monthly.[105] But, in general, pulque producers and vendors did not support changes to how pulque was taxed, and in the early twentieth century, they began to organize. In 1905 some fifty pulque hacendados added their voices to those who were already protesting the regime.[106]

During the same years that pulqueros were complaining about changes to pulque taxes, small landowners in Zacatelco insisted that pulqueros and other hacendados were being afforded tax breaks "out of friendship" because Cahuantzi needed their support around election time.[107] Although there is no direct evidence in the historic record to support Zacatelco residents' claims, given Cahuantzi's history of negotiating residents' tax contributions, they were probably correct. Both before and after the Ley de Hacienda was passed in 1897, residents wrote frequently to the governor to ask him to reduce their tax contributions. This was true regardless of the nature of the tax: head tax, property tax, or a tax on a specific product such as pulque or meat. Cahuantzi sometimes granted these requests. Cahuantzi was also amenable to negotiation when his administration conducted new property surveys to augment land values and property taxes.[108]

Cahuantzi's selective conciliation of residents' demands—to install a new district prefect, to allow villagers to continue to use lands for communal cattle grazing, to build a dam, to lower a property tax rate, to fix a road—helped Cahuantzi to remain in office for twenty-six years. However, over time, Cahuantzi imposed more burdens on the people of Tlaxcala to meet not only their demands but also those of an increasingly powerful authoritarian nation-state, one that was focused on economic growth and its international repute over the quotidian concerns of its impoverished citizens. As Cahuantzi's regime became less flexible, Tlaxcalans of all socioeconomic backgrounds became incensed—both small landowners and pulqueros protested tax hikes. But for poorer residents especially, occasionally conciliating their demands failed to overcome a national and state-level dictatorship that exploited them and left them with no political voice. Many of Tlaxcala's small landowners and villagers took up arms against Díaz and Cahuantzi's authoritarian rule when the Mexican Revolution broke out in 1910.

Conclusion

Governor Cahuantzi used infrastructure and public works as physical manifestations of his power and of his state's capacity to be modern. To make modernization happen, he leveraged the state apparatus—imposing obligations, fiscal and otherwise—on local governments and individual residents.[109] As Cahuantzi's ambition grew, as his and Díaz's regimes became more entrenched, so too did the burdens Cahuantzi's administration placed upon ayuntamientos and residents. At the same time, residents' petitions to state and local officials make clear how Tlaxcalans of all walks of life insisted on improvements to services and spaces that they used regularly. In Tlaxcala, modernization was not simply imposed by elites on a populace who did not see its need. However, because Tlaxcala did not play a critical role in national development schemes, Tlaxcalans were left to manage and fund modernization on their own. Paltry state and local budgets were rarely sufficient to accomplish modernization goals, let alone maintain the status quo. Cahuantzi's efforts to modernize his state and make it more fiscally solvent—as well as to augment state power—precipitated tax increases and the protests and revolutionary dissent that ensued.

Conclusion

In October 1905, a riot broke out in San Miguel Tenancingo during the town's patron saint's day celebration. According to *La Antigua República*, a group of men and women were arrested because they appeared intoxicated and "began to insult local officials." As the revelers became increasingly "scandalous," local police were called on to get matters under control. A few particularly rowdy carousers were thrown in jail. Their imprisonment set off a riot led by a farmer who rallied thirty-some villagers and small landowners to storm the jail and demand the release of the captives. When the group began to throw rocks and fire random shots at the policemen, rurales stationed nearby, along with Governor Cahuantzi—who had boarded an overnight train from Mexico City—were called on to quell the outburst. Together, Cahuantzi and the police "violently reestablished order." According to various journalistic and scholarly sources, among the thirty-four townspeople arrested were "the most ardent proponents" of revolutionary ideas in Tlaxcala.[1]

Toward the end of his rule, Próspero Cahuantzi became less open to negotiation, less tolerant of local autonomy, and more willing to engage with violence. At the same time, small landowners and villagers in Tlaxcala, like those present during the Tenancingo riot, grew increasingly vocal in their protests of Cahuantzi's tax policies in the early twentieth century. Factory workers—some of whom were also farmers—began to strike as well. Connected to and emboldened by labor networks throughout the central Mexican textile corridor, factory workers demanded better pay and working conditions.² Cahuantzi sometimes deflected workers' requests, as he did when the president of El Segundo Círculo de Obreros Libres, based out of Puebla, pleaded with him to intercede on the workers' behalf. In that instance, Cahuantzi encouraged the labor leader to lodge a complaint with the district judge "in order to punish and denounce [workers' maltreatment]."³ By and large, however, Cahuantzi, like most Porfirian leaders, sided with factory owners and arrested suspected strikers.⁴ In 1908, the governor also renewed some factories' tax exemptions for another ten-year period.⁵ With substantial tax breaks, the textile industry was generating more income than the state had ever seen, and Cahuantzi no doubt did not wish to cut off what had become a vital revenue stream as his ambitions to modernize his state expanded.

Cahuantzi and his supporters used different forms of political propaganda to counter rising public discontent with his and Díaz's rule. Reelection clubs that campaigned to reelect Cahuantzi had existed in Tlaxcala as far back as 1892. Between 1892 and 1908, the number of these clubs tripled.⁶ *La Antigua República* boasted that as of 1908, Cahuantzi's last gubernatorial bid, Tlaxcala had thirty-six reelection clubs, all of which came together during a large gathering in early 1909.⁷ Yet many *anti* reelection clubs had also emerged since 1892 in different Mexican regions, including Tlaxcala, to contest the reelection of President Díaz and his cronies. Spearheaded by Francisco Madero, anti-reelection clubs formed the grassroots bases through which the Mexican Revolution was organized. The high number of reelection clubs in 1908, especially as compared to 1892, makes clear how Cahuantzi's administration was making deliberate efforts to counter increasingly public dissent.

Cahuantzi's backers also took advantage of the governor's native-born background to rally support. In 1906, pro-Porfirian newspaper *El Popular*, based in Mexico City, ran a story insisting that Tlaxcalans were "lucky" to have one of their "native sons ... born in this very *pueblo*, familiar with its customs and needs" leading their state.⁸ In Tlaxcala in 1909, *La Antigua República* similarly touted Cahuantzi as "a son of Ixtulco," stressing his humility and local ties.⁹ These same articles emphasized how Cahuantzi was "not just loved, but idolatrized by his *pueblo*" and that the "popular vote" in Tlaxcala had "fairly ... favored the progress-minded Cahuantzi ... who sincerely loves his people who, in turn, trust him."¹⁰ Cahuantzi's supporters exploited the one advantage they had over other Porfirian governors: because Cahuantzi was born there, they could claim that he "represented" their state. By the early twentieth century, Díaz had replaced most state governors with nonmilitary, outsider cronies. The only other governor during the late Porfiriato who could make claims to "represent" state residents by virtue of his birth—Manuel Alarcón of Morelos—died in 1908.

Public protests against Cahuantzi's regime clearly refuted pro-Porfirian sources' obsequiousness. Most Tlaxcalans were acutely aware of how Cahuantzi, albeit locally born, was appointed, not elected, to power. That the governor was a "son of Ixtulco," or even that he celebrated Tlaxcala's Indigenous history at national and international forums, mattered little to Tlaxcalans who could not afford to pay their property taxes or who were not being paid a livable factory wage. Cahuantzi's local knowledge sometimes proved useful to Tlaxcalans—as when he rejected land and factory owners' requests to build deviation dams, knowing that doing so would flood surrounding lands and villages. However, given Tlaxcalans' material struggles during the late Porfiriato, and that the press only began to highlight Cahuantzi's heritage during his last two gubernatorial bids, the emphases on his place of birth seem to have been desperate measures to subdue opposition, rather than effective means to court support.

The same articles that touted Cahuantzi as a native-born Tlaxcalan also countered pejorative and racialized depictions of the governor that were published in the opposition press. When a national newspaper ridiculed the governor for being "a barefoot Indian," *La Antigua República* wrote that Cahuantzi was neither "beautiful" nor "an Adonis" but that he was nevertheless "loved" by the people of Tlaxcala.[11] *El Popular* insisted that Cahuantzi was a "genuine representative of his intelligent race."[12] Cahuantzi and his supporters engaged with Indigenous signifiers as they always had—carefully and discriminately, and in such a way to distance Cahuantzi from depreciatory notions of Indigenousness.

For the elites of Tlaxcala, Cahuantzi's nonelite upbringing had always been a source of consternation. Because of his background, and for myriad other reasons, many hacendados and factory owners had never been happy with Díaz's choice for state leadership. Some believed that Cahuantzi was too undereducated to help Tlaxcala "progress" and modernize. Others, especially Poblanos, grumbled about Cahuantzi's insistence on drawing a clear border between his state and theirs and forcing non-Tlaxcalans who owned properties there to abide by usufruct natural resource practices. Many large land and factory owners resented that Cahuantzi imposed conditions on their water access rights and compelled them to maintain infrastructure, such as dikes and roads, in and around their properties. Dozens of residents who used large quantities of water had petitioned the Secretaría de Fomento in Mexico City to confirm their exclusive water access rights and attempt to skirt the requirements Cahuantzi imposed on water users. A few land and factory owners had gone so far as to call for the governor's ouster. While Díaz listened to these demands, he did not abide by them. Cahuantzi remained in office, and elites' complaints were tempered instead through political patronage, tax breaks, and favors.

However, as the Revolution that would overthrow Díaz's dictatorship in 1911 dawned, and revolutionaries attacked railroads, bridges, and other properties throughout the Tlaxcala-Puebla region, many of Tlaxcala's large land and factory owners looked past their dislike, or at least their indifference, toward Cahuantzi, and backed him outright. During Cahuantzi's last "run" for office, some land and factory owners wrote to and even visited Díaz to express their support for Cahuantzi.[13] Others indicated their public support by joining reelection clubs.[14] Textile bosses gathered antirevolutionary reconnaissance for the governor, sending him lists of names of workers who they suspected of participating in subversive activity.[15] For the elites who did an about-face, Cahuantzi represented stability over chaos. He was a stalwart agent of a national regime that created amenable economic conditions and supported the interests of large land and factory owners over the popular classes, even if this was not always true on the state and local levels. In February 1908, Cahuantzi wrote to Díaz to thank him for receiving his elite supporters, as well as for their "long-standing and loyal friendship" and the "generosity" Díaz had always shown him.[16]

Díaz was forced out of office in May 1911. Days later, so too was Cahuantzi. The official announcement of Cahuantzi's departure published in the *Periódico Oficial* made it seem as though the governor was taking yet another trip to Puebla or Mexico City, as he had done many times during the previous twenty-six years. The newspaper indicated that Cahuantzi's absence was "temporary" and that Diego Kennedy, a hacendado and an Irish-descended American immigrant, would serve as interim governor in his stead.[17] Kennedy had been one of the hacendados and factory owners who had written to Díaz and the Secretaría de Fomento to express his annoyance with Cahuantzi's stipulations about water. No doubt other elites were pleased to see Kennedy—one of their own—ascend to the governorship. Some days later, a merchant, Agustín Sánchez, took Kennedy's place. As Ricardo Ramírez Rancaño notes, "paradoxically, the Revolution gave the reins of power back to Tlaxcala's dominant classes."[18] The main socioeconomic sectors that participated in the Revolution—peasants, workers, and middle-class radicals—never saw one of their own assume the governorship.[19]

While Díaz sailed away to exile in Paris, Cahuantzi, the "old dinosaur of Tlaxcalan politics," continued to fight for his *compañero de armas*.[20] Cahuantzi took up various political posts under Victoriano Huerta, first as Tlaxcala's *jefe de armas* in 1913 and later as a delegate in the state congress. Two years later, amid revolutionary chaos, Cahuantzi was captured by none other than Francisco "Pancho" Villa and thrown in a penitentiary in Chihuahua.[21] At the age of eighty-one, the former governor died not from a bullet, but most likely from hunger and untreated diabetes, which had also caused Cahuantzi to go nearly blind.[22] Between the Tuxtepec Rebellion in 1876 until his death in 1915, Cahuantzi's loyalty to Mexican dictator Porfirio Díaz never wavered.

A Transformative Revolution?

Because of its central location—a railroad hub between Mexico City and Veracruz—Tlaxcala was a locus of the Revolution. By the time the violence subsided in 1920, the Revolution had ushered in a new democratic constitution and a new, more inclusive political party in Mexico. Tlaxcala's revolutionary leaders had diverse backgrounds, political affiliations, and goals. Some, like Juan Cuamatzi and Domingo Arenas, were small landowners, peasants, or herders. Others, like Antonio Hidalgo, were peasants who had taken up textile factory work. Tlaxcalan revolutionaries were well connected to labor movements out of Puebla. Aquiles Serdán, a Poblano labor leader whose ideologies had been shaped by the radical socialism of the Flores Magón brothers, was highly influential in Tlaxcala. Early on, many of Tlaxcala's revolutionaries were Maderistas—followers of Francisco Madero, the northern hacendado who called for and successfully oversaw Díaz's ouster. When Madero abandoned his promise of land redistribution to peasants, many Tlaxcalans switched their allegiance to revolutionary leader Emiliano Zapata of Morelos. Later, some Tlaxcalan revolutionaries joined the Constitutionalists.[23]

Between 1910 and 1920, it was normal for regional revolutionaries' political affiliations to shift with the changing political winds, from year to year or even from month to month. But as historians of the Revolution in Tlaxcala have emphasized, the goals of revolutionaries there were not always tied to or in alignment with the goals of national or other regional movements. Tlaxcalan revolutionaries were also motivated by local needs and demands. Borrowing from their storied Indigenous past, Tlaxcalan revolutionaries dubbed themselves the Brigade Xicohténcatl.[24] When it was first formed, Tlaxcala's Anti-Reelectionist Party, comprised mostly of peasants and workers, had several goals, including, as Raymond Buve writes, "return of stolen lands to communities, the abolition of the land tax for smallholders, the foundation of agricultural colonies for landless peasants on large haciendas, better labor conditions for workers, the transfer of the hated rural police to another state, and . . . the punishment of Porfirista officials guilty of repression and murder."[25] Unlike the Zapatistas of Morelos, who had a common enemy—sugar planters—and a common goal—to reclaim their lands—around which to coalesce, in Tlaxcala, it was less obvious who exactly was to blame for residents' poverty and oppression.[26] Tlaxcalan revolutionaries' grievances, and the people to blame for those grievances, were multitudinous. That diversity risked stifling the revolutionary movement in the area, and after power had shifted hands, hampered the revolutionaries' ability to form a coherent and sustained political party that could carry out reforms.[27]

During the previous decades, that same lack of unity among Tlaxcalans had been invaluable for Cahuantzi, who selectively conciliated residents' demands in ways that helped him to remain in office for twenty-six years. Tlaxcalans were divided by how they earned a living, what they produced, where they lived—many property owners in Tlaxcala did not reside within the state—and their political goals. Despite his nonelite background, Cahuantzi managed to respond to some elite demands through quintessential Porfirian mechanisms of patronage and favors. As for popular class demands—especially those of small landowners and villagers—Cahuantzi strengthened the state apparatus and used it to impose obligations on well-to-do residents to maintain infrastructure and uphold usufruct water and land rights. Cahuantzi's intimate understanding of Tlaxcala's diversity was vital for him to gauge residents' demands and make strategic decisions about how to deal with them effectively.

To be sure, some Tlaxcalans' lots improved because of the Revolution. Particularly in the Nativitas Valley, small landholders and villagers were able to reclaim hacienda lands that had been stolen from their colonial ancestors. Yet, for those who were able to seize, and more challengingly, keep, these lands, the problem of water access continued. In 1910, the Porfirian government declared the *Ley sobre aprovechamientos de aguas de jurisdicción federal*. The law amended the 1888 Federal Waters Law by declaring that the federal government would henceforth grant usage rights along *all* waterways, not just those that were navigable or marked state or national boundaries.[28] Seven years later, Article 27 of the Constitution of 1917 declared all lands and waters property of the Mexican people.[29] The federal government retained jurisdiction. Despite the revolutionary government's progressive proclamation about natural resources, the document contained a caveat: while water itself could not be privatized, *access* to it could.[30] Even after 1917, the federal government, just like ayuntamientos during the centuries before them, retained the right to grant private access to a pipeline, a dam, a well, or any other toma de agua. The constitution's legal proviso all but assured the hierarchizing of water access, which continues in Mexico to this day.[31]

The number of complaints about water access and floods that Tlaxcalans lodged during the Porfiriato, that remained unsolved even after the dictatorship fell, affirm how water problems continued for many Tlaxcalans during and after the Revolution. In the decades following the Revolution, motorized ground pumping and improved flood infrastructure helped Tlaxcalans to access and control water to some extent. But in general, government interventions, regulations, and laws—even a radical new Constitution—could not undo centuries of human abuse of the hydrological landscape. Moreover, agrarian redistribution could only be effective if residents had sufficient water to irrigate their lands as well as infrastructure to deter floods. Examinations of ongoing water conflicts in Mexican regions like Tlaxcala make clear that the Revolution was not an especially transformative event in the history of water politics in Mexico.

A similar argument can be made for postrevolutionary indigenismo. This book has demonstrated how, not only did indigenismo exist prior to the Revolution, it was used by recognizably Indigenous peoples to fulfill their own political goals. Although the popular aim of the Mexican Revolution was to remedy the nation's class, rather than ethnic, divisions, by bringing attention to popular class struggles, the Revolution facilitated increased appreciation for Indigenous cultures and ideas. Whereas the Porfirian administration focused on the Indigenous past, the postrevolutionary state institutionalized indigenismo by creating and funding Indigenous schools, ministries, and myriad other programs to assimilate and integrate contemporary Indians into the nation-state.[32]

And yet, the attitudes of indigenistas toward Indigenous peoples in the postrevolutionary era, while different in some respects, were as fluid, diverse, and often discriminatory as they had been in the nineteenth century. As A. S. Dillingham writes, "[indigenista intellectuals] ostensibly valorized Indigenous cultures while simultaneously presenting them as a problem to be overcome."[33] Writings such as Guillermo Bonfil Batalla's *México Profundo* and political movements such as the Zapatista National Liberation Army (EZLN), which demanded respect and autonomy for Mexican Indigenous peoples, would not come until the late twentieth century.[34] Anti-Indigenous discrimination remains pervasive throughout Mexico, the Mexican diaspora, and Latin America writ large.[35]

In this view of indigenismo, a top-down construction that relied on prejudicial and contextually dependent notions of ethnic difference, Próspero Cahuantzi was a proto-indigenista. What is more, unlike most indigenista intellectuals of the twentieth century, Cahuantzi, to the extent that was allowable for a person who held official power under Díaz, identified himself as Indigenous. Cahuantzi valorized certain aspects of Indigenousness—especially the history and region of Tlaxcala—while distinguishing himself and fellow Tlaxcalans from the sorts of Indians whom the Porfirian regime believed were a threat to Mexico's forward progress. Cahuantzi's supporters emphasized the governor's nativeness and humility but dismissed notions that he was, as one newspaper alleged, "a barefoot Indian."[36] Indubitably, the pro-Porfirian press exalted Cahuantzi while ridiculing Indigenous peoples elsewhere. There is more work to be done to examine indigenismo in Mexico prior to the Revolution, as well as to compare its iterations across different Latin American spaces and among different Indigenous communities and actors in the nineteenth century.[37]

According to historian Paul Garner, Porfirio Díaz's political longevity derived from his ability to borrow elements from nineteenth-century liberalism and the rule of law, while also engaging with personalistic practices such as patronage that typified the boss-style politics of the "Hispanic world."[38] This book has shown how a regional autocrat—one who was not considered elite by any standard of the definition at the time—maneuvered deftly in order to endure in office. Like Díaz, Próspero Cahuantzi's politics were pragmatic and personalistic. Cahuantzi acted as a keeper of regional history, a granter of patronage, an arbiter of natural resources, an urban planner, and a school superintendent, among other roles. Cahuantzi's personalistic reach, and his capacity to use violence, are indisputable. At the same time, the governor did not always use his power to oppress the popular classes and popular needs in favor of modernization, as was so often the case in other regions during the Porfiriato.

To be clear, negotiations between the authoritarian government and residents were possible in Tlaxcala because of circumstances specific to the region. But these negotiations were also possible because Tlaxcalans demanded them. The arguments contained in this book do not contest, nor should they overshadow, the violence and coercion many Mexicans, including Tlaxcalans, experienced under Porfirian rule. As with the seven-decade rule of the Partido Revolucionario Institucional (PRI) that followed it, violence and coercion underpinned much of Porfirian "stability" and "peace." Yet as this book has shown, regional actors and circumstances—historical, political, geographical, economic, and even hydrological—shaped how, and sometimes whether, national authoritarian imperatives were implemented.

NOTES

Introduction

1. A territory of the state of Mexico until 1857, Tlaxcala was the fifth smallest state by area in the Mexican Federation. Its population grew from 154,871 in 1886 to 184,171 in 1910. *Censo y división territorial del Estado de Tlaxcala* (Mexico, 1895 and 1910).

2. French Minister of Mexico to Minister of Foreign Relations of Mexico, Doc. #415 de la sección de Europa y Africa, 12 Dec. 1901, Archivo Histórico del Estado de Tlaxcala (AHET), Sin clasificar siglo diecinueve (SC), Caja (C. [Box]) 1, Expediente (Exp. [File]) 13, Ficha (f. [File number]) 40.

3. See files contained in AHET, SC, C. 1, Exp. 13, fs. 40–56.

4. Memorandum por C. Manuel, 20 Dec. 1901, AHET, SC, C. 1, Exp. 13, f. 52.

5. Testimonio de Juan González, 27 Dec. 1901, AHET, SC, C. 1, Exp. 13, f. 47.

6. Memorandum por C. Manuel, 20 Dec. 1901, AHET, SC, C. 1, Exp. 13, f. 53.

7. Memorandum por C. Manuel, 20 Dec. 1901, AHET, SC, C. 1, Exp. 13, f. 53.

8. Memorandum por C. Manuel, 20 Dec. 1901, AHET, SC, C. 1, Exp. 13, f. 52.

9. Memorandum por C. Manuel, 20 Dec. 1901, AHET, SC, C. 1, Exp. 13, f. 3.

10. French Minister to Minister of Foreign Relations, 12 Dec. 1901, AHET, SC, C. 1, Exp. 13, f. 40.

11. French Minister to Minister of Foreign Relations, 12 Dec. 1901, AHET, SC, C. 1, Exp. 13, f. 40.

12. Historian Enrique Krauze dubbed the nineteenth century in Mexico "the Century of Caudillos." Krauze, *Siglo de caudillos: Biografía política de México (1810–1910)* (Barcelona: Tusquets Editores, 1994). Beginning with Domingo Sarmiento's famous derision of the Argentine gaucho Juan Facundo Quiroga originally published in 1845, to a plethora of contemporary analyses, Latin America's regional strongmen have long captured scholarly and popular imaginations. Classic accounts include Sarmiento, *Facundo; or, Civilization and Barbarism* (New York:

Penguin Classics, 1998), and more contemporarily John Lynch, *Caudillos in Spanish America, 1800–1850* (Oxford: Clarendon Press, 1992) and Richard Graham, *Patronage and Politics in Nineteenth-Century Brazil* (Stanford, CA: Stanford University Press, 1990). Edited volumes have done much to advance our knowledge about Latin America's regional strongmen. These include D. A. Brading, ed., *Caudillo and Peasant in the Mexican Revolution* (Cambridge: Cambridge University Press, 1980); Fernando López-Alves, ed., *State Formation and Democracy in Latin America, 1810–1900* (Durham, NC: Duke University Press, 2000); Friedrich Katz, ed., *Riot, Rebellion, and Revolution: Rural Social Conflict in Mexico* (Princeton, NJ: Princeton University Press, 1988); Alan Knight and W. G. Pansters, eds., *Caciquismo in Twentieth-Century Mexico* (London: Institute for the Study of the Americas, 2005); Benjamin Thomas and William McNellie, eds., *Other Mexicos: Essays on Regional Mexican History, 1876–1911* (Albuquerque: University of New Mexico Press, 1984); Luis Roniger and Tamar Herzog, eds., *The Collective and the Public in Latin America: Cultural Identities and Political Order* (Brighton: Sussex Academic Press, 2000).

13. Summaries of Mexico's economic growth under Díaz can be found in Edward Beatty's work, including *Institutions and Investment: The Political Basis of Industrialization in Mexico before 1911* (Stanford, CA: Stanford University Press, 2001) and *Technology and the Search for Progress in Modern Mexico* (Berkeley: University of California Press, 2015). On infrastructural growth, see Priscilla Connolly, *El contratista de don Porfirio: Obras públicas, deuda y desarrollo desigual* (Mexico City: Fondo de Cultura Económica, Universidad Autónoma Metropolitana-Azcapotzalco, El Colegio de Michoacán, 1997). On the growth of the export economy, see Steven Topik and Allen Wells, eds., *The Second Conquest of Latin America: Coffee, Henequen, and Oil during the Export Boom, 1850–1930* (Austin: Institute of Latin American Studies, University of Texas Press, 1998). A more regionally centered analysis on the export economy is Casey Lurtz, *From the Grounds Up: Building an Export Economy in Southern Mexico* (Stanford, CA: Stanford University Press, 2019).

14. Historians often frame Díaz as the ultimate caudillo—his political practices have been well treated by historians. For a comprehensive historiography on the Porfiriato, see Mauricio Tenorio Trillo and Aurora Gómez Galvarriato, *El Porfiriato* (Mexico City: Centro de Investigación y Docencia Económicas, Fondo de Cultura Económica, 2006).

15. François-Xavier Guerra, *México: Del antiguo régimen a la Revolución*, vol. 1 (Mexico City: Fondo de Cultura Económica, 1988), 64; Paul Garner, *Porfirio Díaz* (Harlow, England: Longman, 2001), 107.

16. National and state elections were always "held" during the Porfiriato, but candidates typically either ran unopposed or electoral outcomes were otherwise predetermined. A summary of gubernatorial elections under Díaz can be found in Carlos Bravo Regidor, "Elecciones de gobernadores durante el Porfiriato," in *Las elecciones y el gobierno representativo en México (1810–1910)*, ed. José Antonio

Aguilar Rivera (Mexico City: Centro de Investigación y Docencia Económica, 2010), 257–81.

17. Ricardo Rendón Garcini, *El Prosperato: El juego de equilibrios de un gobierno estatal* (Mexico City: Siglo Veintiuno, 1993).

18. In the field of history, critical examinations of Rafael Trujillo's regime in the Dominican Republic inspire the book's central questions. See Richard Lee Turits, *Foundations of Despotism: Peasants, the Trujillo Regime, and Modernity in Dominican History* (Stanford, CA: Stanford University Press, 2003); Lauren Hutchinson Derby, *The Dictator's Seduction: Politics and the Popular Imagination in the Era of Trujillo* (Durham, NC: Duke University Press, 2009). Research in political science, especially among scholars who examine the politics of Mexico's official revolutionary party (Partido Revolucionario Institucional or PRI), are also influential. The Porfiriato has been framed by some scholars as a precursor to the PRI, which ruled Mexico for most of the twentieth century. Relevant works include Armando Razo, *Social Foundations of Limited Dictatorship: Networks and Private Protection during Mexico's Early Industrialization* (Stanford, CA: Stanford University Press, 2008); Beatriz Magaloni, *Voting for Autocracy: Hegemonic Party Survival and Its Demise in Mexico* (Cambridge: Cambridge University Press, 2006); Kenneth F. Greene, *Why Dominant Parties Lose: Mexico's Democratization in Comparative Perspective* (Cambridge: Cambridge University Press, 2007); Guillermo Trejo, *Popular Movements in Autocracies: Religion, Repression, and Indigenous Collective Action in Mexico* (New York: Cambridge University Press, 2012); Joy Langston Hawkes and Scott Morgenstern, "Campaigning in an Electoral Authoritarian Regime: The Case of Mexico," *Comparative Politics* 41, no. 2 (2009): 165–82.

19. Relevant examples within this genre include Yanna Yannakakis, *The Art of Being In-Between: Native Intermediaries, Indian Identity, and Local Rule in Colonial Oaxaca* (Durham, NC: Duke University Press, 2008); Jeffrey L. Gould, *To Die in This Way: Nicaraguan Indians and the Myth of Mestizaje, 1880–1965* (Durham, NC: Duke University Press, 1998); Greg Grandin, *The Blood of Guatemala: A History of Race and Nation* (Durham, NC: Duke University Press, 2000); Charles Walker, *Smoldering Ashes: Cuzco and the Creation of Republican Peru, 1780–1840* (Durham, NC: Duke University Press, 1999); Lesley Byrd Simpson, *Many Mexicos* (Berkeley: University of California Press, 1966). The literature on popular liberalism in Mexico, explained further on, also includes relevant discussions about these intermediary actors.

20. The massive body of work on provincial Mexican politics has upended decades-old notions that the Porfiriato was hegemonic, or that Díaz himself was a leviathan figure who controlled regional political operations throughout Mexico. In some part, the Porfiriato as leviathan metaphor reflected postrevolutionary leaders' efforts to demonize Díaz's rule as a means of legitimating the power of the official party of the Revolution.

21. See Peter F. Guardino, *Peasants, Politics, and the Formation of Mexico's National State: Guerrero, 1800–1857* (Stanford, CA: Stanford University Press, 1996);

Guardino, *The Time of Liberty: Popular Political Culture in Oaxaca, 1750–1850* (Durham, NC: Duke University Press, 2005); Karen Deborah Caplan, *Indigenous Citizens: Local Liberalism in Early National Oaxaca and Yucatán* (Stanford, CA: Stanford University Press, 2009); Florencia E. Mallon, *Peasant and Nation: The Making of Postcolonial Mexico and Peru* (Berkeley: University of California Press, 1995); Guy P. C. Thomson, "Popular Aspects of Liberalism in Mexico, 1848–1888," *Bulletin of Latin American Research* 10, no. 3 (1991): 265–92; Michael Ducey, "Liberal Theory and Peasant Practice: Land and Power in Northern Veracruz, Mexico, 1826–1900," in *Liberals, the Church, and Indian Peasants: Corporate Lands and the Challenge of Reform in Nineteenth-Century Spanish America*, ed. Robert H. Jackson (Albuquerque: University of New Mexico Press, 1997), 65-85.

22. Guardino, *Peasants, Politics, and the Formation of Mexico's National State*, 219.

23. Mallon, *Peasant and Nation*, 286, 317.

24. Joaquín Díaz Calderón, "Biografía del Señor Coronel Don Próspero Cahuantzi," in *La Antigua República* (Tlaxcala), 15 Jan. 1905.

25. According to the state census, 60 percent of Tlaxcalans spoke Nahuatl and/or Otomí (and were thus classified as "Indígena"), but only 20 percent of Tlaxcalans spoke exclusively in an Indigenous language. *Censo y división territorial del Estado de Tlaxcala* (México, 1902).

26. Rendón Garcini, *El Prosperato*, 41.

27. Rendón Garcini, *El Prosperato*, 42. The national guard was a common career path for many men during the nineteenth century. See Patrick J. McNamara, *Sons of the Sierra: Juárez, Díaz, and the People of Ixtlán, Oaxaca, 1855–1920* (Chapel Hill: University of North Carolina Press, 2007), 2.

28. Throughout Latin America, Indigenous difference was tied to the historical, geographic, and political contexts in which it was being produced. Generally speaking, "Indian" and "Indigenous" were ambiguous terms that referred to markers of dress, diet, language, and occupation as well as heredity and appearance. These ideas are interrogated more thoroughly in chapter one. See Alan Knight, "Racism, Revolution, and *Indigenismo:* Mexico, 1910–1940," in *The Idea of Race in Latin America, 1870–1940*, ed. Richard Graham (Austin: University of Texas Press, 1990), 72–74; Paula López Caballero with Ariadna Acevedo-Rodrigo, "Introduction: Why beyond Alterity?" in *Beyond Alterity: Destabilizing the Indigenous Other in Mexico*, ed. Paula López Caballero and Ariadna Acevedo-Rodrigo (Tucson: University of Arizona Press, 2018), 6.

29. Rendón Garcini, *El Prosperato*, 41.

30. See exemplary discussions in Nicolas Shumway, *The Invention of Argentina* (Berkeley: University of California Press, 1991); Rebecca Earle, *Return of the Native: Indians and Myth-Making in Spanish America, 1810–1930* (Durham, NC: Duke University Press, 2007); Brooke Larson, *Trials of Nation Making: Liberalism, Race, and Ethnicity in the Andes, 1810–1910* (Cambridge: Cambridge University Press, 2012); Michel Gobat, "The Invention of Latin America: A Transnational History of Anti-Imperialism, Democracy, and Race," *American Historical Review* 118, no. 5 (2013): 1345–75.

31. See, for example, Gilbert Joseph and Allen Wells, *Summer of Discontent, Seasons of Upheaval: Elite Politics and Rural Insurgency in Yucatán, 1876–1915* (Stanford, CA: Stanford University Press, 1996); Evelyn Hu-DeHart, *Yaqui Resistance and Survival: The Struggle for Land and Autonomy, 1821–1910* (Madison: University of Wisconsin Press, 1984); Ricardo León García and Carlos González Herrera, *Civilizar o exterminar: Tarahumaras y apaches en Chihuahua, siglo XIX* (Mexico City: CIESAS, 2000).

32. Earle, *Return of the Native*.

33. For a summary of the attitudes of Mexican nation-builders toward Indigenous peoples, see Earle, *Return of the Native*. This literature is treated in depth in chapter two.

34. See Earle, *Return of the Native*; Mauricio Tenorio-Trillo, *Mexico at the World's Fairs: Crafting a Modern Nation* (Berkeley: University of California Press, 1996); Christina Bueno, *The Pursuit of Ruins: Archeology, History, and the Making of Modern Mexico* (Albuquerque: University of New Mexico Press, 2016).

35. Matthew Restall's work exemplifies contemporary arguments that maintain that the "Spanish Conquest" misrepresents events in which Indigenous peoples greatly outnumbered the Europeans who participated. See Matthew Restall, *Seven Myths of the Spanish Conquest* (Oxford: Oxford University Press, 2003). Primary accounts that discuss Tlaxcalans' role in the "Spanish conquest" include Bernal Díaz del Castillo, *Historia verdadera de la conquista de la nueva España* (Mexico City: Oficina de la Secretaría de fomento, 1904, 1905; [1632]); Miguel León-Portilla, *The Broken Spears: The Aztec Account of the Conquest of Mexico* (Boston: Beacon Press, 1992). See also Charles Gibson, *Tlaxcala in the Sixteenth Century* (Stanford, CA: Stanford University Press, 1952); Stephanie Wood, *Transcending Conquest: Nahua Views of the Spanish Colonial Mexico* (Norman: University of Oklahoma Press, 2003); Jeanne Gillespie, *Saints and Warriors: Tlaxcalan Perspectives on the Conquest of Tenochtitlán* (New Orleans: University Press of the South, 2004). Many theses, dissertations, and articles on Tlaxcala during the colonial era are housed in the library of the Archivo Histórico del Estado de Tlaxcala.

36. On Tlaxcalans in the north, see L. S. Offutt, "Defending Corporate Identity on Spain's Northeastern Frontier: San Esteban de Nueva Tlaxcala, 1780–1810," *The Americas* 64, no. 3 (2007): 351–75; Patricia Martínez, "'Noble Tlaxcalans': Race and Ethnicity in Northeastern New Spain, 1770–1810" (PhD diss., University of Texas at Austin, 2004). In Central America, see Laura E. Matthews, "Whose Conquest? Nahua, Zapoteca, and Mixteca Allies in the Conquest of Central America," in *Indian Conquistadors: Indigenous Allies in the Conquest of Mesoamerica*, ed. Laura E. Matthews and Michel R. Oudijk (Norman: University of Oklahoma Press, 2007), 102–26.

37. These privileges, which were hard-fought and granted only to some, usually elite, Tlaxcalans, are described in Gibson, *Tlaxcala in the Sixteenth Century*; Andrea Martínez Baracs, *Un gobierno de indios: Tlaxcala, 1519–1750* (Mexico City: Fondo Cultural Económica, Centro de Investigaciones y Estudios Superiores en

Antropología Social; Tlaxcala: Fideicomiso Colegio de Historia de Tlaxcala, 2008), 76–102.

38. Bradley Skopyk, *Colonial Cataclysms: Climate, Landscape, and Memory in Mexico's Little Ice Age* (Tucson: University of Arizona Press, 2020), 67.

39. These ideas are addressed in detail in chapter one.

40. Patricia Ybarra, *Performing Conquest: Five Centuries of Theatre, History, and Identity in Tlaxcala, Mexico* (Ann Arbor: University of Michigan Press, 2009).

41. *El Popular* (Mexico City), 8 Aug. 1906.

42. As Paula López Caballero and Ariadna Acevedo-Rodrigo assert, "The category *indigenous* is a permanent field of negotiation and dispute whose meanings are always volatile and elusive," López Caballero with Acevedo-Rodrigo, "Introduction: Why beyond Alterity?" 6.

43. Skopyk, *Colonial Cataclysms*.

44. See chapters contained in Christopher Boyer, ed., *A Land between Waters* (Tucson: University of Arizona Press, 2012); Mikael Wolfe, *Watering the Revolution: An Environmental and Technological History of Agrarian Reform in Mexico* (Durham, NC: Duke University Press, 2017); Matthew Vitz, *A City on a Lake: Urban Political Ecology and the Growth of Mexico City* (Durham, NC: Duke University Press, 2018). Beyond Mexico, see Sarah T. Hines, *Water for All: Community, Property, and Revolution in Modern Bolivia* (Oakland: University of California Press, 2022); Jacob Blanc, *Before the Flood: The Itaipu Dam and the Visibility of Rural Brazil* (Durham, NC: Duke University Press, 2019).

45. Christina M. Jiménez, *Making an Urban Public: Popular Claims to the City in Mexico, 1879–1932* (Pittsburgh: University of Pittsburgh Press, 2019).

46. On Díaz as national patriarch, see Garner, *Porfirio Díaz*; Jason Ruiz, *Americans in the Treasure House: Travel to Porfirian Mexico and the Cultural Politics of Empire* (Austin: University of Texas Press, 2014), 65–101.

47. John Womack, "Mexican Political Historiography," in *Investigaciones contemporáneas sobre historia de México: Memorias de la tercera reunión de historiadores Mexicanos y Norteamericanos, Oaxtepec, Morelos, 4–7 de noviembre de 1969* (Austin: University of Texas Press, 1971), 478–92. This analytical framework is also shaped by David Blackbourn and Geoff Eley, historians who use the phrase "tyranny of hindsight" to criticize perspectives that are determined to uncover continuities between nineteenth-century imperial Germany and the rise of Third Reich in the post–World War I era. Blackbourn and Eley, introduction to *The Peculiarities of German History: Bourgeois Society and Politics in Nineteenth-Century Germany* (Oxford: Oxford University Press, 1984), 33.

Chapter 1

1. The chapter on the "Porfiritos" in the sweeping set *Historia moderna de México* remains the most comprehensive, if dated, account of Porfirian governors. See D. Cosío Villegas et al., *Historia moderna de México*, vol. 9, *El Porfiriato: La vida política interior*, tomo 2 (Mexico City: Hermes, 1972), 52–124, 425–93. See also Guerra, *México*, vol. 1, 59–125. On governors after the Revolution, see Jürgen Bu-

chenau and William H. Beezley, eds., *State Governors in the Mexican Revolution, 1910–1952: Portraits in Conflict, Courage, and Corruption* (Lanham, MD: Rowman and Littlefield, 2009); Andrew Paxman, ed., *Los gobernadores: Caciques del pasado y del presente* (Mexico City: Grijalbo, 2018).

2. Bravo Regidor, "Elecciones de gobernadores durante el Porfiriato," 276.

3. José C. Valadés, *El Porfirismo: Historia de un régimen, el crecimiento*, Nueva biblioteca mexicana 63 (Mexico City: Universidad Nacional Autónoma de México, 1977), 22.

4. These arguments build on the work of scholars who have demonstrated Porfirio Díaz's remarkable, if inherently limited, ability to understand regional conditions and to consider these conditions when making decisions about provincial leadership. See Guerra, *México*, vol. 1; Garner, *Porfirio Díaz*; chapters contained in Thomas and McNellie, eds., *Other Mexicos*; Romana Falcón and Raymundus Thomas Joseph Buve, eds., *Don Porfirio presidente, nunca omnipotente: Hallazgos, reflexiones y debates, 1876–1911* (Mexico City: Universidad Iberoamericana, Departamento de Historia, 1998); Seminario Nacional "Jornadas Porfirianas" and Jane-Dale Lloyd, eds., *Visiones del Porfiriato, visiones de México: Jornadas de investigación sobre el Porfiriato* (Mexico City: Universidad Iberoamericana, Departamento de Historia, 2004).

5. Mario Ramírez Rancaño, "Próspero Cahuantzi: El gobernador porfirista de Tlaxcala," in *Historias*, Instituto Nacional de Antropología e Historia, Dirección de Estudios Históricos 16 (1987), 100–101; Díaz Calderón, "Biografía del Señor Coronel Don Próspero Cahuantzi," in *La Antigua República*, 15 Jan. 1905.

6. Lauro Carrillo in Chihuahua (in office 1887–92) and Rosendo Márquez in Puebla (in office 1884–92) were also among this cohort. Garner, *Porfirio Díaz*, 84, 108; Guerra, *México*, vol. 1, 100; Bravo Regidor, "Elecciones de gobernadores durante el Porfiriato," 270.

7. Ricardo Rendón Garcini, *Tlaxcala: Historia breve* (Mexico City: El Colegio de México, 2011), 80–82.

8. Bravo Regidor, "Elecciones de gobernadores durante el Porfiriato," 264. An overview of Díaz's first gubernatorial appointees can be found in Cosío Villegas, *Historia moderna de México*, vol. 8, 454–69.

9. Díaz appointed military generals in Baja California, Campeche, Coahuila, Chihuahua, Durango, Guanajuato, Guerrero, Hidalgo, Jalisco, México, Michoacán, Morelos, Nuevo León, Oaxaca, Puebla, San Luis Potosí, Tepic, Veracruz, and Zacatecas. Cosío Villegas, *Historia moderna de México*, vol. 9, 425; Guerra, *México*, vol. 1, 64; Garner, *Porfirio Díaz*, 107.

10. Lurtz, *From the Grounds Up*, 68; Bravo Regidor, "Elecciones de gobernadores durante el Porfiriato," 265–67.

11. Lurtz, *From the Grounds Up*, 71; Garner, *Porfirio Díaz*, 83.

12. Lurtz, *From the Grounds Up*, 71; Héctor G. Martínez and Francie Chassen-López, "Elecciones y crisis política en Oaxaca: 1902," *Historia Mexicana*, 39, no. 2 (October–December 1989): 524.

13. Garner, *Porfirio Díaz*, 71; Cosío Villegas, *Historia moderna de México*, vol. 9, 854; Bravo Regidor, "Elecciones de gobernadores durante el Porfiriato," 275–76. I

agree with Paul Garner that historians have overstated the reach of the científicos beyond Mexico City.

14. The científicos have been treated elaborately in Mexican historiography. Comprehensive summaries of Mexican positivism and how it influenced Díaz's científicos can be found in Leopoldo Zea, *El positivismo en México: Nacimiento, apogeo y decadencia* (Mexico City: Fondo de Cultura Económica, 1968); Charles A. Hale, *The Transformation of Liberalism in Late Nineteenth-Century Mexico* (Princeton, NJ: Princeton University Press, 1989). There were some regional Porfiristas such as Governor Bernardo Reyes in Nuevo León, Governor Teodoro Dehesa in Veracruz, and Díaz's nephew Félix, involved in politics in Oaxaca and Mexico state, who opposed Díaz's científicos. The historic record does not make clear whether Cahuantzi did so as well. Martínez and Chassen-López, "Elecciones y crisis política en Oaxaca," 533.

15. Garner, *Porfirio Díaz*, 107, 109–10.

16. Examples include Manuel González, who became Díaz's successor in 1880 after governing Michoacán from 1877 until 1880 (he also served as governor of Guanajuato from 1885 until 1889); Enrique Creel, one of the wealthiest men in Mexico, went on to be secretary of Foreign Relations after serving as governor of Chihuahua before the Revolution swiftly ended his tenure; and Emilio Rabasa, who became senator after serving as governor of Chiapas from 1891 until 1895. See Bravo Regidor, "Elecciones de gobernadores durante el Porfiriato," 269.

17. Rabasa's brief stint as governor of Chiapas was but a blip in a long career as a lawyer and political theorist. Although their backgrounds could not have been more divergent, Rabasa and Cahuantzi advanced Porfirian nation-building and modernizing projects in their own way. Where Rabasa wrote prodigiously to justify Díaz's reelection and helped shape ideas that were eventually enshrined in the 1917 Mexican constitution, Cahuantzi participated in campaigns to create a national patrimony for Mexico by engaging with and promoting Tlaxcala's pre-Hispanic past. Though he was bound by his state-level station, Cahuantzi asserted his influence on a major national enterprise. Rabasa and Cahuantzi were good stewards of the national regime, and Díaz continually rewarded both men for their support and aptitude. Charles Hale, *Emilio Rabasa and the Survival of Porfirian Liberalism: The Man, His Career, and His Ideas, 1856–1930* (Stanford, CA: Stanford University Press, 2008).

18. Guerra, *México*, vol. 1, 65–66. Though Cahuantzi had little formal education, he had tutors who taught him to read. John Kenneth Turner, *Barbarous Mexico*, 3rd ed. (New York: Cassell, 1912; Austin: University of Texas Press, 1968), 268. Citations refer to the 1968 reprint edition.

19. Guerra, *México*, vol. 1, 65. Nearly all the Porfirian officials who did not have significant wealth when they came to office had accumulated fortunes by the time they left office, including Cahuantzi. Guerra, *México*, vol. 1, 69; 20 Sept. 1889, Colección Porfirio Díaz (CGPD), Legajo (L) 14, Caja (C) 19, Documento (d) 9125; Rendón Garcini, *El Prosperato*, 41.

20. Bravo Regidor, "Elecciones de gobernadores durante el Porfiriato," 268.

21. Bravo Regidor, "Elecciones de gobernadores durante el Porfiriato," 267–68.
22. Twenty-five governors died while in office. Bravo Regidor, "Elecciones de gobernadores durante el Porfiriato," 269–70.
23. Turner, *Barbarous Mexico*, 118.
24. Alan Knight, *The Mexican Revolution*, vol. 1 (Cambridge: Cambridge University Press, 1986), 17.
25. Bravo Regidor, "Elecciones de gobernadores durante el Porfiriato," 277.
26. Bravo Regidor, "Elecciones de gobernadores durante el Porfiriato," 277.
27. Francisco Cañedo in Sinaloa (in office 1892–1910) is also included in this group. Garner, *Porfirio Díaz*, 107; Cosío Villegas, *Historia moderna de México*, vol. 9, 483–85.
28. John Womack, *Zapata and the Mexican Revolution* (New York: Knopf, 1969), 14.
29. Womack, *Zapata and the Mexican Revolution*, 16–17.
30. Womack, *Zapata and the Mexican Revolution*, 16–17.
31. Womack, *Zapata and the Mexican Revolution*, 13; Friedrich Katz, "The Liberal Republic and the Porfiriato, 1867–1910," in *Mexico Since Independence*, ed. Leslie Bethell (Cambridge: Cambridge University Press, 1998), 118.
32. Unlike in Morelos, few haciendas in Tlaxcala produced goods for the international export market. See Mario Rancaño Ramírez, *El sistema de haciendas en Tlaxcala* (Mexico City: Consejo Nacional para la Cultura y las Artes, Dirección General de Publicaciones, 1990), 23–24, 33–39; Raymundus Thomas Joseph Buve, *El movimiento revolucionario en Tlaxcala* (Tlaxcala: Universidad Autónoma de Tlaxcala, Secretaría de Extensión Universitaria y Difusión Cultural, 1994), 232–33. On the hacienda system in Morelos, see Womack, *Zapata and the Mexican Revolution*, 41–54.
33. Rosa E. King, *Tempest over Mexico* (Boston: Brown, 1935); quoted in Womack, *Zapata and the Mexican Revolution*, 13.
34. See Womack, *Zapata and the Mexican Revolution*, 70–71; Manuel Gamio, *Forjando Patria*, 3rd ed. (Mexico City: Editorial Porrúa, 1982), 158–60.
35. As Jason Ruiz argues, foreigners engaged with all sorts of tropes to distinguish themselves from Mexico's "strangely appearing people," and these tropes were embedded in their racialized understandings of phenotype, gender, economics, and politics. Ruiz, *Americans in the Treasure House*, 106.
36. Other governors pictured in the illustration are Martín González (Oaxaca), Pedro Rodríguez (Hidalgo), Fransciso Cañedo (Sinaloa), Luis C. Curiel (Jalisco), Teodoro Dehesa (Veracruz), Manuel Alarcón (Morelos), and Luis Torres (Sonora). José Luis Gómez De Lara, "Próspero Cahuantzi en la caricatura política," *Graffylia, Revista de la Facultad de Filosofía y Letras, Benemérita Universidad Autónoma de Puebla*, no. 19 (July–December 2014): 185.
37. Gómez De Lara, "Próspero Cahuantzi en la caricatura política."
38. A summary of Porfirian intellectuals' attitudes toward Indigenous peoples can be found in Hale, *Transformation of Liberalism*, 220–44; Earle, *Return of the Native*.

39. Tenorio-Trillo, *Mexico at the World's Fairs*, 64–178. The literature on late nineteenth-century nation-building is discussed in chapter two.

40. This abuse has been well-documented. See, for example, Joseph and Wells, *Summer of Discontent, Seasons of Upheaval*; Enrique Montalvo Ortega, "Revolts and Peasant Mobilizations in Yucatán: Indians, Peons, and Peasants from the Caste War to the Revolution," in *Riot, Rebellion, and Revolution: Rural Social Conflict in Mexico*, ed. Friedrich Katz (Princeton, NJ: Princeton University Press, 1988), 308–10; Hu-DeHart, *Yaqui Resistance and Survival*; León García and González Herrera, *Civilizar o exterminar*.

41. Hu-DeHart, *Yaqui Resistance and Survival*; Turner, *Barbarous Mexico*, 41–77. On the colonial history of the Yaquis, see Raphael Brewster Folsom, *The Yaquis and the Empire: Violence, Spanish Imperial Power, and Native Resilience in Colonial Mexico* (New Haven, CT: Yale University Press, 2014).

42. Earle, *Return of the Native*, 183.

43. As Paula López Caballero and Ariadna Acevedo-Rodrigo assert, "The category *indigenous* is a permanent field of negotiation and dispute whose meanings are always volatile and elusive." López Caballero with Acevedo-Rodrigo, "Introduction: Why beyond Alterity?" 6. See also Knight, "Racism, Revolution, and Indigenismo," 72–74; Ruiz, *Americans in the Treasure House*, 106.

44. Rendón Garcini, *El Prosperato*, 41.

45. Frederick Starr, *In Indian Mexico: A Narrative of Travel and Labor* (Chicago: Forbes, 1908), 85.

46. Henry Baerlein, *Mexico: The Land of Unrest* (London: Herbert and Daniel, 1914), 123.

47. Turner, *Barbarous Mexico*, 268.

48. Turner, *Barbarous Mexico*, 268.

49. *New York Times*, 7 Oct. 1914.

50. Carleton Beals, *Porfirio Díaz, Dictator of Mexico* (Philadelphia: J. B. Lippincott, 1932), 375.

51. Modesto González Galindo, "Postrimerías del Porfiriato," *El Universal Gráfico*, 17 and 24 Apr., 1932; Antonio Sosa, *Parque nacional Xicohténcatl, Estado de Tlaxcala*, Secretaría de Agricultura y Ganadería, México, 1951, p. 232, cited in Mario Ramírez Rancaño, "Próspero Cahuantzi en la contrarrevolución," *Revista Mexicana de Sociología* 57, no. 3 (July–September 1995): 177–78.

52. Francisco Zempoalteco to Porfirio Díaz (hereafter abbreviated as PD in citations), 3 Sept. 1900, CGPD, L. 25, C. 29, d. 11334.

53. Clement Manuel, "Memorándum que el suscrito presenta respecto de los hechos que motivaron se librará orden de aprehensión en mi contra, por el Juez de primera instancia del Dist. de Apizaco, Estado de Tlaxcala, 20 Dec. 1901, AHET, SC, C. 1, Exp. 13, fs. 52–53.

54. Manuel, "Memorándum."

55. Díaz Calderón, "Biografía del Señor Coronel Don Próspero Cahuantzi," in *La Antigua República*, 15 Jan. 1905, 2.

56. *La Antigua República*, 23 Feb. 1908; Rendon Garcini, *El Prosperato*, 64–65.

57. Although petitioners who wrote to Díaz used self-depreciating terms such as "humble servant" to kowtow to the president, petitioners began to employ terms such as "poor" and "humble" more commonly after the Revolution to emphasize their poverty as a strategic means of making land claims. See Romana Falcón, *El jefe político: Un dominio negociado en el mundo rural del Estado de México, 1856–1911* (Mexico City: El Colegio de México, Centro de Investigaciones y Estudios Sociales en Antropología Social, El Colegio Michoacán, 2015), 34; Christopher R. Boyer, *Becoming Campesinos: Politics, Identity, and Agrarian Struggle in Postrevolutionary Michoacán, 1920–1930* (Stanford, CA: Stanford University Press, 2003).

58. Guy P. C. Thomson and David G. LaFrance, *Patriotism, Politics, and Popular Liberalism in Nineteenth-Century Mexico: Juan Francisco Lucas and the Puebla Sierra* (Wilmington, DE: Scholarly Resources, 1999), 262; Knight, *Mexican Revolution*, vol. 1, 5.

59. Díaz replaced González with the científico-leaning Emilio Pimentel in 1902. Martínez and Chassen-López, "Elecciones y crisis política en Oaxaca," 528, 546–48.

60. Knight, *Mexican Revolution*, vol. 1, 3. Although he did not hold political office, writer Ignacio Manuel Altamirano was recognized as an Indian and had the respect of Porfirian elites. Tenorio-Trillo, *Mexico at the World's Fairs*, 53.

61. Enrique Krauze, *Mexico: Biography of Power; A History of Modern Mexico, 1810–1996*, trans. Hank Heifetz (New York: HarperCollins, 1998), 210; Knight, *Mexican Revolution*, 3–4.

62. Knight, *Mexican Revolution*, vol. 1, 3.

63. Brian Hamnett, *Juárez* (London: Longman, 1994), xii; Gamio, *Forjando Patria*, 38, 159–60.

64. Josefina Zoraida Vázquez, ed., *Juárez: Historia y mito* (Mexico City: El Colegio de México, Centro de Estudios Históricos, 2010); Tenorio-Trillo, *Mexico at the World's Fairs*, 66.

65. Knight, "Racism, Revolution, and *Indigenismo*," 72–74; López Caballero with Acevedo-Rodrigo, "Introduction: Why beyond Alterity?" 6.

66. Erika Pani, "Derribando ídolos: El Juárez de Francisco Bulnes," in *Juárez: Historia y mito*, ed. Josefina Zoraida Vázquez (Mexico City: El Colegio de México, Centro de Estudios Históricos, 2010), 43.

67. Hamnett, *Juárez*, 67–68.

68. Hamnett, *Juárez*, 21–22.

69. Martínez Baracs, *Gobierno de indios*.

70. Sean F. McEnroe, *From Colony to Nationhood in Mexico: Laying the Foundations, 1560–1840* (Cambridge: Cambridge University Press, 2012), 8. See the introduction to this book for a more detailed account of Tlaxcala's pre-Hispanic and colonial histories, including historiographical references.

71. Jannette Amaral-Rodríguez, "Distorsión y silencio en el *Lienzo de Tlaxcala* (1892) de Alfredo Chavero: Notas metodológicas," *Latin American Research Review* 55, no. 2 (2020): 328–29.

72. See Paul Sullivan, *Xuxub Must Die: The Lost Histories of a Murder on the Yucatan* (Pittsburgh: University of Pittsburgh Press, 2004); Wells and Joseph, *Summer of Discontent, Seasons of Upheaval*.

73. Ybarra, *Performing Conquest*, 17–18.

74. See Martínez Baracs, *Gobierno de indios*; Kelly McDonough, "'Love' Lost: Class Struggle among Indigenous Nobles and Commoners of Seventeenth-Century Tlaxcala," *Mexican Studies/Estudios Mexicanos* 32, no. 1 (Winter 2015): 1–28; Jovita Baber, "The Construction of Empire: Politics, Law, and Community in Tlaxcala, New Spain, 1521–1640" (PhD diss., University of Chicago, 2005); Jovita Baber, "Empire, Indians, and the Negotiation for the Status of the City in Tlaxcala, 1521–1550," in *Negotiation within Domination: New Spain's Indian Pueblos Confront the Spanish State*, ed. Ethelia Ruiz Medrano and Susan Kellogg (Boulder: University Press of Colorado, 2010), 19–44; Frederic Hicks, "Land and Succession in the Indigenous Noble Houses of Sixteenth-Century Tlaxcala," *Ethnohistory* 56, no. 4 (2009): 569–88; Ybarra, *Performing Conquest*.

75. Skopyk, *Colonial Cataclysms*, 77–78.

76. See Amaral-Rodríguez, "Distorsión y silencio en el *Lienzo de Tlaxcala* (1892) de Alfredo Chavero." This is further discussed in chapter two.

77. Manuel Gamio's "tripartite continuum" (as described by Alan Knight) of Indigenous peoples, ranging from "pure blood" Indians typified by the Maya, offers a glimpse into how Porfirian and even revolutionary-era Mexican elites viewed differences between and among Indigenous populations. See Gamio, *Forjando Patria*, 155–58; Knight, "Racism, Revolution, and *Indigenismo*," 73–74.

78. Ybarra, *Performing Conquest*, 3.

Chapter 2

1. Bueno, *Pursuit of Ruins*, 25.

2. *Actas del Congreso Internacional de Americanistas: Actas de la Undécima Reunión, México, 1895* (Germany: Kraus-Thomson Organization, 1968), 29. https://archive.org/stream/proceedingsinter1895inte/proceedingsinter1895inte_djvu.txt.

3. *Actas del Congreso Internacional*, 36.

4. The National Museum was opened in 1825. It changed to the National Museum of Archaeology, History, and Ethnology in 1909, and in 1944 it became what it is today, the National Museum of Anthropology. Bueno, *Pursuit of Ruins*, 62–63, 222.

5. Bueno writes, "The purpose of the gallery was to hold the finest pieces from as many of the pre-Hispanic cultures as possible." Christina Bueno, "Forjando Patrimonio: The Making of Archaeological Patrimony in Porfirian Mexico," *Hispanic American Historical Review* 90, no. 2 (May 2010): 236.

6. *Actas del Congreso Internacional*, 37.

7. David Brading, *The First America: The Spanish Monarchy, Creole Patriots, and the Liberal State, 1492–1867* (Cambridge: Cambridge University Press, 2004).

8. On Mexican patrimony, see Bueno, *Pursuit of Ruins*; Tenorio-Trillo, *Mexico*

at the World's Fairs; Larissa Kennedy Kelly, "Waking the Gods: Archeology and State Power in Porfirian Mexico" (PhD diss., University of California, Berkeley, 2011); Barbara A. Tenenbaum, "Streetwise History: The Paseo de la Reforma and the Porfirian State, 1876–1910," in *Rituals of Rule, Rituals of Resistance: Public Celebrations and Popular Culture in Mexico*, ed. William H. Beezley, Cheryl English Martin, and William E. French (Wilmington, DE: Scholarly Resources, 1994), 127–50; Enrique Florescano, *Imágenes de la patria a través de los siglos* (Mexico City: Taurus, 2005), 189–254; Guy Rozat, *Los orígenes de la nación: Pasado indígena e historia nacional* (Mexico City: Universidad Iberoamericana, 2011). On the uses of Incan patrimony, see Earle, *Return of the Native*; Alberto Flores Galindo, *Buscando un inca: Identidad y utopía en los Andes* (Havana, Cuba: Casa de las Américas, 1986); E. Gabrielle Kuenzli, *Acting Inca: Identity and National Belonging in Early Twentieth-Century Bolivia* (Pittsburgh: University of Pittsburgh Press, 2013); Marisol de la Cadena, *Indigenous Mestizos: The Politics of Race and Culture in Cuzco, Peru, 1919–1991* (Durham, NC: Duke University Press, 2000).

9. Bueno, "Forjando Patrimonio," 219; Tenorio-Trillo, *Mexico at the World's Fairs*, 255–61.

10. Tenorio-Trillo, *Mexico at the World's Fairs*, 48–63, 255–61; Bueno, "Forjando Patrimonio," 219.

11. For an examination of how positivism, particularly French positivism, influenced Mexican patrimonial constructions, see Tenorio-Trillo, *Mexico at the World's Fairs*, 20–27, 128.

12. Tenorio-Trillo, *Mexico at the World's Fairs*, 50.

13. Bueno, *Pursuit of Ruins*, 2.

14. Bueno, "Forjando Patrimonio," 224.

15. Earle, *Return of the Native*, 183.

16. Alonso Rodríguez Miramón, *Discurso pronunciado por el C. Diputado Licenciado Alonso Rodríguez Miramón el 26 de noviembre de 1896, ante el gran jurado nacional que conoció del proceso instruido al gobernador del estado l. y s. de Tlaxcala, Coronel Próspero Cahuantzi acusado de violador de la Leyes de Reforma, por algunos periodistas de la Capital de la República* (Tlaxcala: Impr. del gobierno del estado, 1896), 17.

17. Tenorio-Trillo, *Mexico at the World's Fairs*, 103.

18. Earle, *Return of the Native*, 5.

19. Tenorio-Trillo, *Mexico at the World's Fairs*, 52–64.

20. Debates about "Indigenous alterity"—how and why Indigenous peoples are considered "others" and the validity of these distinctions—are superbly interrogated in chapters in the edited volume *Beyond Alterity*, edited by Paula López Caballero and Ariadna Acevedo-Rodrigo.

21. Some indigenistas such as Manuel Gamio held these views after the Revolution, as well. See Gamio, *Forjando Patria*.

22. Earle stresses how nation-builders' reasons for disparaging Indigenous peoples depended on the time period and shifting national ideologies. See Earle, *Return of the Native*, 170–71, 181; Rozat, *Orígenes de la nación*, 413–18.

23. Tenorio-Trillo, *Mexico at the World's Fairs*, 7–8.

24. Ybarra, *Performing Conquest*, 15–17. Tlaxcala's pre-Columbian and colonial histories are summarized in chapter one.

25. Stacie G. Widdifield, *The Embodiment of the National in Late Nineteenth-Century Mexican Painting* (Tucson: University of Arizona Press, 1996), 103–4. See also Earle, *Return of the Native*, 123–25; Tenorio-Trillo, *Mexico at the World's Fairs*, 118–19; Florescano, *Imágenes de la Patria*, 179–83.

26. Ybarra, *Performing Conquest*, 91; Widdifield, *Embodiment of the National*, 103–4; Martínez, "Noble Tlaxcalans."

27. Rebecca Earle uses "acceptably Indigenous" to explain how the Guatemalan government selected an image of an "Indian princess" to depict on a stamp in 1878. Earle, *Return of the Native*, 15.

28. *Periódico Oficial del Estado de Tlaxcala* (Tlaxcala), 19 Sept. 1885.

29. Próspero Cahuantzi (hereafter abbreviated as PC in citations) to PD, 5 Sept. 1885, CGPD, L. 10, C. 18, d. 8828. Even though Díaz denied Cahuantzi's initial solicitation, the president allowed the governor to send someone to Mexico City to make a copy to keep in Tlaxcala.

30. PC to José Y. Limantour, 11 Mar. 1896, El Centro de Estudios de Historia de México Carso (CEHM), Fondo CDLIV, Colección José Y. Limantour, Primera Serie, Año 1883, Carpeta 8, Documento 2181.

31. *Antigua República*, 8 Aug. 1909.

32. See "Introduction to the Lienzo de Tlaxcala: Description," Mesolore, accessed Dec. 15, 2022, www.mesolore.org/tutorials/learn/19/Introduction-to-the-Lienzo-de-Tlaxcala-/53/Description.

33. Today *Lienzo* fragment copies are housed at the Museo Nacional de Antropología in Mexico City; the Benson Latin American Collection in Austin, Texas; the University of Glasgow; and Tulane University in New Orleans, Louisiana. On the mystery behind the disappearance and recovery of the *Lienzo*, see Amaral-Rodríguez, "Distorsión y silencio en el *Lienzo de Tlaxcala* (1892) de Alfredo Chavero"; "Introduction to the Lienzo de Tlaxcala: History and Publications," Mesolore, accessed Dec. 15, 2022, www.mesolore.org/tutorials/learn/19/Introduction-to-the-Lienzo-de-Tlaxcala-/54/History-and-Publications.

34. "Prologue," in Próspero Cahuantzi, ed., *Lienzo de Tlaxcala, manuscrito pictórico mexicano de mediados del siglo XVI* (Mexico City: Librería Anticuaria G. M. Echaniz, 1939), 1.

35. "Prologue."

36. Amaral-Rodríguez, "Distorsión y silencio en el *Lienzo de Tlaxcala*," 325; Diego Muñoz Camargo and Alfredo Chavero, *Historia de Tlaxcala* (Mexico City: Oficina tip. de la Secretaría de Fomento, 1892).

37. Chavero wrote about Tlaxcala throughout the volume and cited the *Lienzo de Tlaxcala* frequently. Alfredo Chavero, *México a través de los siglos*, vol. 1 (Mexico City: Ballescá Espasa y Compañía, 1882; Alicante: Biblioteca Virtual Miguel de Cervantes, 2017), http://www.cervantesvirtual.com/nd/ark:/59851/bmctjom8. For more

on Chavero, see Bueno, *Pursuit of Ruins*, 41–42, 60, 125–26; Tenorio-Trillo, *Mexico at the World's Fairs*, 55, 66–73, 84, 256.

38. Amaral-Rodríguez, "Distorsión y silencio en el *Lienzo de Tlaxcala*," 325.
39. Amaral-Rodríguez, "Distorsión y silencio en el *Lienzo de Tlaxcala*," 324.
40. Alfredo Chavero y Junta colombina de México, *Homenaje á Cristóbal Colón: Antigüedades mexicanas* (Mexico City: Oficina tip. de la Secretaría de Fomento, 1892).
41. Amaral-Rodríguez, "Distorsión y silencio en el *Lienzo de Tlaxcala*," 325.
42. Amaral-Rodríguez, "Distorsión y silencio en el *Lienzo de Tlaxcala*," 325.
43. "Prologue," 1.
44. Amaral-Rodríguez argues that the discrepancies between the two *Lienzo* versions are especially problematic because many colonial scholars use the 1890 edition of the *Lienzo* in their analyses, unknowingly studying a work that is less accurate than the original *Lienzo*. She stresses how the 1892 *Lienzo* should be analyzed less as an "authentic codex" and more as a "product of its time." Amaral-Rodríguez, "Distorsión y silencio en el *Lienzo de Tlaxcala*," 322, 324.
45. *El Diario de Hogar*, 21 Nov. 1888, in Sonia Lombardo, *El pasado prehispánico en la cultura nacional: Memoria hemerográfica, 1877–1911*, vol. I (Mexico City: Instituto Nacional de Antropología e Historia, 1994), 155. These early excavations were limited, and it was not until well into the twentieth century that well-known sites in Tlaxcala like Cacaxtla and Xochitécatl were discovered and excavated.
46. Próspero Cahuantzi, *Memoria de la administración pública del estado de Tlaxcala presentada a la H. Legislatura del mismo, por el gobernador constitucional Coronel Próspero Cahuantzi, el 2 de abril 1893* (Tlaxcala: Imprenta del Gobierno, 1894), 12.
47. AHET, Ayuntamiento (A), 21 Mar. 1888, C. 175, Exp. 1, fs. 70-71; 24 Apr. 1888, C. 175, Exp. 2, fs. 342-3; 13 Feb. 1892, C. 188, Exp. 3, fs. 264-67; 25 Mar. 1892, C. 189, Exp. 1, fs. 29-34; 25 Oct. 1892, C. 192, Exp. 1, fs. 165-8; SC, 1899, C. 1, Exp. 5, f. 111; 1902, C. 1, Exp. 11, fs. 4-5; 23 Feb. 1902, C. 1. Exp. 1, fs. 72-80; Justicia y gobernación (JG), 1 Dec. 1903, C. 34, Exp. 51, f. 49; C. 35, Exp. 42, f. 92; Cahuantzi, *Informe de gobierno*, 1893; *Periódico Oficial del Estado de Tlaxcala*, 1 Sept. 1900.
48. Comité de la Exposición Universal de St. Louis to PC, 19 May 1903, AHET, JG, C. 35, Exp. 42, f. 30.
49. Facturas de los efectos que remite el subscrito á la Sec. de Fomento con destino á la Exposición Universal de St. Louis Missouri, 1904, AHET, SC, C. 1, Exp. 17, fs. 1–12; C. 2, Exp 1, fs. 2–3.
50. Authors illegible, 1 Dec. 1903, AHET, JG, C. 34, Exp. 51, fs. 32–40.
51. *Periódico Oficial del Estado de Tlaxcala*, 8 Apr. 1893.
52. Secretaría de gobierno de Tlaxcala to Prefecto del Distrito de Hidalgo, 29 May 1888, AHET, A, C. 175, Exp. 3, f. 105.
53. Pedro Larrea y Cordero, *Gran cuadro histórico, político, geográfico, industrial, y religioso de la ciudad de Tlaxcala y del Estado de su nombre* (Tlaxcala: Imprenta de gobierno, 1886); Alfonso Luis Velasco, *Geografía y estadística del estado de Tlaxcala*

(Mexico City: Oficina Tip. de la Secretaría de Fomento, 1892). While both authors worked for the *Secretaría de Fomento* (Ministry of Development) in Mexico City, Larrea y Cordero appears to have written only one other territorial study on Veracruz, whereas Mexico City–trained geographer and statistician Velasco conducted twenty separate regional analyses for the Porfirian government.

54. Larrea y Cordero, *Gran cuadro*, 72–73, cited in René Cuéllar Bernal, *Tlaxcala a través de los siglos* (Mexico City: B. Costa-Amic, 1968), 237.

55. Larrea y Cordero, *Gran cuadro*, 72–73.

56. Bueno, *Pursuit of Ruins*, 114.

57. Bueno, *Pursuit of Ruins*, 25–26.

58. Archivo Histórico del Museo Nacional de Antropología, Museo Nacional de Antropología, Mexico City (hereafter cited as AHMNA), vol. 203, exp. 113, fol. 295–96.

59. AHMNA, vol. 203, exp. 113, fol. 295–96.

60. AHMNA, vol. 203, exp. 113, fol. 295–96.

61. *El Universal*, 23 Jun. 1895, 7 Sept. 1895; *El Monitor Republicano*, 10 Nov. 1895, in Lombardo, *El pasado prehispánico*, 1: 275, 284, 291.

62. *Actas del Congreso, 1895*, 28; *El Monitor Republicano*, 10 Nov. 1895, in Lombardo, *El pasado prehispánico*, 1: 291.

63. Bueno, "Forjando Patrimonio," 239–45.

64. *Actas del Congreso, 1895*, 548.

65. *Actas del Congreso, 1895*, 548.

66. *Actas del Congreso, 1895*, 548; *El Universal*, 7 Sept. 1895, in Lombardo, *El pasado prehispánico*, 1: 284; Bueno, *Pursuit of Ruins*, 128.

67. *Actas del Congreso, 1895*, 99.

68. After the Congress, Hunt Cortés went on to publish various works on Nahuatl philology, focusing especially on Tonantzin, the Indigenous cult of the Virgin of Guadalupe. Hunt Cortés's publications are listed in Ascensión Hernández de León-Portilla, *Tepuztlahcuilolli, impresos en náhuatl: Historia y bibliografía*, vol. 2 (Mexico City: Universidad Nacional Autónoma de México, 1988), 189–92. Hunt Cortés also published the short-lived journal *Hunt-Cortés Digest: A Monthly Journal of Things about Mexico, the Egypt of the West and of General Literature* (Mexico City: Imp. de A. Carranza y Comp, 1905).

69. *Actas del Congreso, 1895*, 99.

70. *Indigenismo*, the valorization of Indigenous peoples and cultures by the nation-state, is typically examined as a feature of the postrevolutionary state. (Its practitioners are thusly called indigenistas.) Examples of the rich canon of literature on postrevolutionary Indigenismo and nation-building in Mexico, as well as critiques of Indigenismo, include, but are by no means limited to: Guillermo Bonfil Batalla, *México Profundo: Una civilización negada* (Mexico City: Grijalbo, 1987); Alexander S. Dawson, *Indian and Nation in Revolutionary Mexico* (Tucson: University of Arizona Press, 2004); Paul Gillingham, *Cuauhtémoc's Bones: Forging National Identity in Modern Mexico* (Albuquerque:

University of New Mexico Press, 2011); Natividad Gutiérrez, *Nationalist Myths and Ethnic Identities: Indigenous Intellectuals and the Mexican State* (Lincoln: University of Nebraska Press, 2015); Ruth Hellier-Tinoco, *Embodying Mexico: Tourism, Nationalism, and Performance* (New York: Oxford University Press, 2011); Rick Anthony López, *Crafting Mexico: Intellectuals, Artisans, and the State after the Revolution* (Durham, NC: Duke University Press, 2010); Nathaniel Morris, *Soldiers, Saints, and Shamans: Indigenous Communities and the Revolutionary State in Mexico's Gran Nayar, 1910–1940* (Tucson: University of Arizona Press, 2020); A. S. Dillingham, *Oaxaca Resurgent: Indigeneity, Development, and Inequality in Twentieth-Century Mexico* (Stanford, CA: Stanford University Press, 2021).

71. Bueno, "Forjando Patrimonio," 216–17.
72. Earle, *Return of the Native*, 170.
73. *Actas del Congreso, 1895*, 99.
74. Bueno, "Forjando Patrimonio," 216–17.
75. *El Imparcial* (Mexico City), 17 Sept., 20 Sept. 1896.
76. Garner, *Porfirio Díaz*, 123–27. On the role of the press during the Porfiriato, see Pablo Piccato, *The Tyranny of Opinion: Honor in the Construction of the Mexican Public Sphere* (Durham, NC: Duke University Press, 2010).
77. PD to PC, CPGD, 23 Sept. 1896, L. 21, C. 31, d. 15160–15161.
78. *El Tiempo* (Mexico City), 24 Sept. 1896; *El Mundo* (Mexico City), 14 Oct. 1896. See also CGPD, 2 Oct. 1896, L. 21, C. 36, d. 17598–17599.
79. Rodríguez Miramón, *Discurso pronunciado*, 17.
80. Rodríguez Miramón, *Discurso pronunciado*, 17.
81. Próspero Cahuantzi, *Dictamen formulado por la segunda sección del Gran jurado nacional y presentado a los miembros de este tribunal que conoció de la acusación contra el gobernador del estado de Tlaxcala Coronel Próspero Cahuantzi atribuyéndole la infracción de algunas leyes de reforma* (Tlaxcala: Imprenta del Gobierno del Estado, 1896), 5–6.
82. Indalecio Sánchez Gavito, *Defensa del gobernador del estado libre y soberano de Tlaxcala, Coronel Próspero Cahuantzi, hecha ante la Cámara de Diputados, erigida en gran jurado el día 26 de noviembre de 1896* (Tlaxcala: Imprenta del Gobierno del Estado, 1896), 4, 8–9; Cahuantzi, *Dictamen*, 4.
83. Cahuantzi, *Dictamen*, 4.
84. See, for example, AHET, SC, 7 Dec. 1886, C. 5, Exp. 16, f. 3; AHET, A, 23 Mar. 1897, C. 211, Exp. 3, f. 124; 24 Mar. 1899, C. 221, Exp. 4, d. 2, fs. 146–48. On the tensions between local Catholic movements and the Porfirian state, see Paul J. Vanderwood, *The Power of God against the Guns of Government: Religious Upheaval in Mexico at the Turn of the Nineteenth Century* (Stanford, CA: Stanford University Press, 1998); Edward Wright-Rios, *Revolutions in Mexican Catholicism: Reform and Revelation in Oaxaca, 1877–1934* (Durham, NC: Duke University Press, 2009).
85. For a summary of Díaz's reconciliation with the church, see Garner, *Porfirio Díaz*, 117–23.

86. Rodríguez Miramón, *Discurso*, 21.
87. Cosío Villegas, *Historia moderna de México*, vol. 8, 595; vol. 9, 441; Guerra, *México*, vol. 1, 228.
88. Cahuantzi, *Dictamen*, 10-13.
89. Rodríguez Miramón, *Discurso*, 14, 21.
90. Cahuantzi, *Dictamen*, 15.
91. Cahuantzi, *Dictamen*, 14-15; Adalberto A. Esteua, *Discurso pronunciado en la cámara de diputados el día de 26 de noviembre de 1896 por el diputado miembro de la segunda sección del gran jurado, Lic. Adalberto A. Esteua en pro del dictamen de Tlaxcala Coronel Próspero* (Tlaxcala: Imprenta del Gobierno del Estado, 1896), 7.
92. Rodríguez Miramón, *Discurso*, 17.
93. Sánchez Gavito, *Defensa*, 25.
94. Sánchez Gavito, *Defensa*, 25.
95. Sánchez Gavito, *Defensa*, 25.
96. Sánchez Gavito, *Defensa*, 5.
97. Sánchez Gavito, *Defensa*, 5.
98. Rodríguez Miramón, *Discurso*, 16.
99. Rodríguez Miramón, *Discurso*, 16.
100. Rodríguez Miramón, *Discurso*, 18.
101. Rodríguez Miramón, *Discurso*, 18.
102. Rodríguez Miramón, *Discurso*, 18.
103. Ybarra, *Performing Conquest*, 75.
104. Ybarra, *Performing Conquest*, 3.
105. Rendón Garcini, *El Prosperato*.
106. Written Nahuatl almost never appears in the official documents or personal correspondence between state officials and residents, even among poorer residents who were likely bilingual. Cahuantzi wrote at least one *discurso* in Nahuatl in 1889. See PC to PD, 20 Sept. 1889, CGPD, C. 14, L. 19, ds. 9125-6.

Chapter 3

1. Income from pulque hovered around 10 percent of total state income for most of the Porfiriato, and Tlaxcala produced about 65 percent of Mexico's total pulque output. Economic production by sector in Tlaxcala is detailed in Rendón Garcini, *El Prosperato*, 233-37.
2. Smaller producers in Tlaxcala relied much more on the local market, with very few producing for commercial sale. Rendón Garcini, *El Prosperato*, 114-18; 217-20. See also Rendón Garcini, *Dos haciendas pulqueras en Tlaxcala, 1857-1884* (Tlaxcala: Gobierno del Estado de Tlaxcala, 1990), 214-18.
3. José Juan Juárez Flores and Francisco Téllez Guerrero, "Las finanzas municipales de la ciudad de Tlaxcala durante el segundo imperio," *Siglo XIX, Cuadernos de Historia*, Universidad Autónoma de Nuevo León/Facultad de Filosofía y Letras, UNAM, no. 8 (January–April 1994): 93; Beatty, *Institutions and Investment*, 11; Rendón Garcini, *Dos haciendas pulqueras en Tlaxcala*.

4. Timothy Henderson, *The Worm in the Wheat: Rosalie Evans and Agrarian Struggle in the Puebla-Tlaxcala Valley of Mexico, 1906–1927* (Durham, NC: Duke University Press, 1998), 34.

5. Raymond Buve, *El movimiento revolucionario en Tlaxcala* (Tlaxcala: Universidad Autónoma de Tlaxcala, Secretaría de Extensión Universitaria y Difusión Cultural; Mexico City: Universidad Iberoamericana, Departamento de Historia, 1994), 97, 105.

6. Rancaño Ramírez, *El sistema de haciendas en Tlaxcala*, 47–48.

7. On the differences between hacienda laborers in Tlaxcala-Puebla, see Herbert J. Nickel, "Agricultural Laborers in the Mexican Revolution (1910–40): Some Hypotheses and Facts about the Participation and Restraint in the Highlands of Puebla-Tlaxcala," in *Riot, Rebellion, and Revolution*, ed. Friedrich Katz (Princeton, NJ: Princeton University Press, 1988), 377–78; Henderson, *The Worm in the Wheat*, 29–30.

8. Hectarage and property values varied within the state, and commonly used designations such as *hacienda*, *rancho*, and *finca rústica* did not always correlate to the size or quality of the lands they prescribed. For the purposes of taxation, the state government divided properties into small, middling, and large. Small properties were usually valued less than MXN $200, while large properties were usually at more than $10,000, leaving a large gulf in the middle. In 1892, forty-eight properties in Tlaxcala were valued over $40,000 and only six were valued more than $100,000, all in the north. According to hectarage, a rough division would place ranches between 50 and 250 hectares and haciendas over 250 hectares, but these figures varied widely between localities. Rancaño Ramírez, *El sistema de haciendas en Tlaxcala*, 23–50; Rendón Garcini, *El Prosperato*, 86–95; Buve, *El movimiento revolucionario en Tlaxcala*, 232–33. I use historians Jean Meyer's and Alan Knight's definitions of "small" and "middling" landowners. Meyer defines small landowners as those who have 10 hectares of land or less and who existed predominately in Oaxaca, Guerrero, Jalisco, Michoácan, Veracruz, Morelos, Tlaxcala, and parts of Puebla and México. Jean Meyer, "Haciendas y ranchos, peones y campesinos en el Porfiriato: Algunas falacias estadísticas," *Historia Mexicana* 35, no. 3 (January–March 1986): 480–81. "Middling" landowners are defined by Alan Knight as those "who, despite their subordinate position in rural society, retain a significant degree of control, even ownership, over the land they till." See Alan Knight, "Peasant and Caudillo in Revolutionary Mexico, 1910–1917," in *Caudillo and Peasant in the Mexican Revolution*, ed. D. A. Brading (Cambridge: Cambridge University Press, 1980), 21–22.

9. In 1910, Tlaxcala had a total of six political-administrative districts. Tlaxcala's three districts in the south, Hidalgo, Zaragoza, and Cuauhtémoc, contained 31 percent of Tlaxcala's territory but were approximately 50 percent more populated than the three political-administrative districts in the north, Ocampo, Morelos, and Juárez. *Censo y división territorial del Estado de Tlaxcala*, Mexico, 1895, 1910; Rendón Garcini, *El Prosperato*, 80–81.

10. Tlaxcala's administrative organization is ordered as follows: state (governor), district (governed by *prefecto politico* or *jefe político*), municipality, town, and village (*municipio* or *pueblo* governed by ayuntamiento officials and headed by a *presidente municipal*; some pueblos were their own municipalities), and lastly *barrio* (governed by *agente municipal*). The term *pueblo* translates in English as community or village, but in Tlaxcala pueblo usually denoted independent administrative polities that were created during the colonial or pre-Columbian periods. *Barrio* denoted a specific subsection within a village or town.

11. Rendón Garcini, *Tlaxcala: Historia breve*, 49.

12. The different tax breaks Cahuantzi doled out to factories are summarized in Diana López Martínez, "La construcción de una nueva territorialidad a través de los usos del agua: El caso de la región del Rio Zahuapan (1888–1919)" (Master's thesis, Instituto de Investigaciones Dr. José María Luis Mora, 2013); Rendón Garcini, *El Prosperato*, 251–52.

13. In 1900, Tlaxcala's population density index was 41.6, a distant second from Mexico City (361.3), but high nevertheless as compared to more urbanized regions. Tlaxcala was followed by Mexico state (40.3), Guanajuato (37.4), and Puebla (30.3). The national average was 6.5. The population density of Mexico can be found at: www.lib.utexas.edu/maps/atlas_mexico/population_1900.jpg.

14. On the railroad in Mexico, see John H. Coatsworth, *Growth against Development: The Economic Impact of Railroads in Porfirian Mexico* (DeKalb: Northern Illinois University Press, 1981); Sandra Kuntz Ficker and Paolo Riguzzi, eds., *Ferrocarriles y vida económica en México, 1850–1950: Del surgimiento tardío al decaimiento precoz* (Mexico City: El Colegio Mexiquense/UAM/Ferrocarriles Nacionales de México, 1996); Michael Matthews, *The Civilizing Machine: A Cultural History of Mexican Railroads, 1876–1910* (Lincoln: University of Nebraska Press, 2014); Arthur Schmidt, *The Social and Economic Effect of the Railroad in Puebla and Veracruz, Mexico, 1867–1911* (New York: Garland, 1987).

15. Cosío Villegas et al., *Historia moderna de México*, vol. 2, *La república restaurada: Vida económica*, 563, 567–68, 660.

16. By 1910, forty private lines had been built in the state, totaling 267 kilometers of track, most of which was in the northern regions. Rendón Garcini, *Tlaxcala: Historia breve*, 91.

17. Many pulque haciendas also made aguardiente and produced staple crops such as corn and barley. Still, few of Tlaxcala's larger producers distributed foodstuffs outside of Mexico. Rendón Garcini, *Dos haciendas pulqueras en Tlaxcala*, 214–18; Rendón Garcini, *El Prosperato*, 217–20.

18. Rancaño Ramírez, *El sistema de haciendas en Tlaxcala*, 24.

19. Rendón Garcini, *El Prosperato*, 114–18; 217–20; Rendón Garcini, *Dos haciendas pulqueras en Tlaxcala*, 214–18.

20. José Juan Juárez Flores, "Besieged Forests at Century's End: Industry, Speculation, and Dispossession in Tlaxcala's La Malintzin Woodlands, 1860–

1910," in *A Land between Waters: Environmental Histories of Modern Mexico*, ed. Christopher R. Boyer (Tucson: University of Arizona Press, 2012), 100–123.

21. As exemplified by the dozens of railroad accidents located in the *Causa Criminal o Penal* series in the historical archives of the *Casa de la Cultura Jurídica* in Tlaxcala (CCJT) during this period.

22. Katz, "The Liberal Republic and the Porfiriato, 1867–1910," 83.

23. Katz, "The Liberal Republic and the Porfiriato, 1867–1910," 85; Vanderwood, *Disorder and Progress*.

24. As Thomas Benjamin notes, "three corps, out of a total of ten, protected the Mexico City–Veracruz railway." Benjamin, "Introduction," in *Other Mexicos*, 15; Vanderwood, *Disorder and Progress*, 120.

25. See, for example, *Periódico Oficial del Estado de Tlaxcala*, 16 Oct. 1886, 2 Apr. 1887.

26. Rendón Garcini, *El Prosperato*, 22–23.

27. The historic record does not convey the exact year the district of Cuauhtémoc was created. Próspero Cahuantzi, *Memoria de 1893*, 9; Rendón Garcini, *El Prosperato*, 71, 79–80. See also Cruz María Ochoa Paredes, "Evolución histórico-geografía de las divisiones territoriales del estado de Tlaxcala (1519–1980)," *Boletín del Instituto de Geografía* 15 (Mexico City: UNAM, 1985): 211–53.

28. Rendón Garcini, *El Prosperato*, 79–80.

29. Not all states followed the same path toward political cohesion during the Porfiriato. The Soconusco in Chiapas, a region much more geographically peripheral than Tlaxcala, where the railroad came decades later and governors had much less political influence than Cahuantzi, offers an apropos contrast to state consolidation in Tlaxcala during the Porfiriato. See Lurtz, *From the Grounds Up*, 76, 83–85.

30. *La Opinión* (Puebla), Sept. 1895, cited in *Periódico Oficial del Estado de Tlaxcala*, 28 Sept. 1895.

31. Alcalde Primer Constitucional de Villa de Libres, Puebla to Governor of Tlaxcala, 1 Sept. 1879, AHET, SC, 1887, C. 10, Exp. 9, fs. 27–28. Examples of cross-border robberies can be found in AHET, SC, 1886, C. 3, Exps. 74, 75, 84; "El jefe político de Puebla solicita la aprehensión de Jermin Flores por robo," 8 Mar. 1888, AHET, SC, 1888, C. 8, Exp. 4, fs. 42–43. Examples of cross-border resource disputes can be found in AHET, SC, 1887, C. 10, Exp 9, fs. 1–46.

32. See Sec. de gobernación y milicia de Puebla al jefe político de Juárez, 9 Jul. 1877; Jefe político de Juan de los Llanos, Puebla al Gobernador del Estado de Tlaxcala, 3 Aug. 1877; Testimonio de la Prefectura política de Juárez, Tlaxcala, 1877 (date n/a); "Acuerdo del día 19 de Feb. de 1880," 9 Feb. 1880; Jefe político de Juan de los Llanos al Gobernador del Estado de Tlaxcala, 13 Apr. 1880, AHET, SC, 1887, C. 10, Exp. 9, fs. 16, 31–32, 38, 46.

33. Cahuantzi, *Informe de gobierno*, *Periódico Oficial del Estado de Tlaxcala*, 16 Oct. 1886, 2.

34. Cahuantzi, *Informe de gobierno*, *Periódico Oficial del Estado de Tlaxcala*, 2 Apr. 1887, 2.

35. Cahuantzi, *Informe de gobierno*, *Periódico Oficial del Estado de Tlaxcala*, 8 Oct. 1887.

36. Cahuantzi, *Informe de gobierno*, *Periódico Oficial del Estado de Tlaxcala*, 4 Oct. 1890.

37. Cahuantzi, *Informe de gobierno*, *Periódico Oficial del Estado de Tlaxcala*, 4 Oct. 1890. Cahuantzi reaffirmed that interstate relations were "improving more and more" in his *Discurso* to the state legislature the following October. *Periódico Oficial del Estado de Tlaxcala*, 23 Oct. 1891.

38. *Periódico Oficial del Estado de Tlaxcala*, 23 Oct. 1891.

39. "Contestación al discurso del Ejecutivo," *Periódico Oficial del Estado de Tlaxcala*, 11 Oct. 1890.

40. Thomson and LaFrance, *Patriotism, Politics, and Popular Liberalism in Nineteenth-Century Mexico*, 261; Cosío Villegas, *Historia moderna de México*, vol. 9, 447–49; Garner, *Porfirio Díaz*, 62–64, 108.

41. Garner, *Porfirio Díaz*, 29–31, 108; Knight, *Mexican Revolution*, vol. 1, 16, 32; Cosío Villegas, *Historia moderna de México*, vol. 9, 447–49; Guerra, *México*, vol. 2, 182; Rendón Garcini, *El Prosperato*, 46, 56.

42. Mucio Martínez to PD, 1896, CGPD, L. 21, C. 35, d. n/a; Rendón Garcini, *El Prosperato*, 56.

43. Rancaño Ramírez calculates that La Compañía had the eleventh-highest value among haciendas in the state (valued at MXN $80,000 in 1892). Rancaño Ramírez, *El sistema de haciendas en Tlaxcala*, 38.

44. Archivo Histórico del Agua (AHA), Aprovechamientos superficiales (AS), C. 4573, Exp. 60813, fs. 1–43; Sergio Francisco Rosas Salas, "Agua e industria en Puebla: El establecimiento de la fábrica textil la Covadonga, 1889–1897," *Relaciones* 136 (Fall 2013), 242, 244–45. Díaz Rubín was one of dozens of immigrants who took advantage of liberal agrarian privatization laws to revitalize and build new industry, especially textile factories, in central Mexico. See Aurora Gómez Galvarriato, *Industry and Revolution: Social and Economic Change in the Orizaba Valley, Mexico* (Cambridge, MA: Harvard University Press, 2013), 50; Alba González Jácome, "De las manos tejedoras a las fábricas textiles: El nacimiento de una industria en Tlaxcala," *Tlahcuilo, Boletín del Archivo Histórico del Estado de Tlaxcala*, vol. 2, no. 4 (Jan.–Mar. 2008), 21.

45. Rosas Salas, "Agua e industria en Puebla," 242–45.

46. Cahuantzi, *Informe de gobierno*, *Periódico Oficial del Estado de Tlaxcala*, 2 Apr. 1898, 4.

47. Cahuantzi, *Informe de gobierno*, *Periódico Oficial del Estado de Tlaxcala*, 2 Apr. 1898, 5; see also "Alegato de buena prueba presentado por el señor José Maria Macías en representación del Estado de Tlaxcala," 21 May 1899, AHET, A, 1899, C. 222, Exp. 3, fs. 26–53.

48. Cahuantzi, *Informe de gobierno*, *Periódico Oficial del Estado de Tlaxcala*, 2 Apr. 1898, 5.

49. Cahuantzi, *Informe de gobierno*, *Periódico Oficial del Estado de Tlaxcala*, 2 Apr. 1898, 6.

50. Cahuantzi, *Informe de gobierno, Periódico Oficial del Estado de Tlaxcala*, 2 Apr. 1898, 8.
51. Cahuantzi, *Informe de gobierno, Periódico Oficial del Estado de Tlaxcala*, 2 Apr. 1898, 6.
52. Mucio Martínez to PC, 4 Jan. 1897, cited in *Informe de gobierno, Periódico Oficial del Estado de Tlaxcala*, 2 Apr. 1898, 9–10.
53. Rosas Salas, "Agua e industria en Puebla," 242–45.
54. "Alegato de buena prueba," 21 May 1899, AHET, A, 1899, C. 222, Exp. 3, f. 26. Despite the 1899 agreement, territorial conflicts between Puebla and Tlaxcala continued. See, for example, "Relativo al predio laborio y montuoso de la Malintzi, propiedad del ayuntamiento de esta ciudad," 1899–1902, AHET, A, C. 222, Exp. 2, fs. 136–225. A more recent example is in Tepexco, Puebla, where residents who lived along the border with Tlaxcala solicited protection from Puebla's government after a Tlaxcalan landowner threatened to evict them from their lands. *Periódico Central*, 10 Apr. 2013: www.periodicocentral.mx/municipios/advierten-conflicto-puebla-tlaxcala.
55. Author emphasis. "Relativo al predio laborio y montuoso de la Malintzi, propiedad del ayuntamiento de esta ciudad," 1899–1902, AHET, A, C. 222, Exp. 2, f. 53.
56. "Convenio de límites, Decreto aprobando los que celebraron entre los Estados de Puebla y Tlaxcala," 6 Jan. 1900, AHET, SC, 1901, C. 1, Exp. 10, d. 1, fs. 1–19.
57. Cahuantzi, *Informe de gobierno, Periódico Oficial del Estado de Tlaxcala*, 14 Apr. 1900.
58. Cahuantzi, *Informe de gobierno, Periódico Oficial del Estado de Tlaxcala*, 14 Apr. 1900
59. PC to agentes municipales, 24 Oct. 1899, AHET, SC, 1899, C. 1, Exp. 5, fs. 27–109.
60. The Ayuntamientos of Tlaxcala, Chiautempan, Nativitas, Teolocholco, Xaltocan, and Zacatelco sent delegates to the national congress to argue for statehood. See Enciclopedia de los Municipios y Delegaciones de México, Estado de Tlaxcala, www.inafed.gob.mx/work/enciclopedia/EMM29tlaxcala/historia.html. Anthropologist Hugo Nutini and more recently theater scholar Patricia A. Ybarra are among those who have examined this local sovereignty and how it has manifested and been celebrated in modern times. See Hugo G. Nutini and Betty Bell, *Ritual Kinship: The Structure and Historical Development of the Compadrazgo System in Rural Tlaxcala* (Princeton, NJ: Princeton University Press, 1980); Ybarra, *Performing Conquest*.
61. Xavier-Guerra, *México*, vol. 1, 59–125. On the function of elections in Latin America in the nineteenth century, see various chapters in Antonio Annino, ed., *Historia de las elecciones en Iberoamérica, siglo XIX: De la formación del espacio político nacional* (Buenos Aires: Fondo de Cultura Económica, 1995); José Antonio Aguilar Rivera, ed., *Las elecciones y el gobierno representativo en México (1810–1910)* (Mexico City: Fondo de Cultura Económica, 2010); Carlos Malamud, ed.,

Legitimidad, representación y alternancia en España y América Latina: Las reformas electorales, 1880–1930 (Mexico City: Colegio de México, Fideicomiso Historia de las Américas, 2000); Eduardo Posada Carbó, ed., *Elections before Democracy: The History of Elections in Europe and Latin America* (Houndmills, Basingstoke, Hampshire: Macmillan, 1996); Hilda Sábato, *The Many and the Few: Political Participation in Republican Buenos Aires* (Stanford, CA: Stanford University Press, 2001); David Rock, *State Building and Political Movements in Argentina, 1860–1916* (Stanford, CA: Stanford University Press, 2002); Graham, *Patronage and Politics in Nineteenth-Century Brazil*; Sarah C. Chambers, *From Subjects to Citizens: Honor, Gender, and Politics in Arequipa, Peru, 1780–1854* (University Park: Pennsylvania State University Press, 1999); Paula Alonso, *Between Revolution and the Ballot Box: The Origins of the Argentine Radical Party in the 1890s* (Cambridge: Cambridge University Press, 2000). Beyond Latin America see Tracy Campbell, *Deliver the Vote: A History of Election Fraud, an American Political Tradition, 1742–2004* (New York: Carroll and Graf, 2005).

62. See, for example, Juan Francisco Gaviño to PD, 18 Jan. 1885, CGPD, L. 10, C. 2, d. 606.

63. 21 Dec. 1888, AHET, A, C. 176, Exp. 6, d. 285. Rendón Garcini, *El Prosperato*, 54. Federal constitutional reforms allowing for nonconsecutive presidential reelection passed in 1877, followed by consecutive reelection in 1887, and finally, indefinite reelection in 1890. All states except Campeche passed similar constitutional reforms. Bravo Regidor, "Elecciones de gobernadores durante el Porfiriato," 273–74.

64. Gabriel L. Negretto and José Antonio Aguilar-Rivera, "Rethinking the Legacy of the Liberal State in Latin America," *Journal of Latin American Studies* 32, no. 2 (May 2000): 391.

65. Ruiz, *Americans in the Treasure House*.

66. Various Tlaxcalans to PD, 1892, CGPD, L. 17, C. 25, d. 13495.

67. Members of the "Club Central Tlaxcalteca" to PD, 1 Sept. 1892, CGPD, L. 17, C. 25, d. 13318, 13320.

68. Members of the "Club Central Tlaxcalteca" to PD, 1 Sept. 1892, CGPD, L. 17, C. 25, d. 13318, 13320.

69. Juan González y González to PD, 29 Sept. 1892, 15 Sept. 1892, CGCP, C. 17, L. 29, d. 14019, 13972; Rendón Garcini, *El Prosperato*, 54.

70. Vecinos of Huamantla to PD, 28 July 1892, CGPD, L. 17, C. 25, d. 12038.

71. Falcón, *El jefe político*, 147–92.

72. Negretto and Aguilar-Rivera, "Rethinking the Legacy of the Liberal State in Latin America," 391; *Constitución política del estado libre y soberano de Tlaxcala, 27 de Noviembre de 1884*, Art. 55, 15. Federal law eliminated the position entirely in 1917. Falcón, *El jefe político*, 74.

73. Gregorio Nava to PD, 31 Jul. 1888, L. 13, C. 16, d. 8065; Rendón Garcini, *El Prosperato*, 54.

74. Vecinos of Huamantla to PD, 28 July 1892, CGPD, L. 17, C. 25, d. 12038.

75. Felipe Pulido to PD, 16 Sept. 1892, CGPD, L. 17, C. 29, d. 14447.
76. Montiel was given a new appointment as diputado in the state legislature. Cahuantzi, *Memoria de 1893*, 5–6.
77. PC to PD, 27 Dec. 1892, CGPD, L. 17, C. 38, d. 18893.
78. PD to PC, 27 Dec. 1892, CGPD, L. 17, C. 38, d. 18894.
79. Cahuantzi, *Memoria de 1888*, 5; *Commercial Directory of the American Republics*, vol. 2 (Washington, DC: Governmental Printing Office, 1898), 279.
80. Garner, *Porfirio Díaz*, 79–85.
81. Interim governor Teodoro Rivera wrote concernedly to Díaz after Cahuantzi had informed Rivera before beginning his first term that he would be replacing many positions. Díaz did not respond to Rivera's concerns. Teodoro Rivera to PD, 17 Dec. 1884, CGPD, L. 9, C. 2, d. 850.
82. Cahuantzi, *Memoria de 1888*, 5–7; Cahuantzi, *Memoria de 1893*, 5–6; Ramírez, *Sistema de Haciendas en Tlaxcala*, 43. Placing hacendados as district judges meant that they had significant leverage in local disputes, including those pertaining to land. Agrarian disputes are discussed further in chapter five. Allegations of judges' corruption and abuse during the Porfiriato abound in Tlaxcala's archives and have been corroborated by regional historians. See Evelyne Sanchez, *El juez, el notario, y el caudillo: Análisis de un juicio verbal en Tlaxcala durante la revolución* (Madrid: Casa de Velázquez, 2019), 64–65.
83. Cahuantzi, *Memoria de 1888*, 5–7; Cahuantzi, *Memoria de 1893*, 5–6.
84. Thomson and LaFrance, *Patriotism, Politics, and Popular Liberalism in Nineteenth-Century Mexico*, 261; Cosío Villegas, *Historia moderna de México*, vol. 9, 447–49; Garner, *Porfirio Díaz*, 62–64, 108.
85. Rendón Garcini, *El Prosperato*, 46, 56.
86. AHET, Bandos, decretos, e impresos, Exps. 66–82.
87. 29 Jul. 1892, AHET, Bandos, decretos, e impresos, Exp. 67; Aug. 1892, AHET, Bandos, decretos, e impresos, Exp. 69.
88. Librado López to PD, Aug.–Sept. 1892, CGPD, L. 17, C. 29, ds. 14113–14118; Librado López to PD, 2 Oct. 1896, CGPD, L. 21, C. 34, d. 16953.
89. PC to PD, 24 Aug. 1885, CGPD, L. 10, C. 18, d. 8897; Cahuantzi, *Memoria de 1888*, 7.
90. Juan Francisco Gaviño to PD, 18 Nov. 1890, CGPD, L. 15, C. 27, d. 13479; 27 Dec. 1890, L. 15, C. 30, d. 14847; 2 Jan. 1891, L. 16, C. 2, d. 513. These ventures are discussed in chapter five.
91. PC to PD, 14 Oct. 1891, CGPD, L. 16, C. 25, ds. 12008–12009; PD to PC, 16 Oct. 1891, L. 16, C. 25, d. 12009; Librado López to PD, 17 Nov. 1891, CGPD, L. 16, C. 29, d. 14077.
92. Rendón Garcini, *El Prosperato*, 57–58.
93. 24 June 1899, CGPD, L. 24, C. 15, d. 7376. See also José de Jesus Herrerías et al. to PD, 26 June 1899, CGPD, L. 24, C. 15, d. 7375.
94. José de Jesus Herrerías et al. to PD, 26 June 1899, CGPD, L. 24, C. 15, d. 7375.
95. PC to PD, Nov. 1899, CGPD, L. 24, C. 32, 33, 35, ds. 16434-6.

96. *El Hijo del Ahuizote*, 7 Jan. 1900; Joaquin Calero (district judge) to Díaz, 20 Jan. 1900; PC to PD, 8 Jan. 1900, CGPD, L. 25, C. 2 ds. 728, 773.

97. Katz, "The Liberal Republic and the Porfiriato," 109.

98. The ten towns were: Chimalpan, Tepehitec, Cuahtelulpan, Metepec, Acuitlapilco, Atlahapa, Cuauhtla, Ocotlan, Ixtulco, and Atempan. Circular from Miguel Sandoval, representative of "La Corporación municipal," 29 Dec. 1885, AHET, A, C. 166, Exp. 3, d. 1, f. 60.

99. Vecinos of Metepec to Ayuntamiento of Tlaxcala, 5 Oct. 1886, AHET, A, C. 166, Exp. 3, d. 1, f. 83.

100. Vecinos of Metepec to Ayuntamiento of Tlaxcala, 5 Oct. 1886, AHET, A, C. 166, Exp. 3, d. 1, f. 83.

101. The historic record does not indicate whether Cahuantzi responded to Ayecac's solicitation. Vecinos of San Mateo de Ayecac to PC, 21 Dec. 1885, AHET, SC, C. 2, Exp. 22, fs. 1–33.

102. Juan Nava Zamora to PC, 11 Jan. 1895, SC, C. 3, Exp. 1, fs. 90–91.

103. See Garner, *Porfirio Díaz*, 79–85; see chapters contained in Falcón and Buve, eds., *Don Porfirio presidente, nunca omnipotente*; Seminario Nacional "Jornadas Porfirianas" and Jane-Dale Lloyd, eds., *Visiones del Porfiriato, visiones de México*.

104. These processes are discussed in chapter six.

105. *Cuadro de personal de del Ayuntamiento de Tlaxcala de 1901–2*, 1 Dec. 1901, AHET, A, C. 233, Exp. 2, f. n/a.

106. Cahuantzi, *Memoria de 1893*, 5.

107. 9 Dec. 1902, AHET, SC, C. 1 Exp. 2, f. 110. Curiously, election results in the municipality of Tzompantepec were among the few municipalities whose electoral outcomes were not listed in the *Periódico Oficial*, which announced all the 1902 electoral outcomes. *Periódico Oficial de Tlaxcala*, 29 Nov. 1902.

108. Violence erupted in the municipalities of Zacatelco, Tzompantepec, Teolocholo, Chiautempan, and others. See 13 Dec. 1902, AHET, SC, C. 1 Exp. 2, fs. n/a; Presidente municipal of Zacatelco to Sec. de gobierno, 7 Nov. 1902, AHET, JG, C. 11, Exp. 26, f. 1; Agente municipal of Tetlanohcán to Secretaría de gobierno, 15 Nov. 1902, AHET, JG, C. 11, Exp. 26, f. 2. Examples of residents' opposition to Cahuantzi's regime during 1902–3 can be found in AHET, JG, 1903, C. 33, Exp. 12, fs. 1–24; C. 34, Exp. 8, fs. 1–40.

109. See documents pertaining to Zacatelco, Nov. 1900, CGPD, L. 25, C. 37, ds. 14784–88; Nov. 1902, CGPD, C. 27, L. 33, ds. 12835, 12964–67, 12983–84.

Chapter 4

1. *Periódico Oficial del Estado de Tlaxcala*, 15 Sept. 1888, 1–2.

2. Residents used *terrenos de la corporación* primarily to extract broom root (*zacatón*) or to put cattle out to pasture. Municipal governments extracted resources such as mud and clay to use on public works projects from these lands, as well. Some Tlaxcalan municipalities had been holding onto these properties since colonial, even precolonial, times. Tlaxcala, especially south-central Tlaxcala, had

a higher number of small properties and communally farmed lands that had not yet been forcibly distributed or taken over by larger haciendas compared to other places in central Mexico, such as Morelos, during the Porfirian period. Tlaxcala's agrarian patterns and transformations are discussed in chapter five.

3. *Periódico Oficial del Estado de Tlaxcala*, 15 Sept. 1888, 2.

4. *Rancho* and *hacienda* typically designated larger properties, for which sizes and values varied, sometimes drastically. A hacienda was generally larger than a rancho. These properties were privately and individually owned.

5. *Periódico Oficial del Estado de Tlaxcala*, 6 Oct. 1888, 2.

6. *Periódico Oficial del Estado de Tlaxcala*, 6 Oct. 1888, 2.

7. Italian traveler Giovanni Francesco Gemelli Careri, in his seventeenth century account *Viaje por la Nueva España*, and later, American traveler Frederick Starr, both commented on Tlaxcala's floods while passing through the region. Giovanni Francesco Gemelli Careri and José María de Agreda y Sánchez, *Viaje a la Nueva España* (Mexico City: José Porrúa, 1983), 231; Frederick Starr, *Notes upon the Ethnography of Southern Mexico* (Davenport: Washington Academy of Sciences, 1898, 1899, 1900), 14, cited in Alba González Jácome, "El paisaje lacustre en Tlaxcala," in *Estudios sobre historia y ambiente en América, I: Argentina, Bolivia, Mexico, Paraguay*, ed. Alba González Jácome and Bernardo García Martínez (Mexico City: Instituto Panamericano de Geografía e Historia, 1999), 198–99.

8. Chapters four and five build on the work of scholars who examine water as a window into the history of modernization in Mexico and the relationships between the Mexican people and the environment. For a historiographical outline of the history of Mexico's "modern environmental progression," with a focus on water, see Boyer, "Cycles of Environmental History," in *A Land between Waters*, 6.

9. Barbara Mundy, *The Death of Aztec Tenochtitlán, the Life of Mexico City* (Austin: University of Texas Press, 2018).

10. Skopyk, *Colonial Cataclysms*, 146. Historical investigations of water in colonial era Mexico include, but are certainly not limited to, Michael C. Meyer, *Water in the Hispanic Southwest: A Social and Legal History, 1550–1850* (Tucson: University of Arizona Press, 2016); Vera Candiani, *Dreaming of Dry Land: Environmental Transformation in Colonial Mexico City* (Stanford, CA: Stanford University Press, 2014); Sonya Lipsett-Rivera, *To Defend Our Water with the Blood of Our Veins: The Struggle for Resources in Colonial Puebla* (Albuquerque: University of New Mexico Press, 1999); Celia Salazar Exaire, *Uso y distribución del agua en el valle de Tehuacán: El caso de San Juan Bautista Axalpan, Pue., 1610–1798* (Mexico City: Instituto Nacional de Antropología e Historia, 2000); Louisa Schell Hoberman, "City Planning in Spanish Colonial Government: The Response of Mexico City to the Problem of Floods, 1607–1637" (PhD diss., Columbia University, 1972); Richard E. Boyer, *La gran inundación: Vida y sociedad en México, 1629–1638* (Mexico City: Sepsetentas, 1975); Alain Musset, *El agua en el valle de México: Siglos XVI–XVIII* (Mexico City: Pórtico-CEMC, 1992).

11. Skopyk, *Colonial Cataclysms*, 69.

12. Skopyk, *Colonial Cataclysms*, 68–70.
13. Skopyk, *Colonial Cataclysms*, 146.
14. Mexico's hydrological history during the Porfiriato is understudied relative to periods before and after. There are important exceptions to this historiographical pattern, however. These include the work of Luis Aboites, as well as regional water studies such as those in Puebla and Morelos. See Luis Aboites, *El agua de la nación: Una historia política de México, 1888–1946* (Mexico City: Centro de Investigaciones y Estudios Superiores en Antropología Social, 1998); Rocío Castañeda González, *Las aguas de Atlixco: Estado, haciendas, fábricas y pueblos, 1880–1920* (Mexico City: Centro de Investigaciones y Estudios Superiores en Antropología Social, 2005); Alejandro Tortolero Villaseñor, "Water and Revolution in Morelos, 1850–1915," in *A Land between Waters: Environmental Histories of Modern Mexico*, 124–49; Blanca Estela Suárez Cortez, ed., *Historia de los usos del agua en México: Oligarquías, empresas y ayuntamientos (1840–1940)* (Mexico City: Comisión Nacional del Agua, 1998); Aquiles Omar and Ávila Quijas, eds., *Negociaciones acuerdos y conflictos en México, siglos XIX y XX, agua y tierra* (Zamora: Colegio de Michoacán, 2009); Juan Manuel Durán, Martín Sánchez, and Antonio Escobar Ohmstede, eds., *El agua en la historia de México: Balance y perspectiva* (Guadalajara, Jalisco: Universidad de Guadalajara, Centro Universitario de Ciencias Sociales y Humanidades, 2005).
15. Alejandro Tortolero Villaseñor, "Transforming the Central Mexican Waterscape: Lake Drainage and Its Consequences during the Porfiriato," in *Territories, Commodities, and Knowledges: Latin American Environmental History in the Nineteenth and Twentieth Centuries*, ed. Christian Brannstrom (London: Institute for the Study of the Americas, 2004), 121. For an overview of Porfirian-era public works projects, see Connolly, *El contratista de don Porfirio*.
16. Aboites, *El agua de la nación*; Claudia Agostini, *Monuments of Progress: Modernization and Public Health in Mexico City, 1876–1910* (Calgary: University of Calgary Press, 2003); Connolly, *El contratista de don Porfirio*, 191–304; Tortolero Villaseñor, "Transforming the Central Mexican Waterscape," 121–47; Vitz, *A City on a Lake*, 19–50.
17. Candiani, *Dreaming of Dry Land*, 5.
18. Clifton B. Kroeber, *Man, Land, and Water: Mexico's Farmlands Irrigation Policies, 1885–1911* (Berkeley: University of California Press, 1984); Wolfe, *Watering the Revolution*, 23–57.
19. Later in the twentieth century the Laguna region became a center for dairy production in Mexico. Wolfe, *Watering the Revolution*, 29–34; Kroeber, *Man, Land, and Water*. For an overview of the development of the export economy during the Porfiriato, see Steven Topik and Allen Wells, *Second Conquest of Latin America*; Beatty, *Institutions and Investment*; Lurtz, *From the Grounds Up*.
20. Alba González Jácome has detailed descriptions of south-central Tlaxcala's water ecology in González Jácome, *Humedales en el suroeste de Tlaxcala: Agua y agricultura en el siglo XX* (Mexico City: Universidad Iberoamericana, 2008), 31–72.

21. Luis Aboites, "Relación sociedad-naturaleza desde la historia de los usos del agua en México (1900–1940)," in *Estudios sobre historia y ambiente en America* I, ed. Alba González Jácome and Bernardo García Martínez (Mexico City: Instituto Panamericano de Geografía e Historia: El Colegio de México, 1999), 173–90.

22. Wolfe, *Watering the Revolution*, 34. Flood irrigation was still commonplace throughout the region and most of rural Mexico during this period. As of 1905, Tlaxcala had nineteen aguardiente factories and nine wheat mills. *La Antigua República*, 29 Jul. 1906, 48.

23. Most factories and mills used steam power, regardless of their size. Textile factories' production and water use dwarfed that of aguardiente factories and mills. Except for three mills, aguardiente and wheat manufacturers used significantly less horsepower (HP) than textile factories. The average textile factory used 112 HP, much more than wheat mills, which averaged 12 HP. Most aguardiente factories used one HP. See *La Antigua República*, 29 Jul. 1906, 48.

24. Wolfe, *Watering the Revolution*, 3. Many of the cases discussed in chapters four and five remained open at the end of the Porfirian period. Potable water is further discussed as part of the state's modernization plans in chapter six.

25. A summary of colonial water laws can be found in Oscar Cruz Barney, *Historia del derecho en México* (Mexico City: Oxford University Press, 1999), 423–25; and José Trinidad Lanz Cardenas, *Legislación de aguas en México* (Mexico City: Consejo Editorial del Gobierno del Estado de Tabasco, 1982).

26. Benjamin T. Smith, "Rewriting the Moral Economy: Agricultural Societies and Economic Change in Oaxaca's Mixtec Baja, 1830–1910," in *Mexico in Transition/México y sus transiciones*, ed. Antonio Escobar Ohmstede and Matthew Butler (Mexico City: CIESAS, 2013), 84. The idea of a moral economy, originated by E. P. Thompson and elaborated by political scientist James C. Scott, has been repurposed by historians such as Smith to describe a "system of mutual obligations and expectations" that existed between agricultural elites and nonelites in some Mexican regions, especially those less dominated by commercial agriculture after independence. Christina Jiménez also has a useful discussion of how moral economies functioned in Mexican neighborhoods in *Making an Urban Public*, 19–21.

27. José Esteban Castro, *Water, Power, and Citizenship: Social Struggle in the Basin of Mexico* (Basingstoke, England: Palgrave Macmillan, 2006). An exception to this pattern was in the Valley of Mexico, where the colonial government claimed jurisdiction over water there to carry out the Desagüe project. See Vera Candiani, "The Desagüe Reconsidered: Environmental Dimensions of Class Conflict in Mexico," *Hispanic American Historical Review* 92, no. 1, Environmental History (February 2012): 12.

28. Candiani, *Dreaming of Dry Land*, xxvi–xxix; Aboites, *El agua de la nación*, 26–35.

29. López Martínez, "La construcción de una nueva territorialidad a través de los usos del agua," 29.

30. Aboites, *El agua de la nación*, 31.

31. See files contained in AHET, SC, 1888, C. 9, Exp. 3, fs. 1–228; 23 Oct. 1885, AHET, A, C. 165, Exp. 3, fs. 165–67.

32. Vecinos y labradores de Zacatelco to PC, Apr.–May 1886, AHET, SC, C. 6, Exp. 52, fs. 3–7.

33. Vecinos y labradores de Zacatelco to PC, Apr.–May 1886.

34. Declaraciones de Mariano Grajales a las habitantes del Estado de Tlaxcala, 15 Jun. 1881, AHET, SC, C. 10, Exp. 1, fs. 186–91.

35. *Periódico Oficial del Estado de Tlaxcala*, 8 May 1886, 1–3.

36. *Periódico Oficial del Estado de Tlaxcala*, 12 Mar. 1887.

37. Circular from Cahuantzi to Ayuntamientos, 18 June 1888, AHET, A, C. 175, Exp. 4, f. 65.

38. Circular from Ayuntamiento de Tlaxcala to agentes municipales, 1 Aug. 1890, AHET, A, C. 180, Exp. 3, f. 6.

39. Aboites, *El agua de la nación*, 31.

40. Aboites, *El agua de la nación*, 31.

41. Francisco Sela to PC, 5 Feb. 1887, AHET, SC, 1887, C. 4, Exp. 35, f. 2.

42. Francisco Sela to PC, 5 Feb. 1887, f. 2.

43. Francisco Sela to PC, 5 Feb. 1887, f. 3. Boyer, *Political Landscapes*, 27.

44. Plinio Petricioli to PC, 12 Feb. 1887, AHET, SC, C. 4, Exp. 35, f. 4.

45. Plinio Petricioli to PC, 12 Feb. 1887.

46. Plinio Petricioli to PC, 12 Feb. 1887.

47. Plinio Petricioli to PC, 12 Feb. 1887.

48. Carlos Lenox Kennedy, representing Plinio Petricioli, to PC, 12 Jul. 1887, AHET, SC, C. 3, Exp. 5, f. 178–79.

49. Carlos Lenox Kennedy, representing Plinio Petricioli, to PC, 12 Jul. 1887.

50. Concepción Petricioli to Sec. de fomento, 23 June 1902, AHA, AS, C. 1231, Exp. 17042, f. 2.

51. See files contained in AHA, AS, C. 1073, Exp. 15073, fs. 1–210; C. 1231, Exp. 17042, fs. 1–119.

52. A full articulation of the law as well as all of Mexico's water-related legislation can be found in Lanz Cardenas, *Legislación*, 357–60. Wolfe also includes a helpful summation of the law. See Wolfe, *Watering the Revolution*, 41.

53. Aboites, *El agua de la nación*. Mikael Wolfe explains how Congress passed the law to grant "a major water concession from the Nazas [River]" in the Laguna region to boost cotton production there, the likes of which had dire environmental and human consequences. Wolfe, *Watering the Revolution*, 33.

54. Given the environmental, economic, and human impact of large water infrastructure projects in Mexico City and the Laguna region, scholars have examined the effects of the Waters Law in these regions more than others.

55. La Tlaxcalteca and la Josefina factories, as well as various haciendas including Dolores, Santa Elena, Santa Agueda, Santa Ana Portales, Santo Tomás, Santa Apolonia, Mixco and others unnamed were among those who took water

from the Zahuapan during the dry season. Ramón de Ibarrola to Sec. de Fomento, 1 Sept. 1904, AHA, AS, C. 272, Exp. 6557, fs. 23–24.

56. Gerardo Emilio Herrerias to Sec. de Fomento, 12 Aug. 1896, AHA, AS, C. 4574, Exp. 60833, f. 7.

57. The Caso brothers' farms that drew from the Atoyac were Santa Clara, San Antonio, and Santa Barbara, while their farm Santo Tomás drew from the Zahuapan River. See AHA, AS, C. 1311, Exp. 17871, fs. 1–11; C. 1247, Exp. 17178, fs. 1–73.

58. Lanz Cárdenas, *Legislación*, 359–60. For further explanation of the 1888 law, see Aboites, *El agua de la nación*, 12, 83–89; Martín Sánchez Rodríguez, "La herencia del pasado: La centralización de los recursos acuíferos durante el Porfiriato, 1888–1910," *Universidad Michoacana* 7 (Enero–Marzo 1993): 50–60.

59. Sec. de Fomento to Gerardo Emilio Herrerias, 30 Jan. 1896, AHA, AS, C. 4574, Exp. 60833, f. 7. In this case Herrerias demanded an explanation for why the Zahuapan did not fall under federal jurisdiction, especially given that the water would be used "to advance an industry so new . . . [for] the Republic." Herrerias went on to petition the Fomento Ministry in 1903 and 1905 over the same issue. Gerardo Emilio Herrerias to Sec. de Fomento, 12 Aug. 1896, 30 Jan. 1903, 14 Nov. 1905, AHA, AS, C 4574, Exp. 60833, fs. 11–13.

60. For example, in la Laguna, the federal government passed new water use regulations on three separate occasions during the Porfiriato after they took more accurate water flow measurements of the Nazas River. Wolfe, *Watering the Revolution*, 41, 64. See also Vitz, *A City on a Lake*, 20; Connolly, *Contraista de Don Porfirio*; Kroeber, *Man, Land, and Water*, 62–86; It should be noted that these authors also emphasize how federalization did not preclude local parties, even poorer residents, from shaping development.

61. López Martínez, "La construcción," 72. Likewise, the organization of the Tlaxcala state archives suggests that Tlaxcala state did not begin to systematically track water-related documentation until the 1920s. The first document in the "hydraulic resources" series under the "development" section in the Archivo Histórico del Estado de Tlaxcala is recorded as 1921. Prior to this period, water-related documentation is scattered throughout various collections.

62. Sebastian Mier to the Sec. de Fomento, 8 Apr. 1899, AHA, AS, C. 4569, Exp. 60765, f. 7. See also López Martínez, "La construcción," 70.

63. Sebastian Mier to the Sec. de Fomento, 8 Apr. 1899.

64. Sebastian Mier to the Sec. de Fomento, 8 Apr. 1899.

65. Mier served various diplomatic positions under Díaz, including as the Mexican Ministry's representative in London and Paris. See Castañeda González, *Las aguas de Atlixco*, 133.

66. Castañeda González, *Las aguas de Atlixco*, 137; Gutiérrez Álvarez, *Experiencias contrastadas*, 120; Cosío Villegas, *Historia moderna de México*, vol. 9, 381.

67. Señores Gavito y Villa, Pellón Germanos, A. Couttolene, Salceda Méndez,

and A. Vivanco to Sec. de Fomento, 12 Jan. 1904, AHA, AS, C. 272, Exp. 6557, f. 2.

68. Señores Gavito y Villa, Pellón Germanos, A. Couttolene, Salceda Méndez, and A. Vivanco to Sec. de Fomento, 12 Jan. 1904.

69. Señores Gavito y Villa, Pellón Germanos, A. Couttolene, Salceda Méndez, and A. Vivanco to Sec. de Fomento, 12 Jan. 1904.

70. Señores Gavito y Villa, Pellón Germanos, A. Couttolene, Salceda Méndez, and A. Vivanco to Sec. de Fomento, 12 Jan. 1904.

71. A dispute between Sebastian Mier and residents prompted Ibarrola to inspect the Atoyac River in Puebla. See Castañeda González, *Las aguas de Atlixco*, 141. On Ibarrola's work in the Laguna, see Kroeber, *Man, Land, and Water*, 109–33.

72. Ramón de Ibarrola to Sec. de Fomento, 14 Apr. 1904, AHA, AS, C. 272, Exp. 6557, f. 10.

73. Ramón de Ibarrola to Sec. de Fomento, 14 Apr. 1904, f. 10.

74. Ramón de Ibarrola to Sec. de Fomento, 14 Apr. 1904, f. 11.

75. Ramón de Ibarrola to Sec. de Fomento, 14 Apr. 1904, f. 12.

76. Ramón de Ibarrola to Sec. de Fomento, 1 Sept. 1904, AHA, AS, C. 272, Exp. 6557, fs. 23–24.

77. Ramón de Ibarrola to Sec. de Fomento, 1 Sept. 1904.

78. Manuel Vera to Sec. de Fomento, 7 Jul. 1904, AHA, AS, C. 272, Exp. 6557, f. 16.

79. Ramón de Ibarrola to Sec. de Fomento, 1 Sept. 1904, AHA, AS, C. 272, Exp. 6557, fs. 23–24.

80. Ruíz, Santibañez, & Co to Sec. de Fomento, 30 Sept. 1904, AHA, AS, C. 272, Exp. 6557, f. 30.

81. Ruíz, Santibañez, & Co to Sec. de Fomento, 30 Sept. 1904.

82. Kroeber, *Man, Land, and Water*, 82.

83. Engineer (name unclear) to Sec. de Fomento, 10 Aug. 1907, AHA, AS, C. 272, Exp. 6557, f. 53.

84. Later in the twentieth century, most of Tlaxcala's factories closed.

85. Gerardo Emilio Herrerias to Sec. de Fomento, 12 Aug. 1896, AHA, AS, C. 4574, Exp. 60833, f. 7; Gerardo Emilio Herrerias to Sec. de Fomento, 30. Jan. 1903, 14 Nov. 1905, AHA, AS, C. 4574, Exp. 60833, fs. 11–13.

Chapter 5

1. Full text of the Ley Lerdo can be found in the online archive of the Biblioteca Jurídica Virtual del Instituto de Investigaciones Jurídicas de la UNAM: https://archivos.juridicas.unam.mx/www/bjv/libros/12/5625/17.pdf.

2. George McBride, "Los sistemas de propiedad rural en México," 94, cited in Jean Meyer, "Haciendas y ranchos, peones y campesinos en el Porfiriato," 487.

3. The new canon of scholarship on agrarian reform in Mexico has forced historians to rethink Mexico's national narrative and to contemplate the extent to which land privatization sparked the Revolution in certain regions. A summation

of the historiography on nineteenth-century agrarian reform in Mexico can be found in Emilio Kourí, "Interpreting the Expropriation of Indian Pueblo Lands: The Unexamined Legacies of Andrés Molina Enríquez,"*The Hispanic American Historical Review* 82, no. 1 (February 2002): 69–117. Examples of the contemporary canon on agrarian reform include Kourí, *A Pueblo Divided: Business, Property, and Community in Papantla, Mexico* (Stanford, CA: Stanford University Press, 2004), as well as contributions to Antonio Escobar Ohmstede and Matthew Butler, eds., *Mexico in Transition/México y sus transiciones* and Escobar Ohmstede, Martín Sánchez, and Ana María Graciela Gutiérrez Rivas, eds., *Agua y Tierra en México, Siglos XIX y XX*.

4. In Tlaxcala, *sociedades agrícolas,* in which every head of household owned a portion of what was previously a collective property, also went by *colonias* and *compañías agrícolas*. Rendón Garcini, *El Prosperato*, 118. Terms used in other regions include *rancherías, condueñazgos,* and *grandes lotes*. Kourí, *A Pueblo Divided*, 138–39. When sociedades agrícolas purchased lands, they often had no choice but to take out a mortgage through the state, as opposed to a private lender or credit institution, an option more possible for wealthier landowners who already owned properties. Thus, through state-owned mortgages, the state government had even more control over the disentailment process there. Rendón Garcini, *El Prosperato*, 108–13.

5. Examples of disputes over forestlands and shared spaces are scattered through the Sin clasificar (siglo XIX), Ayuntamiento, and Justicia y gobernación files in the Archivo Histórico del Estado de Tlaxcala. Demand for broom root and timber increased significantly during the Porfiriato. See Juárez Flores, "Besieged Forests at Century's End." On the transformation of ejido forestlands in this region after the Revolution, see Emily Wakild, *Revolutionary Parks: Conservation, Social Justice, and Mexico's National Parks, 1910–1940* (Tucson: University of Arizona Press, 2011), 94–121.

6. Examples of *despojos* during the Porfirian period can be found in various sections of the Archivo Histórico del Estado de Tlaxcala. See also Rendón Garcini, *Breve Historia*, 90; Juárez Flores, "Besieged Forests at Century's End." The number of "localities"—cities, towns, villages, and neighborhoods, as well as haciendas and ranchos—diminished from 506 in 1886 to 416 in 1910, a decline that undoubtedly reflected disentailment taking place in Tlaxcala. Rendón Garcini, *El Prosperato*, 87.

7. On agrarian reform in Tlaxcala during the Porfiriato, see Rendón Garcini, *El Prosperato*, 114–26, 133–39. The Tlaxcalan state archive was relocated and reorganized since Rendón Garcini undertook his research. I have found most of the documentation on "adjudicaciones de terrenos de comunidad" to be housed in the *Sin clasificar, Siglo XIX and Justicia Civil* sections of the Archivo Histórico del Estado de Tlaxcala.

8. Through this process some regions saw anywhere between 19 and 47 percent of lands expropriated and privatized. The first law authorizing the collection of

terrenos baldíos was passed under Juárez in 1863 and was then reformed and renewed under the González administration in 1883. Robert Holden, *Mexico and the Survey of Public Lands: The Management of Modernization, 1876–1911* (DeKalb: Northern Illinois University Press, 1994), 7–24.

9. Holden, *Mexico and the Survey of Public Lands*, 23.

10. Cahuantzi, *Memoria de 1893*, 9; Rendón Garcini, *El Prosperato*, 173.

11. Rendón Garcini, *El Prosperato*, 173.

12. Rendón Garcini, *El Prosperato*, 55, 171–73; *El C. Coronel Próspero Cahuantzi, Gob. Constitucional del Estado Libre y Soberano de Tlaxcala certifica: que en el archivo de la Sec. de este gobierno existen dos expedientes relativos a composiciones de tierras de este Estado, y con ellos se comprueba que no hay en él, baldíos, huecas ni demasías, y las cuales constancias extendidas en el papel correspondiente, son a la letra como siguen . . . ,*" AHET, 1891, SC (siglo XIX); Holden, *Mexico and the Survey of Public Lands*, 34.

13. Kourí explains why and how historians have erroneously conflated disentailment and the expropriation of land through terrenos baldíos. See Kourí, "Interpreting the Expropriation of Indian Pueblo Lands."

14. Declaración no. 8, 25 May 1897, AHET, BDI, Exp. 91.

15. Vecinos de San Tadeo Huilopan to PC, 7 Mar. 1901, AHET, SC, 1901, C. 2, Exp. 15, fs. 1–3.

16. PC to C. Juez de Distrito del Estado, CGPD, 8 Dec. 1891, L. 17, C. 1, d. 432.

17. "Juan de la Rosa Cuamatzi y socios entablaron demanda de amparo ante el Juzgado de Distrito de Tlaxcala, contra el Gobernador . . ." Sj, 1892, vol. 5 (3ª época), pp. 490–97, in *Seminario Judicial de la Federación*, cited in Robert James Knowlton, "Tribunales federales y terrenos rurales en el México del siglo xix: El Semanario judicial de la Federación," *Historia mexicana* 46, no. 1 (1996): 91–93. Historian Elsie Rockwell reports how Juan de la Rosa Cuamatzi's descendants retain copies of the amparo to this day. See Rockwell, "Todos tenemos la crisma de dios: Engaging Spanish Literacy in a Tlaxcalan Pueblo," in *Beyond Alterity*, 133.

18. See Tortolero Villaseñor, "Water and Revolution in Morelos, 1850–1915," 141.

19. Though not in this case, agrarian conflicts sometimes broke out in Tlaxcala because the occupant of a given territory lacked a formal property title. Take, for example, the dispute among the Tlilayatzin family of Contla in which one family member accused another family member of occupying a terreno illegally and bribing a local official so that they could continue to work the land without legal title. 27 Dec. 1908, AHET, JG, C. 93, Exp. 61, d. 3.

20. Knowlton, "Tribunales federales y terrenos rurales en el México del siglo XIX; Timothy James, *Mexico's Supreme Court: Between Liberal Individual and Revolutionary Social Rights, 1867–1934* (Albuquerque: University of New Mexico Press, 2013), 91–92.

21. PC to C. Juez de Distrito del Estado, CGPD, 8 Dec. 1891, L. 17, C. 1, d. 432.

22. PC to C. Juez de Distrito del Estado, CGPD, 8 Dec. 1891, L. 17, C. 1, d. 432.

23. Rendón Garcini, *El Prosperato*, 52–53.

24. See chapter six; Buve, *El movimiento revolucionario en Tlaxcala*.
25. "Juan de la Rosa Cuamatzi y socios entablaron demanda de amparo ante el Juzgado de Distrito de Tlaxcala, contra el Gobernador . . ." cited in Knowlton, "Tribunales federales y terrenos rurales en el México del siglo XIX," 91–93.
26. "Juan de la Rosa Cuamatzi."
27. Juan de la Rosa Cuamatzi et al. to C. Juez de Distrito del Estado, CGPD, 8 Dec. 1891, L. 17, C. 1, d. 432.
28. Rendón Garcini describes Cahuantzi's actions in this case as "somewhat exceptional." But cases like these occurred more regularly than Rendón Garcini's description implies. *El Prosperato*, 136.
29. Rendón Garcini, *El Prosperato*, 120–30.
30. Rendón Garcini, *El Prosperato*. Friedrich Katz points out how, "Repeatedly Díaz wrote to governors and local officials asking them to respect Indians' property rights when the latter could show titles to them, or even to respect *de facto* property rights of Indians." Katz, "The Liberal Republic and the Porfiriato," 98; Kourí, "Interpreting," 86.
31. Rendón Garcini, *El Prosperato*, 197–213. Examples of these conflicts can be found in the Justicia civil section of the Archivo Histórico del Estado de Tlaxcala, boxes 168–219. See also Buve, *El movimiento revolucionario en Tlaxcala*, 113; Rendón Garcini, *Breve Historia*, 88.
32. Antonio Escobar Ohmstede, "El oriente de San Luis Potosí visto a través de la conflictividad del agua y la tierra, ¿ciclos que se abrieron?" in *Mexico in Transition/México y sus transiciones*, 186. Although the Ley Lerdo did not mention water, a water law from December 1902 clarifies how access to a canal or dam did not grant the water user ownership over the lands from where the water was taken, that the water user's access rights were "temporary and revocable," and that the water user was "subject to lose [water usage rights] if they did not use the water consecutively for five years or for the exact purpose for which the user was granted access to that water." "Art. 2 de Ley 18 de Dic de 1902 sobre clasificación de bienes federales," in *Oficial contrato entre Sec. de Fomento y Francisco Sela para concesión de agua*, 7 Oct. 1909, AHA, C. 1073, Exp. 15073, f. 100.
33. See chapter four. It is important to distinguish here between land use and ownership. Whereas individuals could own land privately, individuals could not own water. Instead, they leased exclusive water access rights from municipal governments (after 1888, leases along federalized waterways were granted by the federal government).
34. Agencia Municipal de Ayecac to Prefecto Político de Tlaxcala, 7 Jan. 1903, AHET, SC, C. 1, Exp. 1, fs. 1, 15; AHA, C. 1231, Exp. 17042, fs. 1–119; González Jácome, *Humedales en el Suroeste de Tlaxcala*, 158–60. After the municipal president indicated to the agente municipal that he supported Petricioli rather than the villagers, the agente municipal wrote to the district prefect directly to plead that the prefect contact the governor on the village's behalf.
35. Concepción Petricioli to Sec. de Fomento, 23 Jun. 1902, AHA, C. 1231, Exp.

17042, f. 2; Sec. de comunicaciones y obras públicas to Concepción Petricioli, 5 Jul. 1902, fs. 3–4.

36. Eng. Joaquin Lorenz to Sec. de Fomento, 31 Oct. 1902, AHA, C. 1231, Exp. 17042, fs. 53–62.

37. Eng. Joaquin Lorenz to Sec. de Fomento, 20 Jun. 1903, AHA, C. 1231, Exp. 17042, fs. 63–64.

38. Eng. Luis Guerrero y Romero to Sec. de Fomento, 14 Dec 1908, AHA, C. 1073, Exp. 15073, f. 74.

39. See documents contained in AHA, C. 1231, Exp. 17042, fs. 1–119.

40. Vecinos del Ayuntamiento de Tlaxcala to the Ayuntamiento de Tlaxcala, 30 Aug. 1888, AHET, A, C. 176, Exp. 3, f. 102.

41. Trinidad Vela Farfán to Prefecto político de Tlaxcala, 31 Aug. 1888, AHET, A, C. 176, Exp. 4, f. 112.

42. Trinidad Vela Farfán to Prefecto político de Tlaxcala, 31 Aug. 1888.

43. Declaración del Patriótico Ayuntamiento de Tlaxcala, 25 Sept. 1888, AHET, A, C. 176, Exp. 4, fs. 113–14.

44. Prefecto político de Tlaxcala to PC, AHET, SC, 2 Sept. 1902, C. 1, Exp. 12, fs. 57–58.

45. See files contained in AHET, SC, 1903, C. 1, Exp. 12, fs. 1–88.

46. Other examples of these conflicts are littered throughout the Archivo Nacional de Agua and the Tlaxcalan state archives. In the Archivo Histórico del Estado de Tlaxcala, water-related documentation for years prior to 1921 is scattered throughout different sections, whereas documentation from 1921 onward can be found in the Fomento section under the series *Recursos Hidráulicos y administrativos*.

47. These two communities were Santa Elena and Santo Tomás Xoxtla, both in Nativitas. *Periódico Oficial del Estado de Tlaxcala*, 2 Apr. 1887; Rendón Garcini, *El Prosperato*, 92–93.

48. *Periódico Oficial del Estado de Tlaxcala*, 2 Apr. 1887.

49. Tlaxcala City vecinos to Ayuntamiento of Tlaxcala, 5 Jan. 1886, Land commission of Tlaxcala City to the Ayuntamiento of Tlaxcala, 25 Dec. 1888, AHET, A, C. 166, Exp. 3, fs. 94–96.

50. In the late nineteenth century, water conservation was conceived as conservation for human use in dams, reservoirs, and such. It is only in the past few decades that conservation has come to signify the environmental protection and preservation of free-flowing waterways. Wolfe, *Watering the Revolution*, 14. During the Porfirian period, conversations about environmental conservation usually centered on forests. See, for example, Emily Wakild's chapter on conservation of la Malintzin National Park in Tlaxcala in *Revolutionary Parks*, 94–121. See also Boyer, *Political Landscapes*.

51. See chapter four.

52. *Periódico Oficial del Estado de Tlaxcala*, 7 Oct. 1893.

53. *Periódico Oficial del Estado de Tlaxcala*, 7 Apr. 1894.

54. *Periódico Oficial del Estado de Tlaxcala*, 7 Apr. 1894.

55. Eng. Rafael Serrano to Sec. de Fomento, 2 Aug. 1907, AHA, C. 290, Exp. 6953, f. 8.

56. Eng. Rafael Serrano to Sec. de Fomento, 2 Aug. 1907.

57. *Periódico Oficial del Estado de Tlaxcala*, 25 Aug. 1894; Rendón Garcini, *El Prosperato*, 143; Carlos Bustamante López, "Un perfil urbano del Prosperato," *Entorno urbano*, Revista de Historia Instituto de Investigaciones Dr. José Ma. Luis Mora UAM—Iztapalapa, vol. 2: 4 (Julio–Dic 1996), 73.

58. SCJN, Archivo Histórico, Serie Tribunal Pleno, 1898, Legajo (L) 11, Expediente (Exp) 521, Número (N) 20; Bustamante López, "Un perfil urbano del Prosperato," 73; Rendón Garcini, *El Prosperato*, 142–43.

59. José Cuesta Mendizabal to Sec. de Fomento, 20 Dec. 1898, AHA, AS, C. 4572, Exp. 60793, fs. 2–3; Ignacio Morales y Benítez to Sec. de Fomento, 30 Jan. 1899, AHA, AS, C. 4572, Exp. 60793, f. 32; *Diario Oficial* (Mexico), 14 Jan. 1899; *Periódico Oficial de Tlaxcala*, 4 Feb. 1899.

60. See various files contained in AHA, AS, C. 4572, Exp. 60793, fs 1–86.

61. PC to Sec. de Fomento Francisco Martínez López, 14 Mar. 1899, AHA, AS, C. 4572, Exp. 60793, fs. 61–62.

62. PC to Sec. de Fomento Francisco Martínez López, 14 Mar. 1899.

63. José Cuesta Mendizabal to Sec. de Fomento, 7 Jun. 1905, AHA, AS, C. 4572, Exp. 60793, f. 82.

64. Cahuantzi also intervened in other natural resource disputes that were brought about by privatization and development. For example, the governor intervened in a few instances to protect ejido forestlands against developers. He also forced hacendado and rancho owners to keep public roads accessible and in good condition for passersby. See Presidente municipal de Santa Cruz Tlaxcala to PC, 26 Mar. 1885, AHET, SC, 1885, C. 3, Exp. 17; Presidente municipal de San Bernardino de Contla a PC, 9 Jan. 1897, AHET, SC, C. 2, Exp. 1, fs. 1–9; Mariano Muñoz al Administrator de la Hacienda de San. Nicolás, 26 Jul. 1887, SC, Exp. 8, C. 35, fs. 1–5; Rendón Garcini, 143–47.

65. Informe del Dept. de Legislación al Sec. de Fomento, 11 Oct. 1897, AHA, AS, C. 4574, Exp. 60827, fs. 1–7. See also González Jácome, "El paisaje lacustre en Tlaxcala," 115–16.

66. PC to Sec. de Fomento, 22 Nov. 1901, AHA, AS, C. 4574, Exp. 60827, fs. 13–14.

67. PC to Sec. de Fomento, 22 Nov. 1901, 14.

68. AHET, SC, 1897, C. 2, Exp. 1, fs. 166–67; "Decreto sobre los vecinos del pueblo Tepeyanco y las aguas de Acuitlapilco, permite hacer el desagüe de esas aguas," *Periódico Oficial de Tlaxcala*, 30 Dec. 1899. President Álvaro Obregón declared Lake Acuitlapilco private property in 1923. See copy of the declaration of privatization of Lake Acuitlapilco by the President of the Republic, 20 Jan. 1923, AHET, Fomento (F), Recursos hidráulicos (RH), C. 1, Exp. 2, fs.1–4.

69. "Expediente formado con motivo de la queja que hacen los vecinos de Tepeitec [*sic*] contra el Ciudadano Ricardo Carvajal," 7 Jan. 1895, AHET, SC, C. 2,

Exp. 9, fs. 63–73; Vecinos de Tepeihtec to PC, 28 Dec. 1895, AHET, SC, C. 3, Exp. 1, f. 2.

70. "Expediente formado con motivo de la queja que hacen los vecinos de Tepeitec [sic] contra el Ciudadano Ricardo Carvajal," 7 Jan. 1895, AHET, SC, C. 2, Exp. 9, fs. 68–72.

71. *Periódico Oficial de Tlaxcala*, 10 Apr. 1886; Luis Velasco, *Geografía y estadística del Estado de Tlaxcala*, 18.

72. Vecinos and labradores de Zacatelco to PC, 6 May 1886, AHET, SC, C. 6, Exp. 52, f. 3.

73. *Periódico Oficial de Tlaxcala*, 10 Apr. 1886.

74. Name illegible, 13 May 1886, AHET, SC, C. 6, Exp. 52, fs. 3–4.

75. *Periódico Oficial de Tlaxcala*, 2 Apr. 1887.

76. González Jácome, *Humedales*, 94–103.

77. Vecinos de la laguna el Rosario to Sec. de Fomento, *Date unclear*; PC to Sec. de Fomento, 25 Mar. 1900, AHA, AS, C. 4577, Exp. 60910, fs. 1–106.

78. Municipal President of Lardizabal to PC, 14 May 1901, AHET, SC, C. 2, Exp. 3, fs 1–3; Vecinos of Tepetitla, Ayecac, and Villa Alta to Sec. de Fomento, 30 Aug. 1909, AHA, AS, C. 4578, Exp. 60902, fs. 2–3.

79. Vecinos of Tepetitla, Ayecac, and Villa Alta to Sec. de Fomento, 30 Aug. 1909, AHA, AS, C. 4578, Exp. 60902, f. 2.

80. PC to Sec. de Fomento, 27 Oct. 1909, AHA, AS, C. 4578, Exp. 60902, f. 8.

81. PC to Sec. de Fomento, 27 Oct. 1909, 9.

82. PC to Sec. de Fomento, 27 Oct. 1909, 9.

83. Andrés Matienzo to Sec. de Fomento, 23 June 1909, AHA, AS, C. 4578, Exp. 60902, f. 28.

84. Eng. Rafael Serrano to Sec. de Fomento, 26 Jul. 1910, AHA, AS, C. 4578, Exp. 60902, fs. 39–40.

85. Eng. Rafael Serrano to Sec. de Fomento, 26 Jul. 1910, fs. 39–40.

86. Sec. de Fomento, Colonización, é Industria to Eng. Rafael Serrano, 6 Aug. 1910, AHA, AS, C. 4578, Exp. 60902, fs. 41–42.

87. Felipe A. Berna to Sec. de Fomento, 14 Aug. 1908, AHA, AS, C. 4573, Exp. 60815, f. 2. See also files contained in AHA, AS, C. 1236, Exp. 17089, fs. 2–97.

88. Presidente municipal de Ixtacuixtla to Prefecto de Tlaxcala, 29 Jun. 1901, AHET, JG, C. 10, Exp. 25, fs. 1–4.

89. Ricardo Carvajal to PD, 4 Jul. 1900, CGPD, L. 25, C. 23, d. 8937.

90. See files contained in CGPD, Nov. 1891, L. 16, C. 29, ds. 14076, 14077, 14112.

91. See chapter three.

92. Prefectura de Hidalgo to the Mun. President of Tlaxcala, 23 Dec. 1892, AHET, A, C. 192, Exp. 2, f. 2; files contained in AHET, SC, C. 1, Exp. 12, fs. 57—unmarked; Vecinos of Panotla to the Sec. de Fomento, 28 Sept. 1917, AHA, AS, C. 652, Exp. 9450, fs. 1–2.

93. Trinidad Vela Farfán to José Yves Limantour, 3 Dec. 1901, CEHM, Colección José Y. Limantour, Fondo CDLIV, Segunda Serie, Año 1901, Carpeta 19, Documento 27985.

94. Vela Farfán to Limantour, 27 Mar. 1903, CEHM, Col. José Y. Limantour, Fondo CDLIV, Segunda Serie, Año 1903, Carpeta 18, Documento 235.
95. Vela Farfán to Limantour, 27 Mar 1903.
96. Vela Farfán to Limantour, 17 Sept. 1901, CEHM, Col. José Y. Limantour, Fondo CDLIV, Segunda Serie, Año 1901, Carpeta 18, Documento 27596; Vela Farfán to Limantour, 13 Apr. 1902, Fondo CDLIV, Segunda Serie, Año 1902, Carpeta 15, Documento 325.
97. Vecinos de Panotla to Sec. de Fomento, 28 Sept. 1917, AHA, AS, C. 652, Exp. 9450, f. 2.
98. Vecinos de Panotla to Sec. de Fomento, 28 Sept. 1917.
99. Manuel López to Sec. de Fomento, 29 Oct. 1917, AHA, AS, C. 652, Exp. 9450, f. 15.
100. Manuel López to Sec. de Fomento, 8 Feb. 1918, AHA, AS, C. 652, Exp. 94508, f. 36.
101. Manuel López to Sec. de Fomento, 8 Feb. 1918, f. 37.
102. Manuel López to Sec. de Fomento, 8 Feb. 1918, f. 37.

Chapter 6

1. *La Antigua República*, 4 Oct. 1908.
2. *La Voz de México*, 1871, cited in Daniel Cosío Villegas et al., *Historia moderna de México*, vol. 3, *La república restaurada: Vida social* (Mexico City: Editorial Hermes, 1956), 95.
3. The idea of imprinting modernity onto a physical landscape is borrowed from Geraldo L. Cadava, "Borderlands of Modernity and Abandonment: The Lines within Ambos Nogales and the Tohono O'odham Nation," *Journal of American History* 98, no. 2 (September 2011): 363, 380.
4. Discurso pronunciado por el c. Gobernador Próspero Cahuantzi, *Periódico Oficial del Estado de Tlaxcala*, 4 Apr. 1891. See also López Martínez, "La construcción," 56.
5. James R. Scobie, "The Growth of Latin American Cities, 1870–1930," in *The Cambridge History of Latin America*, ed. Leslie Bethell (Cambridge: Cambridge University Press, 1986), 233–66.
6. Recent examinations of modernization have challenged previous ideas that elites in Mexico City imposed modernization projects on a populace who opposed them, or otherwise did not desire them or see their need. See, for example, Jiménez, *Making an Urban Public*; Anna Rose Alexander, *City on Fire: Technology, Social Change, and the Hazards of Progress in Mexico City, 1860–1910* (Pittsburgh: University of Pittsburgh Press, 2016); Mark Overmyer-Velázquez, *Visions of the Emerald City: Modernity, Traditions, and the Formation of Porfirian Oaxaca, Mexico* (Durham, NC: Duke University Press, 2009). Beyond the Latin American context, see Lisa Keller, *Triumph of Order: Democracy and Public Space in New York and London* (New York: Columbia University Press, 2010).
7. On modernization in Mexico City, see Connolly, *El contratista de don Porfirio*; Tenorio-Trillo, *Mexico at the World's Fairs*; Tenorio-Trillo, *I Speak of the City:*

Mexico City at the Turn of the Twentieth Century (Chicago: University of Chicago Press, 2012); Paul Garner, *British Lions and Mexican Eagles: Business, Politics, and Empire in the Career of Weetman Pearson in Mexico, 1889–1919* (Stanford, CA: Stanford University Press, 2011).

8. Beatty, *Institutions and Investment*; Kennett S. Cott, "Porfirian Investment Policies, 1876–1910" (PhD diss., University of New Mexico, 1978); Graciela Márquez, "The Political Economy of Mexican Protectionism, 1868–1911" (PhD diss., Harvard University, 2002); S. Kuntz Ficker, "La contribución económica de las exportaciones en México: Un acercamiento desde las finanzas estatales (1880–1926)," *América Latina en la Historia Económica* 21, no. 2 (2013): 7–39.

9. "Roads" during the Porfirian period usually meant any route that was passable by horse and cart. Tarmac or asphalt highways did not come about until the decades after the Revolution. See Michael Bess, *Routes of Compromise: Building Roads and Shaping the Nation in Mexico, 1917–1962* (Lincoln: University of Nebraska Press, 2017).

10. A good summary of state rail lines can be found in *La Antigua República*, 29 Jul. 1906. See also López Martínez, "La construcción," 55–56; Rendón Garcini, *Breve Historia*, 89–91.

11. This was true of most places even with federal highways. See Coatsworth, *Growth against Development*, 20.

12. Coatsworth, *Growth against Development*, 20–24.

13. Sec. de gobierno to Pres. mun. de Tlaxcala, 7 Jan. 1886, AHET, A, C. 166, Exp. 4, f. 145.

14. Examples of these complaints are housed in the Sin clasificar (siglo XIX), Ayuntamiento, and Justicia y gobernación sections of the Archivo Histórico del Estado de Tlaxcala.

15. *Diario Oficial de la Federación*, 8 Dec. 1890, quoted in Paolo Riguzzi, "Los Caminos de Atraso: Tecnología, instituciones, e inversión en los ferrocarriles mexicanos, 1850–1900," in *Ferrocarriles y vida económica en México, 1850–1950*, ed. Sandra Kuntz Ficker and Paolo Riguzzi (Mexico City: El Colegio Mexiquense, 1996), 38; Beatty, *Institutions and Investment*, 37.

16. Riguzzi, "Los Caminos de Atraso," 38; Beatty, *Institutions and Investment*, 37; Rendón Garcini, *El Prosperato*, 230–31.

17. See various files contained in AHET, 1902, SC, Exp. 2, fs. 1–16.

18. Presidente municipal de Tlaxco to Prefecto político de Tlaxco, 6 Mar. 1897, AHET, SC, C. 2, Exp. 1, f. 59.

19. Presidente municipal de Tlaxco to Prefecto político de Tlaxco, 6 Mar. 1897.

20. PC, Circular no. 58, 16 May 1885, AHET, SC, C. 1, Exp. 35, f. 1.

21. See, for example, Prefecto político de Tlaxco to el administrador de la hacienda San Nicolás, 25 Jul. 1887, AHET, SC, C. 8, Exp. 35, fs. 3–4.

22. PC, Circular no. 107, AHET, 7 Nov. 1885; *La Antigua República*, 14 Feb. 1902. See also González Jácome, *Humedales en el Suroeste de Tlaxcala*, 61.

23. See, for example, Presidente municipal de Tlaxco to Sec. de Gobierno, 18

Apr. 1887, AHET, SC, C. 4, Exp. 3, f. 8; PC to prefecto político de Tlaxcala, 13 Mar. 1886, AHET, 1886, C. 4, Exp. 5, f. 6.

24. 17 Jan. 1907, AHET, Sec. Grl. de Gobierno, C. 1, Exp. 52, f. 1; *Periódico oficial del Estado de Tlaxcala*, 6 Jan. 1906.

25. Esteban Sánchez de Tagle, *Los Dueños de la Calle: Una estudia de la vía pública en la época colonial* (Mexico City: Instituto Nacional de Antropología e Historia, 1997).

26. Thomson and LaFrance, *Patriotism, Politics, and Popular Liberalism*, 13.

27. Thomson and LaFrance, *Patriotism, Politics, and Popular Liberalism*, 13. See also Benjamin T. Smith, "Communal Work, Forced Labor, and Road Building in Mexico, 1920–1958," in *State Formation in the Liberal Era: Capitalism and Claims of Citizenship in Mexico and Peru*, ed. Ben Fallaw and David Nugent (Tucson: University of Arizona Press, 2020), 273–93; Bess, *Routes of Compromise*.

28. Presidente municipal de Contla to PC, 25 Jan. 1897, AHET, SC, 1897, C. 2, Exp. 1.

29. Ciudadanos de Calpulalpan to PC, 19 Sept. 1901, AHET, SC, C. 2, Exp. 10, fs. 6–12.

30. Ciudadanos de Calpulalpan to PC, 19 Sept. 1901.

31. See, for example, vecinos de Nativitas to PC, 11 Feb. 1886, AHET, SC, C. 5, Exp. 51, fs. 1–6; Smith, "Communal Work, Forced Labor, and Road Building in Mexico."

32. See, for example, Anne G. Hanley, *The Public Good and the Brazilian State: Municipal Finance and Public Services in São Paulo, 1822–1930* (Chicago: University of Chicago Press, 2019); Carlos Contreras, "The Tax Man Cometh: Local Authorities and the Battle over Taxes in Peru, 1885–1906," in *Political Cultures in the Andes, 1750–1950*, ed. Nils Jacobsen and Cristóbal Aljovín de Losada (Durham, NC: Duke University Press, 2005), 116–36.

33. Circular de PC a los Ayuntamientos, 7 Nov. 1885, 14 Feb. 1902, cited in González Jácome, *Humedales en el Suroeste de Tlaxcala*, 61.

34. Mariano Fortuño to PC, 11 Feb. 1887, AHET, SC, C. 4, Exp. 44, f. 14.

35. Mariano Fortuño to PC, 11 Feb. 1887.

36. Tepeyanco residents to PD, 19 Nov. 1900, CGPD, C. 25, L. 37, d. 14783.

37. Tepeyanco residents to PD, 19 Nov. 1900.

38. Tepeyanco residents to PD, 19 Nov. 1900.

39. Bustamante López, "Un perfil urbano del Prosperato," 75; Carlos Bustamante, "Historia urbana del Prosperato: Historiografía, Fuentes y Métodos," *Enlace Histórico*, Órgano de difusión histórica del Archivo General del Estado de Tlaxcala, 2, no. 2 (1996): 5.

40. Eng. Juan Arellano to PC, 2 Oct. 1888, AHET, A, C. 176, Exp. 5, f. 238.

41. Eng. Juan Arellano to PC, 2 Oct. 1888.

42. PC to PD, CGPD, 25 Apr. 1890, L. 15, C. 8, Exps. 3659, 3630; Bustamante López, "Un perfil urbano del Prosperato," 73.

43. Eng. Juan Arellano to PC, 2 Oct. 1888, AHET, A, C. 176, Exp. 5, f. 238.

44. Bustamante López, "Un perfil urbano del Prosperato," 75.

45. Rendón Garcini, *El Prosperato*, 234.

46. Aprobación de gastos del Ayuntamiento de Tlaxcala, 2 Jan. 1888, AHET, A, C. 174, Exp. 1, f. 3; Plan de arbitrarios del mun. de Tlaxcala para el año 1889, 11 Dec. 1888, AHET, A, C. 177, Exp. 2, d. 4.

47. In the Ayuntamiento section of the Tlaxcalan state archives, files that contain lists of public works and infrastructure costs are found alongside lists of debts residents owed to the Ayuntamiento. Circular a Matias Viñas et. al. from Tesorería municipal de Tlaxcala, 11 Oct. 1890, AHET, A, C. 182, Exp. 2, fs. 121–22; Créditos activos y pasivos que existen en el Tesoreria de Tlaxcala, Dec. 1890, C. 183, Exp. 1, d. 5, fs. 166–72. The Ayuntamiento announced plans to collect on a debt that Mariano Muñoz, a hacendado, supposedly owed to the municipality to cover bridge costs, but there is no record of this transaction in the historic record. See Bustamante López, "Un perfil urbano del Prosperato," 75.

48. Relativo al presupuesto y plan de arbitrarios en el mun. de Tlaxcala en al año 1891, 6 Oct. 1890, AHET, A, C. 182, Exp. 2, fs. 105–12.

49. 20 May 1887, AHET, SC, C. 4, Exp. 50, f. 21.

50. See chapter three; Bustamante López, "Un perfil urbano del Prosperato," 86–88.

51. Luis Aboites, "The Illusion of National Power: Water Infrastructure in Mexican Cities," in *A Land between Waters*, 219–21.

52. Aboites, *El agua de la nación*, 35.

53. Bustamante López, "Un perfil urbano del Prosperato," 76.

54. Bustamante López, "Un perfil urbano del Prosperato," 76.

55. Dec. 1890, AHET, A, C. 183, Exp. 1, fs. 166–72; Mar. 1901, C. 234, Exp. 1, f. 2.

56. Sec. de gobierno al Prefecto político del dist. de Hidalgo, 17 Apr. 1888, AHET, A, C. 176, Exp. 3, f. 93; PC al pres. mun. de Tlax., 13 Sept. 1892, AHET, A, C. 191, Exp. 2, fs. 8–9.

57. Aboites, *El agua de la nación*, 37.

58. In nearby Puebla City, for example, the private Empresa de Cañerías took on this job. Aboites, *El agua de la nación*, 35; Diana Birrichaga Gardida, "Las empresas de agua potable en México," in *Historia de los usos del agua en México*, ed. Blanca Estela Suárez Cortez (Mexico City: Comisión Nacional del Agua, 1998), 200–205.

59. Ricardo Agüero to Tesorero municipal de Tlax., 21 Jun. 1904, AHET, A, C. 178, Exp. 1, f. 74.

60. José María Pérez to Pres. mun. de Tlax., 29 Jul. 1890, AHET, A, C. 181, Exp. 3, f. 268.

61. Tesorero municipal to presidente municipal de Tlax., 4 Aug. 1901, AHET, A, C. 234, Exp 1, f. 6.

62. Tesorero municipal to presidente municipal de Tlax., 4 Aug. 1901.

63. See files contained in AHET, A, 1889, C. 178, Exp. 1, f. 68; 1888, C. 177, Exp. 2, fs. 60–62, 139–45; 1890, C. 181, Exp. 3, fs. 265–69; 1901, C. 234, Exp. 1, fs. 1–7.

64. Gerardo Martínez Delgado, "La era de las redes: Servicios públicos,

grandes empresas y finanzas internacionales en las ciudades mexicanas a principios del siglo XX," *Historia Mexicana* 70, no. 4 (2021): 1607. On electricity in Mexico City, see Diana J. Montaño, *Electrifying Mexico: Technology and the Transformation of a Modern City* (Austin: University of Texas Press, 2021).

65. Circular del Ayuntamiento de Calpulalpan, 19 Sept. 1901, AHET, SC, C. 2, Exp. 10, fs. 24–27; Juárez Flores, "Alumbrado público en Puebla y Tlaxcala y deterioro ambiental en los bosques de La Malintzi, 1820–1870," *Historia Crítica*, no. 30 (2005): 13–38.

66. Juárez Flores, "Tlaxcala's La Malintzin Woodlands," 109.

67. Correspondencia entre PC y La Compañia Mexicana de Luz Blanca, 1901, AHET, SC, C. 2, Exp. 28, fs. 1–16.

68. Presidente municipal de Tlax. to Prefecto político de Tlax., 23 Dec. 1902, AHET, JG, C. 12, Exp. 13, f. 1.

69. See files contained in AHET, SC, 1904, C. 1, Exp. 26, fs. 1–17.

70. Bustamante López, "Un perfil urbano," 77.

71. *La Antigua República*, 29 Jul. 1906.

72. Rendón Garcini, *El Prosperato*, 234.

73. Rendón Garcini, *El Prosperato*, 234.

74. Acuerdo dictado por el Ayuntamiento de Tlax., 22 Mar. 1907, AHET, A, C. 262, Exp. 3, f. 87.

75. See files contained in AHET, A, C. 262, Exp. 3, fs. 2–178, Contrato entre Ayuntamiento de Tlaxcala y los Señores Schondube y Neugebauer, fs. 19–22; Bustamante López, "Un perfil urbano del Prosperato," 76–78.

76. Martínez Delgado, "La era de las redes."

77. Presidente municipal de Tlax. to PC, 19 Dec. 1907, AHET, A, C. 262, Exp. 3, f. 129.

78. Acuerdo dictado por el Ayuntamiento de Tlax., 22 Mar. 1907, AHET, A, C. 262, Exp. 3, f. 87.

79. Gruening, *Mexico and Its Heritage*, 472, cited in Rendón Garcini, *El Prosperato*, 236.

80. Rendón Garcini, *El Prosperato*, 240.

81. Rendón Garcini, *El Prosperato*, 234–35.

82. *Informe de gobierno*, 1909; Bustamante López, "Un perfil urbano del Prosperato," 78. See also Vecinos de Zacatelco to PD, Nov. 1900, CGPD, L. 25, C. 37, d. 14785.

83. Elsie Rockwell, "Schools of the Revolution: Enacting and Contesting State Forms in Tlaxcala, 1910–1930," in *Everyday Forms of State Formation: Revolution and the Negotiation of Rule in Modern Mexico*, ed. Gilbert M. Joseph and Daniel Nugent (Durham, NC: Duke University Press, 1994), 207.

84. Rockwell, "Schools of the Revolution," 207.

85. Rockwell, "Schools of the Revolution," 177.

86. Rockwell, "Schools of the Revolution," 177.

87. Agente municipal de Tepehitec to Sec. del Ayuntamiento de Tlaxcala, 18 Jan. 1897, AHET, A, C. 210, Exp. 3, f. 68.

88. Elsie Rockwell, *Hacer Escuela, Hacer Estado: La educación posrevolucionaria vista desde Tlaxcala* (Zamora, Michoacán: El Colegio de Michoacán, 2007), 182–83.

89. Rockwell notes how these positions were often occupied by the hacienda owners themselves. Rockwell, "Schools of the Revolution," 177.

90. See files contained in AHET, Sección Educación (E), 1901–1903, C. 4–19; AHET, Sin clasificar (Siglo XIX).

91. *Periódico Oficial del Estado de Tlaxcala*, 10 Apr. 1886.

92. *Periódico Oficial del Estado de Tlaxcala*, 10 Apr. 1886.

93. *Periódico Oficial del Estado de Tlaxcala*, 10 Apr. 1886.

94. See "Acuerdos que dió a conocer Rafael Anzures, pres. del Ayuntamiento de Tlaxcala . . . ," 14 May 1906, 24 Sept. 1906, 11 Jan. 1907, 12 Jan. 1907, 2 Oct. 1907, AHET, BDI, Exps. 105, 106, 107, 108, 113.

95. México and Guadalupe Villers, *La hacienda pública de los estados: Trabajo hecho por el empleado de la Secretaría de hacienda y crédito público M. Guadalupe Villers* (Mexico City: Tip. de la oficina impresora de estampillas, 1911), 343–54; Rendón Garcini, *El Prosperato*, 234–35.

96. The Ley de Hacienda stipulated that property owners whose land was valued at MXN $100 or more would now pay *8 al millar* instead of the previous *6 al millar* to the state, while those whose properties were valued between $50 and $100 would pay the same tax, but to their respective ayuntamientos. In 1902, those who previously paid 8 al millar were now ordered to pay 10 al millar. Ley de Hacienda, 6 Feb. 1897, 24 May 1897, AHET, A, C. 212, Exp. 2, d. 4, fs. 116–17. See also Rendón Garcini, *El Prosperato*, 19.

97. "Relativo al asunto de sedición ocasionado por el individuo Andrés García," 30 Dec. 1899, AHET, SC, C. 3, Exp. 1, fs. 31–53. García had previously been arrested for disturbing the peace in 1895. See "Partes relativos a movimiento de policía y cárcel," 3 Jan. 1895, AHET, SC, C. 1, Exp. 1, d. 3, f. 204.

98. *El Hijo del Ahuizote*, 7 Jan. 1900.

99. *El Hijo del Ahuizote*, 7 Jan. 1900; Joaquin Calero (district judge) to Díaz, 20 Jan. 1900; PC to PD, 8 Jan. 1900, CGPD, L. 25, C. 2 ds. 728, 773; Nov. 1900, CGPD, L. 25, C. 37, ds. 14784–88; Nov. 1902, CGPD, C. 27, L. 33, ds. 12835, 12964–67, 12983–84; "Varios vecinos pueblos de Tlaxcala solicitan la no reeleccion del Sr. Coronel Próspero Cahuantzi," 1903, AHET, JG, C. 33, Exp. 12, fs. 1–24.

100. Date unknown, 1905, AHET, JG, C. 67, Exp. 55, f. 20; *Periódico Oficial del Estado de Tlaxcala*, 18 Feb. 1905, 27 Aug. 1905; Rendón Garcini, "Una oposición reprimida: El caso de Andrés García," in *Historia y sociedad en Tlaxcala: Memorias del 40. y 50. Simposios Internacionales de Investigaciones Socio-Históricas sobre Tlaxcala, octubre de 1988, octubre de 1989* (Tlaxcala: Gobierno del Estado de Tlaxcala, Instituto Tlaxcalteca de Cultura, 1991), 219–26; Rendón Garcini, *El Prosperato*, 23–37.

101. Buve, *El movimiento revolucionario en Tlaxcala*; Buve, "Neither Carranza nor Zapata!: The Rise and Fall of a Peasant Movement That Tried to Challenge

Both, Tlaxcala, 1910–1919," in *Riot, Rebellion, and Revolution: Rural Social Conflict in Mexico*, ed. Friedrich Katz (Princeton, NJ: Princeton University Press, 1988), 338–75; Jaime S. Sánchez, *Los antirreeleccionistas de Tepehítec, Tlax., y la Revolución en Tlaxcala, 1906–1915* (Tlaxcala: Congreso del Estado de Tlaxcala, LV Legislatura, 1999); Porfirio Del Castillo, *Puebla y Tlaxcala en los días de la revolución* (Mexico City: Imp. "Zavala," 1953); Cuéllar Bernal, *Tlaxcala a través de los siglos*; Luis Nava Rodríguez, *Tlaxcala contemporánea, de 1822 a 1977* (Mexico City: Editorial Progreso, 1978); *Tlaxcala en la historia* (Tlaxcala: [s.n.], 1972); Henderson, *The Worm and the Wheat*. Biographies of these leaders include Candelario Reyes, *Biografía de Juan Cuamatzi* (Tlaxcala: Difusión Cultural del Gobierno del Estado, 1961); Crisanto Cuéllar Abaroa, *Juan Cuamatzi, indio tlaxcalteca, precursor de la revolución mexicana; apuntes para la historia* (Tlaxcala, 1935); *Paz o terror? Inquietudes en 1910* (Tlaxcala: Talleres Gráficos, 1952); *Domingo Arenas: Caudillo agrarista* (Tlaxcala: Difusión Cultural del Estado, 1961).

102. See Archivo Histórico del Tribunal Superior de Justicia del Estado de Tlaxcala (AHJT), Fondo Procuradora General de Justicia (PGJ), Sección Suprema Tribunal de Justicia (STJ), 1905, C. 17, Exp. 14, fs. 1–14; "Varios vecinos pueblos de Tlaxcala solicitan la no reeleccion del Sr. Coronel Próspero Cahuantzi," 1903, AHET, JG, C. 33, Exp. 12, fs. 1–24; *La Antigua República*, 22 Oct. 1905; Cuéllar Bernal, *Tlaxcala a través de los siglos*, 245.

103. Rafael Galicia to PC, 12 Dec. 1906, AHET, JG, C. 79, Exp. 20, f. 2. See also files contained in "Varios negocios de ramo de hacienda," 1895, AHET, SC, C. 1, Exp. 1, fs. 140–200; Vecinos de Chiautempan to PC, 21 Jun. 1897, AHET, SC, C. 2, Exp. 4, f. 39.

104. "Tesorería gen. solicita del H. Congreso del estado se reforme el Art. 37 de la Ley de Hacienda, en virtud de que los dueños de casillas de pulque jamás se producen con verdad," 17 Nov. 1905, AHET, SC, C. 1, Exp. 1, fs. 6–14.

105. Rendón Garcini, *El Prosperato*, 159.

106. *El Tiempo*, 15 Mar. 1905, 30 Mar. 1905; Rendón Garcini, *El Prosperato*, 61.

107. Vecinos de Zacatelco to PD, Nov. 1900, CGPD, L. 25, C. 37, d. 14785.

108. See files contained in Ayuntamiento, Sin clasificar Siglo XIX, Justicia y gobernación, in the Archivo General del Estado de Tlaxcala, 1885–1909; Rendón Garcini, *El Prosperato*, 105–8.

109. On taxation as a form of state-making, see Charles Tilly, *Coercion, Capital, and European States, AD 990–1992* (Cambridge, MA: Blackwell, 1990). In the context of Latin America and the developing world, see, for example, Barbara Geddes, *Politician's Dilemma: Building State Capacity in Latin America* (Berkeley: University of California Press, 1994); Evan S. Lieberman, *Race and Regionalism in the Politics of Taxation in Brazil and South Africa* (Cambridge: Cambridge University Press, 2003); Deborah Brautigam, Odd-Helge Fjeldstad, and Mick Moore, eds., *Taxation and State-Building in Developing Countries: Capacity and Consent* (Cambridge: Cambridge University Press, 2008).

Conclusion

1. *La Antigua República*, 22 Oct. 1905; René Cuéllar Bernal, *Tlaxcala a través de los siglos* (Mexico City: B. Costa-Amic, 1968), 245.

2. See Gómez Galvarriato, *Industry and Revolution*; Jeff Bortz, *Revolution within the Revolution: Cotton Textile Workers and the Mexican Labor Regime, 1910–1923* (Stanford, CA: Stanford University Press, 2008); John Lear, *Workers, Neighbors, and Citizens: The Revolution in Mexico City* (Lincoln: University of Nebraska Press, 2001); Rodney D. Anderson, *Outcasts in Their Own Land: Mexican Industrial Workers, 1906–1911* (DeKalb: Northern Illinois University Press, 1976); Alan Knight, "The Working Class and the Mexican Revolution, c. 1900–1920," *Journal of Latin American Studies* 16, no. 1 (May 1984): 51–79; Coralia Gutiérrez Álvarez, *Experiencias contrastadas: Industrialización y conflictos en los textiles del centro-oriente de México, 1884–1917* (Mexico City: El Colegio de México, Centro de Estudios Históricos: Benemérita Universidad de Puebla, Instituto de Ciencias Sociales y Humanidades, 2000); Blanca Santibáñez Tijerina, "Industria y trabajadores textiles en Tlaxcala: Convergencias y divergencia en los movimientos sociales, 1906–1919" (PhD diss., University of Leiden, 2010).

3. AHET, JG, 1907, C. 97, Exp. 7, f. 6. See also CCJT, Serie Penal, 1907, Exp. 3, d. 4796.

4. See, for example, "Re: a la huelga de los operarios de la fábrica de Estrella," Mar. 1903, AHET, JG, C. 39, Exp. 14, fs. 1–4; "Re: a la huelga de operarios en las fábricas de Río Blanco y Santa Rosa," May 1906, C. 74, Exp. 33, fs. 1–3; "Re: a las huelgas de los operarios de las fábricas en el estado," 1907, C. 78, Exp. 25, fs. 1–200; "Obrero de la fábrica 'La Josefina' se quejó del atentado que sufrió por al administador de La Tlaxcalteca, 1907, C. 97, Exp. 7, fs. 1–6; C. 100, Exp. 42, fs. 1–4; "Re: a la aprehensión de Antonio, Emilio, and Juan Velasco por creerse participar en la huelga de los obreros de Río Blanco," 1907, C. 99, Exp. 10, fs. 1–13; "Huelga de operarios en la fábrica la Tlaxcalteca," 1908, C. 104, Exp. 33, fs. 1–3.

5. AHET, JG, 1906, C. 76, Exp. 23, f. 7; *La Antigua República*, 15 Nov. 1908. Santibáñez Tijerina, "Industria y Trabajadores Textiles en Tlaxcala."

6. *La Antigua República*, nearly every edition for the year 1908.

7. *La Antigua República*, 1 Mar. 1909, 7 Mar. 1909.

8. *El Popular*, 8 Aug. 1906.

9. *La Antigua República*, 8 Aug. 1909. Similar characterizations are found in the biography that *La Antigua República* ran of the governor referenced in chapter one. *La Antigua República*, 23 Feb. 1908.

10. *El Popular*, 8 Aug. 1906; *La Antigua República*, 15 Aug. 1909.

11. *La Antigua República*, 27 Dec. 1908.

12. *El Popular*, 8 Aug. 1906.

13. See letters from hacendados and businessmen to PD in CGPD, 25 Jan. 1908, L. 33, C. 1, d. 317; 8 Feb. 1908, L. 33, C. 4, ds. 1446–1447; Jan. 1908, L. 33, C. 6, ds. 2389–2399. A list of those who visited Díaz in 1908 can be found in *La Antigua República*, 16 Feb. 1908; Ramírez Rancaño, "Próspero Cahuantzi," 110.

14. *La Antigua República*, 2 Feb. 1908, 9 Feb. 1908, 31 May 1908; CGPD, 25 Jan.

1908, L. 33, C. 1, d. 317; 8 Feb. 1908, L. 33, C. 4, ds. 1446–1447; Jan. 1908, L. 33, C. 6, ds. 2389–2399; *La Antigua República*, 2, 9 Feb. 1908, 31 May 1908; Rendón Garcini, *El Prosperato*, 65.

15. PC to name unclear, CGPD, 1910, L. 35, C. 33, ds. 1633–34; Réndon Garcini, *El Prosperato*, 267.

16. PC to PD, CGPD, 11 Feb. 1908, L. 33, C. 7, d. 2584.

17. *Periódico Oficial de Tlaxcala*, 3 Jun. 1911; Ramírez Rancaño, "Próspero Cahuantzi," 113.

18. Ramírez Rancaño, "Próspero Cahuantzi," 114.

19. Ramírez Rancaño, "Próspero Cahuantzi," 114.

20. Ramírez Rancaño, "Prospero Cahuantzi en la contrarrevolución," 180.

21. Ramírez Rancaño, "Prospero Cahuantzi en la contrarrevolución," 180.

22. *New York Times*, 7 Oct. 1914; Ramírez Rancaño, "Próspero Cahuantzi en la contrarrevolución," 179; Cosío Villegas, *Historia moderna de México*, vol. 9, 441.

23. On the Revolution in Tlaxcala, see Sánchez, *El Juez, El Notario y el Caudillo*; Buve, *El movimiento revolucionario en Tlaxcala*; Buve, "Neither Carranza nor Zapata!," 338–75; Sánchez S., *Los antirreeleccionistas de Tepehítec, Tlax., y la Revolución en Tlaxcala, 1906–1915*; Del Castillo, *Puebla y Tlaxcala en los días de la revolución* (Mexico City: Imp. "Zavala," 1953); Cuéllar Bernal, *Tlaxcala a través de los siglos*; Nava Rodríguez, *Tlaxcala contemporánea, de 1822 a 1977*; Henderson, *The Worm and the Wheat*.

24. Buve, "Neither Carranza nor Zapata!," 344.

25. Buve, "Neither Carranza nor Zapata!," 343.

26. Henderson, *The Worm in the Wheat*, 51.

27. Buve, "Neither Carranza nor Zapata!"

28. Lanz Cardenas, *Legislación*, 425–27.

29. For excerpts translated into English, see "The Constitution of 1917: Articles 27 and 123," in *The Mexico Reader*, ed. Gilbert M. Joseph and Timothy J. Henderson (Durham, NC: Duke University Press, 2002), 398–402. For the full text of Article 27 in the original Spanish, see: www.juridicas.unam.mx/legislacion/ordenamiento/constitucion-politica-de-los-estados-unidos-mexicanos, accessed June 5, 2020.

30. As Wolfe asserts, unless the state "determined they were of 'public utility' . . . [Article 27] clearly upheld private ownership of natural resources." Wolfe, *Watering*, 15; "The Constitution of 1917," in *Mexico Reader*, 400.

31. Wolfe, *Watering the Revolution*, 18.

32. Dawson, *Indian and Nation in Revolutionary Mexico*; Dillingham, *Oaxaca Resurgent*; Gillingham, *Cuauhtémoc's Bones*; Gutiérrez, *Nationalist Myths and Ethnic Identities*; Knight, "Racism, Revolution, and *Indigenismo*"; López, *Crafting Mexico*; Morris, *Soldiers, Saints, and Shamans*.

33. Dillingham, *Oaxaca Resurgent*, 45.

34. Bonfil Batalla, *México Profundo*. The literature on the EZLN is expansive. For an exemplary collection, see Thomas Hayden, ed., *The Zapatista Reader* (New York: Thunder's Mouth Press/Nation Books, 2002).

35. In addition to the EZLN in Chiapas, Mexico, Bolivia and Ecuador have become essential sites in the struggle for Indigenous autonomy and citizenship in twentieth- and twenty-first-century Latin America. See Nancy Grey Postero, *Now We Are Citizens: Indigenous Politics in Postmulticultural Bolivia* (Stanford, CA: Stanford University Press, 2007); Deborah J. Yashar, *Contesting Citizenship in Latin America: The Rise of Indigenous Movements and the Postliberal Challenge* (Cambridge: Cambridge University Press, 2005).

36. *La Antigua República*, 27 Dec. 1908.

37. On nineteenth-century indigenismo, see Earle, *Return of the Native*; Kuenzli, *Acting Inca;* Jaclyn Ann Sumner, "The Indigenous Governor of Tlaxcala and Acceptable Indigenousness in the Porfirian Regime," *Mexican Studies/Estudios Mexicanos* 35, no. 1 (Winter 2019): 61–87.

38. Paul Garner, "Porfirian Politics in Mexico, 1876–1911," in *The Oxford Encyclopedia of Mexican History and Culture*, ed. William H Beezley (Oxford: Oxford University Press, 2019).

BIBLIOGRAPHY

Archives and Archival Collections
Mexico City
AGA   Archivo General Agrario de la Nación
AGN   Archivo General de la Nación
AHA   Archivo Histórico del Agua
          Aprovechamientos superficiales (AS)
          Aguas Nacionales (AN)
AHMNA   Archivo Histórico del Museo Nacional de Antropología
CEHM   Centro de Estudios de Historia de México "Carso"
CGPD   Colección General de Porfirio Díaz, Universidad Iberoamericana
HNM   Hemeroteca Nacional de México
SCJN   Suprema Corte de Justicia de la Nación

Puebla
AGNP   Archivo General de Notarías del Estado de Puebla

Tlaxcala
AGNT   Archivo General de Notarías del Estado de Tlaxcala
AHET   Archivo Histórico del Estado de Tlaxcala
          Ayuntamiento (A)
          Bandos, decretos, e impresos (BDI)
          Educación (E)
          Fomento (F)
          Justicia Civil (JC)
          Justicia Criminal (JCM)
          Justicia y gobernación (JG)
          Recursos Hidráulicos (RH)

	Secretaría General de Gobierno (SG)
	Sin clasificar, Siglo diecinueve (SC)
AHJT	Archivo Histórico del Tribunal Superior de Justicia del Estado de Tlaxcala
CCJT	Casa de la Cultura Jurídica Tlaxcala, Suprema Corte de Justicia de la Nación, Archivo Histórico

Newspapers
Mexico City
El Diario de Hogar
El Hijo del Ahuizote
El Imparcial
El Mensajero
El Monitor Republicano
El Mundo
El Obrero Mexicano
El País
El Popular
El Tiempo
El Universal
El Universal Gráfico
La Voz de México

Puebla
La Opinión
La Patria de Xicoténcatl
Periódico Central
El Silbato

Tlaxcala
La Antigua República
El Periódico Oficial del Estado de Tlaxcala

United States
New York Times

Published Primary Sources
Baerlein, Henry. *Mexico: The Land of Unrest*. London, 1914.
Becher, H. C. R. *A Trip to Mexico*. Toronto: Willing and Williamson, 1880.
Cahuantzi, Próspero. *Dictamen formulado por la segunda sección del Gran jurado nacional y presentado a los miembros de este tribunal que conoció de la acusación contra el gobernador del estado de Tlaxcala Coronel Próspero Cahuantzi atribuyéndole la infracción de algunas leyes de reforma*. Tlaxcala: Imprenta del Gobierno del Estado, 1896.

Bibliography

———. *Informes de gobierno.* 1885–1909.

———. *Memoria de la administración pública del estado presentada a la H. Legislatura por el gobernador constitucional del mismo, ciudadano Coronel Próspero Cahuantzi, el día 1 de abril 1887.* Tlaxcala: Imprenta del Gobierno, 1888.

———. *Memoria de la administración pública del estado de Tlaxcala presentada a la H. Legislatura del mismo, por el gobernador constitucional Coronel Próspero Cahuantzi, el 2 de abril 1893.* Tlaxcala: Imprenta del Gobierno, 1894.

———. "Prólogo." *Lienzo de Tlaxcala, manuscrito pictórico mexicano de mediados del siglo XVI.* Mexico City: Librería Anticuaria G. M. Echaniz, 1939.

Chavero, Alfredo. *México a través de los siglos*, vol. 1. Mexico City: Ballescá Espasa y Compañía, 1882; Alicante: Biblioteca Virtual Miguel de Cervantes, 2017. www.cervantesvirtual.com/nd/ark:/59851/bmctjom8.

Chavero, Alfredo y Junta colombina de México. *Homenaje á Cristóbal Colón: Antigüedades Mexicanas.* Mexico City: Oficina tip. de la Secretaría de Fomento, 1892.

Commercial Directory of the American Republics, vol. 2. Washington, DC: Governmental Printing Office, 1898.

Enciclopedia de los Municipios y Delegaciones de México, Estado de Tlaxcala. www.inafed.gob.mx/work/enciclopedia/EMM29tlaxcala/historia.html.

Esteua, Adalberto A. *Discurso pronunciado en la cámara de diputados el día de 26 de noviembre de 1896 por el diputado miembro de la segunda sección del gran jurado, Lic. Adalberto A. Esteua en pro del dictamen de Tlaxcala Coronel Próspero.* Tlaxcala: Imprenta del Gobierno del Estado, 1896.

Gemelli Careri, Giovanni Francesco, and José María de Agreda y Sánchez. *Viaje a la Nueva España.* Mexico City: José Porrúa, 1983.

Gruening, Ernest. *Mexico and Its Heritage.* New York: Appleton-Century, 1928.

Hernández de León-Portilla, Ascensión. *Tepuztlahcuilolli, impresos en náhuatl: Historia y bibliografía*, vol. 2. Mexico City: Universidad Nacional Autónoma de México, 1988.

Hunt-Cortés, Agustín. *Hunt-Cortés Digest: A Monthly Journal of Things about Mexico, the Egypt of the West and of General Literature.* Mexico City: Imprenta de A. Carranza y Comp, 1905.

International Congress of Americanists. *Actas del Congreso Internacional de Americanistas: Actas de la Undécima Reunión, México,* 1895. Germany: Kraus-Thomson Organization Limited, 1968.

King, Rosa E. *Tempest over Mexico: A Personal Chronicle.* Boston: Little, Brown, 1935.

Larrea y Cordero, Pedro. *Gran Cuadro Histórico, Político, Geográfico, Industrial, y Religioso de la Ciudad de Tlaxcala y del Estado de su nombre.* Tlaxcala: Imprenta de Gobierno, 1886.

Lombardo, Sonia. *El pasado prehispánico en la cultura nacional: Memoria hemerográfica, 1877–1911*, vol. 1. Mexico City: Instituto Nacional de Antropología e Historia, 1994.

Luis Velasco, Alfonso. *Geografía y estadística del estado de Tlaxcala.* Mexico City: Oficina Tip. de la Secretaría de Fomento, 1892.

Mexico and Antonio Peñafiel. *Anuario estadístico de la República Mexicana.* Mexico City, 1898.

Mexico. *Constitución Política del Estado Libre y Soberano de Tlaxcala.* Mexico City, 1857, 1884.

Mexico, Dirección General de Estadística, and Moisés González Navarro. *Estadísticas sociales del Porfiriato: 1877–1910.* Mexico City: Talleres Gráficos de la Nación, 1956.

Mexico, Estado de Tlaxcala. *Geografía y estadística del Estado de Tlaxcala.* Mexico City: Oficina Tip. de la Secretaría de Fomento, 1892.

Mexico and Guadalupe Villers. *La hacienda pública de los estados: Trabajo hecho por el empleado de la secretaria de hacienda y crédito público M. Guadalupe Villers.* Mexico City: Tip. de la oficina impresora de estampillas, 1911.

Mexico, Ministerio de Fomento. *Censo general de la República Mexicana,* 1895, 1900, 1910. Mexico City: Gobierno Federal, 1897–1911.

Mexico, Ministerio de Fomento. *Geografía y estadística de la República Mexicana.* Mexico City, 1890.

Mexico, Ministerio de Fomento, Colonización e Industria. *Censo y División Territorial del Estado de Tlaxcala* (1895, 1902, 1910). Mexico City: Gobierno Federal, 1897–1911.

Muñoz Camargo, Diego, and Alfredo Chavero. *Historia de Tlaxcala.* Mexico City: Oficina tip. de la Secretaría de Fomento, 1892.

Pavía, Lázaro. *Breves apuntes biográficos de los miembros más notables del ramo de hacienda de la república mexicana.* Mexico City: E. Duelan, 1895.

Rodríguez Miramón, Alonso. *Discurso pronunciado por el C. Diputado Licenciado Alonso Rodríguez Miramón el 26 de noviembre de 1896, ante el gran jurado nacional que conoció del proceso instruido al gobernador del estado l. y s. de Tlaxcala, Coronel Próspero Cahuantzi acusado de violador de la Leyes de Reforma, por algunos periodistas de la Capital de la República.* Tlaxcala: Impr. del gobierno del estado, 1896.

Sánchez, Enrique. *Informe que rinde al gobernador del Estado de Tlaxcala Coronel Próspero Cahuantzi, el c. Enrique Sánchez.* Tlaxcala: Imprenta del Gobierno, 1897.

Sánchez Gavito, Indalecio. *Defensa del gobernador del estado libre y soberano de Tlaxcala, Coronel Próspero Cahuantzi, hecha ante la Cámara de Diputados, erigida en gran jurado el día 26 de noviembre de 1896.* Tlaxcala: Imprenta del Gobierno del Estado, 1896.

Sosa, Antonio. *Parque nacional Xicohténcatl, Estado de Tlaxcala.* Mexico City: Secretaría de Agricultura y Ganadería, 1951.

Starr, Frederick. *In Indian Mexico: A Narrative of Travel and Labor.* Chicago: Forbes, 1908.

———. *Notes upon the Ethnography of Southern Mexico.* Davenport: Washington Academy of Sciences, 1898, 1899, 1900.

Tlaxcala. *Constitución Política del Estado Libre y Soberano de Tlaxcala* (1919). Tlaxcala: Imprenta de gobierno del estado, 1918.

Turner, John Kenneth. *Barbarous Mexico,* 3rd ed. New York: Cassell, 1912; Austin: University of Texas Press, 1968.

Books and Articles

Aboites, Luis. *El agua de la nación: Una historia política de México (1888–1946)*. Mexico City: Centro de Investigaciones y Estudios Superiores en Antropología Social, 1998.

——. "The Illusion of National Power: Water Infrastructure in Mexican Cities." In *A Land between Waters: Environmental Histories of Modern Mexico*, edited by Christopher Boyer, 218–44. Tucson: University of Arizona Press, 2012.

——. "Relación sociedad-naturaleza desde la historia de los usos del agua en México (1900–1940)." In *Estudios sobre historia y ambiente en America I*, edited by Alba González Jácome and Bernardo García Martínez, 173–90. Mexico City: Instituto Panamericano de Geografía e Historia : El Colegio de México, 1999.

Agostini, Claudia. *Monuments of Progress: Modernization and Public Health in Mexico City, 1876–1910*. Calgary: University of Calgary Press, 2003.

Aguilar Rivera, José Antonio, ed. *Las elecciones y el gobierno representativo en México (1810–1910)*. Mexico City: Fondo de Cultura Económica; Consejo Nacional para la Cultura y las Artes; Instituto Federal Electoral; Consejo Nacional de Ciencia y Tecnología, 2010.

Alexander, Anna Rose. *City on Fire: Technology, Social Change, and the Hazards of Progress in Mexico City, 1860–1910*. Pittsburgh: University of Pittsburgh Press, 2016.

Almandoz Marte, Arturo, ed. *Planning Latin America's Capital Cities, 1850–1950*. New York: Routledge, 2002.

Alonso, Paula. *Between Revolution and the Ballot Box: The Origins of the Argentine Radical Party in the 1890s*. Cambridge: Cambridge University Press, 2000.

Amaral-Rodríguez, Jannette. "Distorsión y silencio en el *Lienzo de Tlaxcala* (1892) de Alfredo Chavero: Notas metodológicas." *Latin American Research Review* 55, no. 2 (June 2020): 322–37.

Anderson, Margaret Lavinia. *Practicing Democracy: Elections and Political Culture in Imperial Germany*. Princeton, NJ: Princeton University Press, 2000.

Anderson, Rodney D. *Outcasts in Their Own Land: Mexican Industrial Workers, 1906–1911*. DeKalb: Northern Illinois University Press, 1976.

Annino, Antonio, ed. *Historia de las elecciones en Iberoamérica, siglo XIX: De la formación del espacio político nacional*. Buenos Aires: Fondo de Cultura Económica, 1995.

Ávila Quijas, Aquiles Omar, Jesús Gómez Serrano, Antonio Escobar Ohmstede, and Martín Sánchez Rodríguez, eds. *Negociaciones, acuerdos y conflictos en México, siglos XIX y XX: Agua y tierra*. Zamora: Colegio de Michoacán; Mexico City: CIESAS; Aguascalientes: Universidad Autónoma de Aguascalientes, 2009.

Baber, R. Jovita. "The Construction of Empire: Politics, Law, and Community in Tlaxcala, New Spain, 1521–1640." PhD diss., University of Chicago, 2005.

——. "Empire, Indians, and the Negotiation for the Status of the City in Tlaxcala, 1521–1550." In *Negotiation within Domination: New Spain's Indian Pueblos*

Confront the Spanish State, edited by Ethelia Ruiz Medrano and Susan Kellogg, 19–44. Boulder: University Press of Colorado, 2010.

Bastian, Jean Pierre. "Metodismo y rebelión política en Tlaxcala, 1874–1920." In *Historia y Sociedad en Tlaxcala: Memorias del Primer Simposio Internacional de Investigaciones Socio-Históricos sobre Tlaxcala, octubre 1985, 109–118.* Tlaxcala: Gobierno del Estado de Tlaxcala, Instituto Tlaxcalteca de Cultura, 1986.

Bazant S., Jan. *Historia de la deuda exterior de México (1823–1946).* Mexico City: El Colegio de México, 1968.

Beals, Carleton. *Porfirio Diaz, Dictator of Mexico.* Philadelphia: J. B. Lippincott, 1932.

Beatty, Edward. *Institutions and Investment: The Political Basis of Industrialization in Mexico before 1911.* Stanford, CA: Stanford University Press, 2001.

———. *Technology and the Search for Progress in Modern Mexico.* Berkeley: University of California Press, 2015.

Beezley, William H. *Judas at the Jockey Club and Other Episodes of Porfirian Mexico.* Lincoln: University of Nebraska Press, 1987.

Benjamin, Thomas, and William McNellie, eds. *Other Mexicos: Essays on Regional Mexican History, 1876–1911.* Albuquerque: University of New Mexico Press, 1984.

Benjamin, Thomas, and Marcial Ocasio-Meléndez. "Organizing the Memory of Modern Mexico: Porfirian Historiography in Perspective, 1880s–1980s." *Hispanic American Historical Review* 64, no. 2 (May 1984): 323–64.

Bess, Michael. *Routes of Compromise: Building Roads and Shaping the Nation in Mexico, 1917–1962.* Lincoln: University of Nebraska Press, 2017.

Bethell, Leslie. *Mexico since Independence.* Cambridge: Cambridge University Press, 1991.

Bieber, Judy. *Power, Patronage, and Political Violence: State Building on a Brazilian Frontier, 1822–1889.* Lincoln: University of Nebraska Press, 1999.

Birrichaga Gardida, Diana. "Las empresas de agua potable en México." In *Historia de los usos del agua en México,* edited by Blanca Estela Suárez Cortez, 183–228. Mexico City: Comisión Nacional del Agua, 1998.

Blackbourn, David, and Geoff Eley. *The Peculiarities of German History: Bourgeois Society and Politics in Nineteenth-Century Germany.* Oxford: Oxford University Press, 1984.

Blanc, Jacob. *Before the Flood: The Itaipu Dam and the Visibility of Rural Brazil.* Durham, NC: Duke University Press, 2019.

Bonfil Batalla, Guillermo. *México Profundo: Una civilización negada.* Mexico City: Grijalbo, 1987.

Bortz, Jeff. *Revolution within the Revolution: Cotton Textile Workers and the Mexican Labor Regime, 1910–1923.* Stanford, CA: Stanford University Press, 2008.

Bortz, Jeff, and Stephen H. Haber, eds. *The Mexican Economy, 1870–1930: Essays on the Economic History of Institutions, Revolution, and Growth.* Stanford, CA: Stanford University Press, 2002.

Boyer, Christopher R. *Becoming Campesinos: Politics, Identity, and Agrarian Strug-*

gle in Postrevolutionary Michoacán, 1920–1935. Stanford, CA: Stanford University Press, 2003.
Boyer, Christopher R., ed. *A Land between Waters: Environmental Histories of Modern Mexico*. Tucson: University of Arizona Press, 2012.
Boyer, Christopher R. *Political Landscapes: Forests, Conservation, and Community in Mexico*. Durham, NC: Duke University Press, 2015.
Boyer, Richard E. *La gran inundación: Vida y sociedad en México, 1629–1638*. Mexico City: Secretaría de Educación Pública, 1975.
Brading, D. A. *The First America: The Spanish Monarchy, Creole Patriots, and the Liberal State, 1492–1867*. Cambridge: Cambridge University Press, 2004.
———. "Manuel Gamio and Official Indigenismo in Mexico." *Bulletin of Latin American Research* 7, no. 1 (January 1988): 75–89.
Brading, D. A., ed. *Caudillo and Peasant in the Mexican Revolution*. Cambridge: Cambridge University Press, 1980.
Brautigam, Deborah, Odd-Helge Fjeldstad, and Mick Moore, eds. *Taxation and State-Building in Developing Countries: Capacity and Consent*. Cambridge: Cambridge University Press, 2008.
Bravo Regidor, Carlos. "Elecciones de gobernadores durante el Porfiriato." In *Las elecciones y el gobierno representativo en México (1810–1910)*, edited by José Antonio Aguilar Rivera, 257–81. Mexico City: Centro de Investigación y Docencia Económicas, 2010.
Brown, Jonathan C. *Oil and Revolution in Mexico*. Berkeley: University of California Press, 1993.
Buchenau, Jürgen, and William H. Beezley, eds. *State Governors in the Mexican Revolution, 1910–1952: Portraits in Conflict, Courage, and Corruption*. Lanham, MD: Rowman and Littlefield, 2009.
Bueno, Christina. "Forjando Patrimonio: The Making of Archaeological Patrimony in Porfirian Mexico." *Hispanic American Historical Review* 90, no. 2 (March 2010): 215–45.
———. *The Pursuit of Ruins: Archaeology, History, and the Making of Modern Mexico*. Albuquerque: University of New Mexico Press, 2016.
Bueno de Mesquita, Bruce, and Hilton L. Root, eds. *Governing for Prosperity*. New Haven, CT: Yale University Press, 2000.
Bulnes, Francisco. *El verdadero Díaz y la revolución*. Mexico City: E. Gomez de la Puente, 1920.
Bustamante López, Carlos. "Historia urbana del Prosperato: Historiografía, fuentes y métodos." *Enlace Histórico*, Órgano de difusión histórica del Archivo General del Estado de Tlaxcala, 2, no. 2 (1996): 1–18.
———. "Un perfil urbano del Prosperato." *Entorno urbano*, Revista de Historia Instituto de Investigaciones Dr. José Ma. Luis Mora, 2, no. 4 (1996): 65–91.
Buve, Raymundus Thomas Joseph. *Amores y odios compartidos: Puebla y Tlaxcala, 1800–1920*. Mexico City: Ediciones de Educación y Cultura: Benemérita, Universidad Autónoma de Puebla, 2010.
———. *El movimiento revolucionario en Tlaxcala*. Tlaxcala; Mexico City: Univer-

sidad Autónoma de Tlaxcala, Secretaría de Extensión Universitaria y Difusión Cultural; Universidad Iberoamericana, Departamento de Historia, 1994.

———. "Neither Carranza nor Zapata!: The Rise and Fall of a Peasant Movement That Tried to Challenge Both, Tlaxcala, 1910–1919." In *Riot, Rebellion, and Revolution: Rural Social Conflict in Mexico*, edited by Friedrich Katz, 338–75. Princeton, NJ: Princeton University Press, 1988.

———. "Peasant Movements, Caudillos, and Land Reform during the Revolution (1910–1917) in Tlaxcala, Mexico." *Boletín de Estudios Latinoamericanos y del Caribe*, no. 18 (June 1975): 112–52.

———. "Political Patronage and Politics at the Village Level in Central Mexico: Continuity and Change in Patterns from the Late Colonial Period to the End of the French Intervention (1867)." *Bulletin of Latin American Research* 11, no. 1 (January 1992): 1–28.

———. "Política y sociedad en Tlaxcala: Unos interrogantes y unos hilos conductores a través de su historia, entre 1810–1910." In *Historia y Sociedad en Tlaxcala, Memoria del 7o Simposio Internacional de Investigaciones Socio-históricas sobre Tlaxcala, oct 1992*. Mexico City: Gobierno del Estado de Tlaxcala, Universidad Autónoma de Tlaxcala, Instituto Nacional de Antropología e Historia y Universidad Iberoamericana, 1992.

Cadava, Geraldo L. "Borderlands of Modernity and Abandonment: The Lines within Ambos Nogales and the Tohono O'odham Nation." *Journal of American History* 98, no. 2 (September 2011): 362–83.

Campbell, Tracy. *Deliver the Vote: A History of Election Fraud, an American Political Tradition, 1742–2004*. New York: Carroll and Graf, 2005.

Candiani, Vera. "The Desagüe Reconsidered: Environmental Dimensions of Class Conflict in Colonial Mexico." *Hispanic American Historical Review* 92, no. 1 (February 2012): 5–39.

———. *Dreaming of Dry Land: Environmental Transformation in Colonial Mexico City*. Stanford, CA: Stanford University Press, 2014.

Caplan, Karen Deborah. *Indigenous Citizens: Local Liberalism in Early National Oaxaca and Yucatán*. Stanford, CA: Stanford University Press, 2009.

Cárdenas, Enrique. "A Macroeconomic Interpretation of Nineteenth-Century Mexico." In *How Latin America Fell Behind: Essays on the Economic Histories of Brazil and Mexico, 1800–1914*, edited by Stephen H. Haber, 34–64. Stanford, CA: Stanford University Press, 1997.

Castañeda González, Rocío. *Las aguas de Atlixco: Estado, haciendas, fábricas y pueblos, 1880–1920*. Mexico City: Centro de Investigaciones y Estudios Superiores en Antropología Social, 2005.

Castillo, Porfirio del. *Puebla y Tlaxcala en los días de la revolución*. Mexico City: Imprenta "Zavala," 1953.

Castro, José Esteban. *Water, Power, and Citizenship: Social Struggle in the Basin of Mexico*. Basingstoke, England: Palgrave Macmillan, 2006.

Centeno, Miguel Angel. *Blood and Debt: War and the Nation-State in Latin America*. University Park: Pennsylvania State University Press, 2002.

Cerutti, Mario. *Burguesía y capitalismo en Monterrey, 1850–1910*. Mexico City: Claves Latinoamericanas, 1983.
Cerutti, Mario, and Carlos Marichal. *La banca regional en México, 1870–1930*. Mexico City: Colegio de México; Fondo de Cultura Económica, 2003.
Chambers, Sarah C. *From Subjects to Citizens: Honor, Gender, and Politics in Arequipa, Peru, 1780–1854*. University Park: Pennsylvania State University Press, 1999.
Chassen de López, Francie R. *From Liberal to Revolutionary Oaxaca: The View from the South, Mexico, 1867–1911*. University Park: Pennsylvania State University Press, 2004.
Chávez, Alicia Hernández. "Mexican Presidentialism: A Historical and Institutional Overview." *Mexican Studies/Estudios Mexicanos* 10, no. 1 (January 1994): 217–25.
Coatsworth, John H. *Growth against Development: The Economic Impact of Railroads in Porfirian Mexico*. DeKalb: Northern Illinois University Press, 1981.
———. "Obstacles to Economic Growth in Nineteenth-Century Mexico." *American Historical Review* 83, no. 1 (February 1978): 80–100.
Coatsworth, John H., and Alan M. Taylor, eds. *Latin America and the World Economy since 1800*. Cambridge, MA: Harvard University/David Rockefeller Center for Latin American Studies, 1998.
Connolly, Priscilla. *El contratista de don Porfirio: Obras públicas, deuda y desarrollo desigual*. Mexico City: Fondo de Cultura Económica, 1997.
"The Constitution of 1917: Articles 27 and 123." In *The Mexico Reader*, edited by Gilbert M. Joseph and Timothy J. Henderson, 398–402. Durham, NC: Duke University Press, 2002.
Contreras, Carlos. "The Tax Man Cometh: Local Authorities and the Battle over Taxes in Peru, 1885–1906." In *Political Cultures in the Andes, 1750–1950*, edited by Nils Jacobsen and Cristóbal Aljovín de Losada, 116–36. Durham, NC: Duke University Press, 2005.
Cosío Villegas, Daniel, et al. *Historia moderna de México*. Vol. 2, *La república restaurada: La vida económica*. Mexico City: Editorial Hermes, 1965.
Cosío Villegas, Daniel, et al. *Historia moderna de México*. Vol. 8, *El Porfiriato: La vida política interior*. Tomo 1. Mexico City: Editorial Hermes, 1970.
Cosío Villegas, Daniel, et al. *Historia moderna de México*. Vol. 9, *El Porfiriato: La vida política interior*. Tomo 2. Mexico City: Editorial Hermes, 1972.
Costeloe, Michael P. *Bonds and Bondholders: British Investors and Mexico's Foreign Debt, 1824–1888*. Westport, CT: Praeger, 2003.
Cott, Kennett S. "Porfirian Investment Policies, 1876–1910." PhD diss., University of New Mexico, 1979.
Cruz Barney, Oscar. *Historia del derecho en México*. Mexico City: Oxford University Press, 1999.
Cuéllar Abaroa, Crisanto. *Antonio Carbajal: Caudillo liberal tlaxcalteca*. Mexico City: Sociedad Mexicana de Geografía y Estadística, Sección de Historia, 1962.

---. *Domingo Arenas: Caudillo agrarista.* Tlaxcala: Difusión Cultural del Estado, 1961.

---. *Juan Cuamatzi, indio tlaxcalteca, precursor de la revolución mexicana; apuntes para la historia.* Tlaxcala, 1935.

---. *Paz o terror? inquietudes en 1910.* Tlaxcala: Talleres Gráficos, 1952.

Cuéllar Bernal, René. *Tlaxcala a través de los siglos.* Mexico City: B. Costa-Amic, 1968.

Dawson, Alexander S. "From Models for the Nation to Model Citizens: Indigenismo and the 'Revindication' of the Mexican Indian, 1920–40." *Journal of Latin American Studies* 30, no. 2 (May 1998): 279–308.

---. *Indian and Nation in Revolutionary Mexico.* Tucson: University of Arizona Press, 2004.

De la Cadena, Marisol. *Indigenous Mestizos: The Politics of Race and Culture in Cuzco, Peru, 1919–1991.* Durham, NC: Duke University Press, 2000.

De la Fuente, Ariel. *Children of Facundo: Caudillo and Gaucho Insurgency during the Argentine State-Formation Process (La Rioja, 1853–1870).* Durham, NC: Duke University Press, 2000.

Derby, Lauren Hutchinson. *The Dictator's Seduction: Politics and the Popular Imagination in the Era of Trujillo.* Durham, NC: Duke University Press, 2009.

Díaz del Castillo, Bernal. *The Discovery and Conquest of Mexico, 1517–1521.* New York: Farrar, Straus, and Cudahy, 1956.

---. *Historia verdadera de la conquista de la Nueva España.* 4 vols. Mexico City: Oficina de la Secretaría de fomento, 1904, 1905; [1632].

Dillingham, A. S. *Oaxaca Resurgent: Indigeneity, Development, and Inequality in Twentieth-Century Mexico.* Stanford, CA: University of Stanford Press, 2021.

Domínguez Pérez, Olivia. "El Puerto de Veracruz: La modernización a finales de Siglo XIX." *Anuario* 7 (1990): 87–102.

Ducey, Michael. "Liberal Theory and Peasant Practice: Land and Power in Northern Veracruz, Mexico, 1826–1900." In *Liberals, the Church, and Indian Peasants: Corporate Lands and the Challenge of Reform in Nineteenth-Century Spanish America,* edited by Robert H. Jackson, 65–85. Albuquerque: University of New Mexico Press, 1997.

Durán, Juan Manuel, Martín Sánchez, and Antonio Escobar Ohmstede, eds. *El agua en la historia de México: Balance y perspectiva.* Guadalajara, Jalisco: Universidad de Guadalajara, Centro Universitario de Ciencias Sociales y Humanidades; Zamora: Colegio de Michoacán, 2005.

Earle, Rebecca. *Return of the Native: Indians and Myth-Making in Spanish America, 1810–1930.* Durham, NC: Duke University Press, 2007.

Enge, Kjell, and Scott Whiteford. *The Keepers of Water and Earth: Mexican Rural Social Organization and Irrigation.* Austin: University of Texas Press, 1989.

Escobar Ohmstede, Antonio. "El oriente de San Luis Potosí visto a través de la conflictividad del agua y la tierra, ¿ciclos que se abrieron?" In *Mexico in Transition/México y sus transiciones,* edited by Antonio Escobar Ohmstede and Matthew Butler, 85–224. Mexico City: CIESAS, 2013.

Esposito, Matthew D. *Funerals, Festivals, and Cultural Politics in Porfirian Mexico.* Albuquerque: University of New Mexico Press, 2010.
Evans, Peter B., Dietrich Rueschemeyer, and Theda Skocpol, eds. *Bringing the State Back In.* Cambridge: Cambridge University Press, 1985.
Falcón, Romana. *El agrarismo en Veracruz: La etapa radical (1928–1935).* Colección Centro de Estudios Internacionales. Mexico City: El Colegio de México, 1977.
———. "La Desaparición de jefes políticos en Coahuila: Una paradoja Porfirista." *Historia Mexicana* 37, no. 3 (January 1988): 423–67.
———. *El jefe político: Un dominio negociado en el mundo rural del Estado de México, 1856–1911.* Mexico City: El Colegio de México, Centro de Investigaciones y Estudios Sociales en Antropología Social, El Colegio Michoacán, 2015.
Falcón, Romana, and Raymundus Thomas Joseph Buve, eds. *Don Porfirio presidente, nunca omnipotente: Hallazgos, reflexiones y debates, 1876–1911.* Mexico City: Universidad Iberoamericana, Departamento de Historia, 1998.
Filatti, Rosa, Manuel Muñoz Lumbier, Luciano López Sorcini, Mexico, and Oficina de Geografía Económica. *Bosquejo geográfico-económico del estado de Tlaxcala.* Mexico City: Talleres Gráficos de la Nación, 1933.
Florescano, Enrique. *Imágenes de la patria a través de los siglos.* Mexico City: Taurus, 2005.
Flores Galindo, Alberto. *Buscando un inca: Identidad y utopía en los Andes.* Havana, Cuba: Casa de las Américas, 1986.
Folsom, Raphael Brewster. *The Yaquis and the Empire: Violence, Spanish Imperial Power, and Native Resilience in Colonial Mexico.* New Haven, CT: Yale University Press, 2014.
French, William E. *A Peaceful and Working People: Manners, Morals, and Class Formation in Northern Mexico.* Albuquerque: University of New Mexico Press, 1996.
Gamboa Ojeda, Leticia. *Los empresarios de ayer: El grupo dominante en la industria textil de Puebla, 1906–1929.* Puebla, Mexico: Universidad Autónoma de Puebla, 1985.
Gamio, Manuel. *Forjando Patria.* 3rd ed. Mexico City: Editorial Porrúa, 1982.
Gandhi, Jennifer. *Political Institutions under Dictatorship.* New York: Cambridge University Press, 2008.
Gandhi, Jennifer, and Adam Przeworski. "Cooperation, Cooptation, and Rebellion under Dictatorships." *Economics and Politics* 18, no. 1 (2006): 1–26.
Garner, Paul. *British Lions and Mexican Eagles: Business, Politics, and Empire in the Career of Weetman Pearson in Mexico, 1889–1919.* Stanford, CA: Stanford University Press, 2011.
———. *Porfirio Díaz.* New York: Longman, 2001.
Geddes, Barbara. *Politician's Dilemma: Building State Capacity in Latin America.* Berkeley: University of California Press, 1994.
Gibson, Charles. *Tlaxcala in the Sixteenth Century.* Stanford, CA: Stanford University Press, 1952.
Gibson, Edward L. *Boundary Control: Subnational Authoritarianism in Federal*

Democracies. Cambridge Studies in Comparative Politics. Cambridge: Cambridge University Press, 2012.

Gillespie, Jeanne. *Saints and Warriors: Tlaxcalan Perspectives on the Conquest of Tenochtitlan*. New Orleans: University Press of the South, 2004.

Gillingham, Paul. *Cuauhtémoc's Bones: Forging National Identity in Modern Mexico*. Albuquerque: University of New Mexico Press, 2011.

Gobat, Michel. "The Invention of Latin America: A Transnational History of Anti-Imperialism, Democracy, and Race." *American Historical Review* 118, no. 5 (December 2013): 1345–75.

Goemans, Henk E., Kristian Skrede Gleditsch, and Giacomo Chiozza. "Introducing Archigos: A Dataset of Political Leaders." *Journal of Peace Research* 46, no. 2 (March 2009): 269–83.

Gómez De Lara, José Luis. "Próspero Cahuantzi en la caricatura política." *Graffylia, Revista de la Facultad de Filosofía y Letras, Benemérita Universidad Autónoma de Puebla*, no. 19 (July–December 2014): 179–92.

Gómez Galvarriato, Aurora. "The Evolution of Prices and Real Wages in Mexico from the Porfiriato to the Revolution." In *Latin America and the World Economy since 1800*, edited by John Coatsworth and John H. Taylor, 347–78. Cambridge, MA: Harvard University/David Rockefeller Center for Latin American Studies, 1998.

———. "The Impact of Revolution: Business and Labor in the Mexican Textile Industry, Orizaba, Veracruz, 1900–1930." PhD diss., Harvard University, 2000.

———. *Industry and Revolution: Social and Economic Change in the Orizaba Valley, Mexico*. Cambridge, MA: Harvard University Press, 2013.

Gonzales, Michael J. "Imagining Mexico in 1910: Visions of the Patria in the Centennial Celebration in Mexico City." *Journal of Latin American Studies* 39, no. 3 (August 2007): 495–533.

Gonzaléz Jácome, Alba. "De las manos tejedoras a las fábricas textiles: El nacimiento de un industria en Tlaxcala." *La Industria textil en Tlaxcala, Tlahcuilo 4, Boletín del Archivo Histórico del Estado de Tlaxcala*, 2, no. 4 (January–March 2008): 9–24.

———. "Evolución de la industria textil en Tlaxcala siglo XIX y primera mitad de XX." In *Historia y sociedad de Tlaxcala*, 86–107. Tlaxcala: Gobierno del Estado de Tlaxcala, Instituto Tlaxcalteca de Cultura, Universidad Autónoma de Tlaxcala; Mexico City: Universidad Iberoamericana, 1990.

———. *Humedales en el suroeste de Tlaxcala: Agua y agricultura en el siglo XX*. Mexico City: Universidad Iberoamericana, 2008.

———. "El paisaje lacustre en Tlaxcala." In *Estudios sobre historia y ambiente en America*, 1: *Argentina, Bolivia, Mexico, Paraguay*, edited by Alba González Jácome and Bernardo García Martínez, 191–218. Mexico City: Instituto Panamericano de Geografía e Historia, 1999.

González Jácome, Alba, and Bernardo García Martínez, eds. *Estudios sobre historia y ambiente en America*: I, *Argentina, Bolivia, México, and Paraguay*. Mexico

City: Instituto Panamericano de Geografía e Historia; El Colegio de México, 1999.
Gould, Jeffrey L. *To Die in This Way: Nicaraguan Indians and the Myth of Mestizaje, 1880–1965*. Durham, NC: Duke University Press, 1998.
Graham, Richard. *Patronage and Politics in Nineteenth-Century Brazil*. Stanford, CA: Stanford University Press, 1990.
Graham, Richard, Thomas E. Skidmore, Aline Helg, and Alan Knight, eds. *The Idea of Race in Latin America, 1870–1940*. Austin: University of Texas Press, 1990.
Grandin, Greg. *The Blood of Guatemala: A History of Race and Nation*. Durham, NC: Duke University Press, 2000.
Greene, Kenneth F. *Why Dominant Parties Lose: Mexico's Democratization in Comparative Perspective*. Cambridge: Cambridge University Press, 2007.
Guardino, Peter F. *Peasants, Politics, and the Formation of Mexico's National State: Guerrero, 1800–1857*. Stanford, CA: Stanford University Press, 1996.
———. *The Time of Liberty: Popular Political Culture in Oaxaca, 1750–1850*. Durham, NC: Duke University Press, 2005.
Guerra, François Xavier. *México: Del Antiguo Régimen a la Revolución*, Tomos 1, 2. Mexico City: Fondo de Cultura Económica, 1988.
Gutiérrez Álvarez, Coralia. *Experiencias contrastadas: Industrialización y conflictos en los textiles del centro-oriente de México, 1884–1917*. Mexico City: El Colegio de México, Centro de Estudios Históricos; Benemérita Universidad de Puebla, Instituto de Ciencias Sociales y Humanidades, 2000.
Gutiérrez, Natividad. *Nationalist Myths and Ethnic Identities: Indigenous Intellectuals and the Mexican State*. Lincoln: University of Nebraska Press, 1999.
Haber, Stephen H., ed. *How Latin America Fell Behind: Essays on the Economic Histories of Brazil and Mexico, 1800–1914*. Stanford, CA: Stanford University Press, 1997.
Haber, Stephen, and Armando Razo. "Industrial Prosperity under Political Instability: An Analysis of Revolutionary Mexico." In *Governing for Prosperity*, edited by Bruce Bueno de Mesquita and Hilton L. Root, 106–52. New Haven, CT: Yale University Press, 2000.
Haber, Stephen, Noel Maurer, and Armando Razo, eds. *The Politics of Property Rights: Political Instability, Credible Commitments, and Economic Growth in Mexico, 1876–1929*. Cambridge: Cambridge University Press, 2003.
Hale, Charles A. *Emilio Rabasa and the Survival of Porfirian Liberalism: The Man, His Career, and His Ideas, 1856–1930*. Stanford, CA: Stanford University Press, 2008.
———. "The Liberal Impulse: Daniel Cosío Villegas and the Historia Moderna de México." *Hispanic American Historical Review* 54, no. 3 (August 1974): 479–98.
———. *Mexican Liberalism in the Age of Mora, 1821–1853*. New Haven, CT: Yale University Press, 1968.
———. *The Transformation of Liberalism in Late Nineteenth-Century Mexico*. Princeton, NJ: Princeton University Press, 1989.

Hale, Charles R. "Does Multiculturalism Menace? Governance, Cultural Rights, and the Politics of Identity in Guatemala." *Journal of Latin American Studies* 34, no. 3 (August 2002): 485–524.

Hamnett, Brian. *Juárez*. London: Longman, 1994.

Hanley, Anne G. "A Failure to Deliver: Municipal Poverty and the Provision of Public Services in Imperial Sao Paulo, Brazil, 1822–1889." *Journal of Urban History* 39, no. 3 (May 2013): 513–35.

———. *Native Capital: Financial Institutions and Economic Development in São Paulo, Brazil, 1850–1920*. Stanford, CA: Stanford University Press, 2005.

———. *The Public Good and the Brazilian State: Municipal Finance and Public Services in São Paulo, 1822–1930*. Chicago: University of Chicago Press, 2019.

Hayden, Thomas, ed. *The Zapatista Reader*. New York: Thunder's Mouth Press/Nation Books: 2002.

Hellier-Tinoco, Ruth. *Embodying Mexico: Tourism, Nationalism, and Performance*. New York: Oxford University Press, 2011.

Henderson, Timothy. *The Worm in the Wheat: Rosalie Evans and Agrarian Struggle in the Puebla-Tlaxcala Valley of Mexico, 1906–1927*. Durham, NC: Duke University Press, 1998.

Herbst, Jeffrey Ira. *States and Power in Africa: Comparative Lessons in Authority and Control*. Princeton, NJ: Princeton University Press, 2000.

Hicks, Frederic. "Land and Succession in the Indigenous Noble Houses of Sixteenth-Century Tlaxcala." *Ethnohistory* 56, no. 4 (2009): 569–88.

Hines, Sarah T. *Water for All: Community, Property, and Revolution in Modern Bolivia*. Oakland: University of California Press, 2022.

Historia y Sociedad en Tlaxcala: Memoria del 1er Simposio Internacional de Investigaciones Socio-históricas sobre Tlaxcala, octubre, 1985. Tlaxcala: Gobierno del Estado de Tlaxcala, Instituto Tlaxcalteca de Cultura, Universidad Autónoma de Tlaxcala; Mexico City: Universidad Iberoamericana, 1986.

Historia y Sociedad en Tlaxcala: Memoria del Tercer Simposio Internacional de Investigaciones Socio-históricas sobre Tlaxcala, octubre, 1987. Tlaxcala: Gobierno del Estado de Tlaxcala, Instituto Tlaxcalteca de Cultura, Universidad Autónoma de Tlaxcala; Mexico City: Universidad Iberoamericana, 1990.

Historia y Sociedad en Tlaxcala: Memorias del 40. y 50. Simposios Internacionales de Investigaciones Socio-históricas sobre Tlaxcala, octubre de 1988, octubre de 1989. Tlaxcala: Gobierno del Estado de Tlaxcala, Instituto Tlaxcalteca de Cultura, Universidad Autónoma de Tlaxcala; Mexico City: Universidad Iberoamericana, 1991.

Hoberman, Louisa Schell. "City Planning in Spanish Colonial Government: The Response of Mexico City to the Problem of Floods, 1607–1637." PhD diss., Columbia University, 1972.

Holden, Robert H. *Mexico and the Survey of Public Lands: The Management of Modernization, 1876–1911*. DeKalb: Northern Illinois University Press, 1994.

Hu-DeHart, Evelyn. *Yaqui Resistance and Survival: The Struggle for Land and Autonomy, 1821–1910*. Madison: University of Wisconsin Press, 1984.

Jacobsen, Nils, and Cristóbal Aljovín de Losada. *Political Cultures in the Andes, 1750–1950*. Durham, NC: Duke University Press, 2005.
James, Timothy. *Mexico's Supreme Court: Between Liberal Individual and Revolutionary Social Rights, 1867–1934*. Albuquerque: University of New Mexico Press, 2013.
Jiménez, Christina M. *Making an Urban Public: Popular Claims to the City in Mexico, 1879–1932*. Pittsburgh: Pittsburgh University Press, 2019.
Joseph, G. M, and Daniel Nugent. *Everyday Forms of State Formation: Revolution and the Negotiation of Rule in Modern Mexico*. Durham, NC: Duke University Press, 1994.
Juárez Flores, José Juan. "Alumbrado público en Puebla y Tlaxcala y deterioro ambiental en los bosques de La Malintzi, 1820–1870." *Historia Crítica*, no. 30 (July–December 2005): 13–38.
———. "Besieged Forests at Century's End: Industry, Speculation, and Dispossession in Tlaxcala's La Malintzin Woodlands, 1860–1910." In *A Land between Waters*, edited by Christopher R. Boyer, 100–123. Tucson: University of Arizona Press, 2012.
Juárez Flores, José Juan, and Francisco Téllez Guerrero. "Las finanzas municipales de la ciudad de Tlaxcala durante el segundo imperio." *Siglo XIX, Cuadernos de Historia*, Universidad Autónoma de Nuevo León/Facultad de Filosofía y Letras, UNAM, no. 8 (January–April 1994): 79–121.
Katz, Friedrich. "The Liberal Republic and the Porfiriato, 1867–1910." In *Mexico since Independence*, edited by Leslie Bethell, 49–124. Cambridge: Cambridge University Press, 1998.
———. *The Life and Times of Pancho Villa*. Stanford, CA: Stanford University Press, 1998.
Katz, Friedrich, ed. *Riot, Rebellion, and Revolution: Rural Social Conflict in Mexico*. Princeton, NJ: Princeton University Press, 1988.
Katz, Friedrich, Jane-Dale Lloyd, and Luz Elena Galván de Terrazas, eds. *Porfirio Díaz frente al descontento popular regional, 1891–1893: Antología documental*. Mexico City: Universidad Iberoamericana, 1986.
Keller, Lisa. *Triumph of Order: Democracy and Public Space in New York and London*. New York: Columbia University Press, 2010.
Kelly, Larissa Kennedy. "Waking the Gods: Archeology and State Power in Porfirian Mexico." PhD diss., University of California, Berkeley, 2011.
Knight, Alan. "El liberalismo mexicano desde la Reforma hasta la Revolución (una interpretación)." *Historia Mexicana* 35, no. 1 (July 1, 1985): 59–91.
———. *The Mexican Revolution*. Vol. I. Cambridge Latin American Studies, 54–55. Cambridge: Cambridge University Press, 1986.
———. "Peasant and Caudillo in Revolutionary Mexico, 1910–1917." In *Caudillo and Peasant in the Mexican Revolution*, edited by David A. Brading, 17–58. Cambridge: Cambridge University Press, 1980.
———. "Racism, Revolution, and Indigenismo: Mexico, 1870–1910." In *The Idea of Race in Latin America, 1870–1940*, edited by Richard Graham, Thomas E.

Skidmore, Aline Helg, and Alan Knight, 71–114. Austin: University of Texas Press, 1990.

———. "The Working Class and the Mexican Revolution, c. 1900–1920." *Journal of Latin American Studies* 16, no. 1 (May 1984): 51–79.

Knight, Alan, and Wil Pansters, eds. *Caciquismo in Twentieth-Century Mexico*. London: Institute for the Study of the Americas, 2005.

Knowlton, Robert James. "Tribunales federales y terrenos rurales en el México del siglo XIX: El Semanario judicial de la Federación." *Historia mexicana* 46, no. 1 (1996): 71–98.

Kourí, Emilio. "Interpreting the Expropriation of Indian Pueblo Lands in Porfirian Mexico: The Unexamined Legacies of Andrés Molina Enríquez." *Hispanic American Historical Review* 82, no. 1 (February 2002): 69–117.

———. *A Pueblo Divided: Business, Property, and Community in Papantla, Mexico*. Stanford, CA: Stanford University Press, 2004.

Krauze, Enrique. *Daniel Cosío Villegas, una biografía intelectual*. Mexico City: J. Mortiz, 1980.

———. *Mexico, Biography of Power: A History of Modern Mexico, 1810–1996*, trans. Hank Heifetz. New York: HarperCollins, 1998.

———. *Siglo de caudillos: Biografía política de México (1810–1910)*. Barcelona: Tusquets Editores, 1994.

Kroeber, Clifton B. *Man, Land, and Water: Mexico's Farmlands Irrigation Policies, 1885–1911*. Berkeley: University of California Press, 1983.

Kuenzli, E. Gabrielle. *Acting Inca: Identity and National Belonging in Early Twentieth-Century Bolivia*. Pittsburgh: University of Pittsburgh Press, 2013.

Kuntz Ficker, Sandra. "La contribución económica de las exportaciones en México: Un acercamiento desde las finanzas estatales (1880–1926)." *América Latina en la Historia Económica* 21, no. 2 (August 2013): 7–39.

———. "Ferrocarriles y mercado: Tarifas, precios, y tráfico ferroviario en el Porfiriato." In *Ferrocarriles y vida económica en México*, edited by Sandra Kuntz Ficker and Paolo Riguzzi, 99–160. Mexico City: El Colegio Mexiquense; Ferrocarriles Nacionales de México; Universidad Autónoma Metropolitana Xochimilco, 1996.

Kuntz Ficker, Sandra, and Paolo Riguzzi, eds. *Ferrocarriles y vida económica en México, 1850–1950: Del surgimiento tardío al decaimiento precoz*. Mexico City: El Colegio Mexiquense; Ferrocarriles Nacionales de México; Universidad Autónoma Metropolitana Xochimilco, 1996.

LaFrance, David G. *The Mexican Revolution in Puebla, 1908–1913: The Maderista Movement and the Failure of Liberal Reform*. Wilmington, DE: SR Books, 1989.

———. *Revolution in Mexico's Heartland: Politics, War, and State Building in Puebla, 1913–1920*. Wilmington, DE: SR Books, 2003.

Langston, Joy, and Scott Morgenstern. "Campaigning in an Electoral Authoritarian Regime: The Case of Mexico." *Comparative Politics* 41, no. 2 (January 2009): 165–81.

Lanz Cardenas, José Trinidad. *Legislación de aguas en México*. Mexico City: Consejo Editorial del Gobierno del Estado de Tabasco, 1982.

Larson, Brooke. *Trials of Nation Making: Liberalism, Race, and Ethnicity in the Andes, 1810–1910*. Cambridge: Cambridge University Press, 2012.
Leal, Victor Nunes. *Coronelismo: The Municipality and Representative Government in Brazil*. Cambridge: Cambridge University Press, 1977.
Lear, John. *Workers, Neighbors, and Citizens: The Revolution in Mexico City*. Lincoln: University of Nebraska Press, 2001.
León García, Ricardo, and Carlos González Herrera. *Civilizar o exterminar: Tarahumaras y apaches en Chihuahua, siglo XIX*. Mexico, City: CIESAS, 2000.
León-Portilla, Miguel. *The Broken Spears: The Aztec Account of the Conquest of Mexico*. Boston: Beacon Press, 1992.
Lewin, Linda. *Politics and Parentela in Paraíba: A Case Study of Family-Based Oligarchy in Brazil*. Princeton, NJ: Princeton University Press, 1987.
Lewis, Stephen. *The Ambivalent Revolution: Forging State and Nation in Chiapas, 1910–1945*. Albuquerque: University of New Mexico Press, 2005.
———. "Mestizaje." In *Encyclopedia of Mexico: History, Society, and Culture*, 2, edited by Michael S. Werner, 838–42. Chicago: Fitzroy Dearborn, 1997.
Lieberman, Evan S. *Race and Regionalism in the Politics of Taxation in Brazil and South Africa*. Cambridge: Cambridge University Press, 2003.
Lipsett-Rivera, Sonya. *To Defend Our Water with the Blood of Our Veins: The Struggle for Resources in Colonial Puebla*. Albuquerque: University of New Mexico Press, 1999.
Lloyd, Jane-Dale, ed. *Visiones del Porfiriato, visiones de México: Jornadas de investigación sobre el Porfiriato*. Mexico City: Universidad Iberoamericana, Departmento de Historia; Morelia: Universidad Michoacana de San Nicolás de Hidalgo, Instituto de Investigaciones Históricas, 2004.
Lockhart, James. *Nahuas and Spaniards: Postconquest Central Mexican History and Philology*. Stanford, CA; Stanford University Press; UCLA Latin American Center Publications, University of California, Los Angeles, 1991.
Lomnitz-Adler, Claudio. *Deep Mexico, Silent Mexico: An Anthropology of Nationalism*. Minneapolis: University of Minnesota Press, 2001.
———. *Exits from the Labyrinth: Culture and Ideology in the Mexican National Space*. Berkeley: University of California Press, 1992.
López, Rick Anthony. *Crafting Mexico: Intellectuals, Artisans, and the State after the Revolution*. Durham, NC: Duke University Press, 2010.
López-Alves, Fernando. *State Formation and Democracy in Latin America, 1810–1900*. Durham, NC: Duke University Press, 2000.
López Caballero, Paula, with Ariadna Acevedo-Rodrigo. "Introduction: Why beyond Alterity?" In *Beyond Alterity: Destabilizing the Indigenous Other in Mexico*, edited by Paula López Caballero and Ariadna Acevedo-Rodrigo, 3–28. Tucson: University of Arizona Press, 2018.
López Martínez, Diana. "La construcción de una nueva territorialidad a través de los usos del agua: El caso de la región del Rio Zahuapan (1888–1919)." Master's thesis, Instituto de Investigaciones Dr. José María Luis Mora, 2013.
Ludlow, Leonor, and Carlos Marichal. *Un siglo de deuda pública en México*. Mexico

City: Instituto Mora, Colegio de Michoacán, Colegio de México, Instituto de Investigaciones Históricas-UNAM, 1998.

Lurtz, Casey. *From the Grounds Up: Building an Export Economy in Southern Mexico.* Stanford, CA: Stanford University Press, 2019.

Lynch, John. "Bolivar and the Caudillos." *Hispanic American Historical Review* 63, no. 1 (February 1983): 3–35.

———. *Caudillos in Spanish America, 1800–1850.* Oxford: Clarendon Press; New York: Oxford University Press, 1992.

Magaloni, Beatriz. *Voting for Autocracy: Hegemonic Party Survival and Its Demise in Mexico.* Cambridge: Cambridge University Press, 2006.

Mainwaring, Scott, and Christopher Welna, eds. *Democratic Accountability in Latin America.* Oxford: Oxford University Press, 2003.

Malamud, Carlos, ed. *Legitimidad, representación y alternancia en España y América Latina: Las reformas electorales, 1880–1930.* Mexico City: Colegio de México, Fideicomiso Historia de las Américas, Fondo de Cultura Económica, 2000.

Mallon, Florencia E. *Peasant and Nation: The Making of Postcolonial Mexico and Peru.* Berkeley: University of California Press, 1995.

Mariátegui, José Carlos. *Seven Interpretive Essays on Peruvian Reality.* Austin: University of Texas Press, 1971.

Marichal, Carlos. *A Century of Debt Crises in Latin America: From Independence to the Great Depression, 1820–1930.* Princeton, NJ: Princeton University Press, 1989.

———. "Obstacles to the Development of Capital Markets in Nineteenth-Century Mexico." In *How Latin America Fell Behind: Essays on the Economic Histories of Brazil and Mexico, 1800–1914*, edited by Stephen H. Haber, 80–100. Stanford, CA: Stanford University Press, 1997.

Márquez Colin, Graciela. "The Political Economy of Mexican Protectionism, 1868–1911." PhD diss., Harvard University, 2002.

———. "Tariff Protection in Mexico, 1892–1909." In *Latin America and the World Economy since 1800*, edited by John H. Coatsworth and Alan M. Taylor, 407–42. Cambridge, MA: Harvard University/David Rockefeller Center for Latin American Studies, 1998.

Martínez, Héctor G., and Francie Chassen-López. "Elecciones y crisis política en Oaxaca: 1902." *Historia Mexicana* 39, no. 2 (October–December 1989): 523–54.

Martinez, Patricia. "'Noble' Tlaxcalans: Race and Ethnicity in Northeastern New Spain, 1770–1810." PhD diss., University of Texas at Austin, 2004.

Martínez Baracs, Andrea. *Un gobierno de indios: Tlaxcala, 1519–1750.* Mexico City: Fondo de Cultura Económica; Fideicomiso Colegio de Historia de Tlaxcala; Centro de Investigaciones y Estudios Superiores en Antropología Social, 2008.

Martínez Delgado, Gerardo. "La era de las redes: Servicios públicos, grandes empresas y finanzas internacionales en las ciudades mexicanas a principios del siglo XX." *Historia Mexicana* 70, no. 4 (April–June 2021): 1599–660.

Matthews, Laura E. "Whose Conquest? Nahua, Zapoteca, and Mixteca Allies in the Conquest of Central America." In *Indian Conquistadors: Indigenous Allies in the Conquest of Mesoamerica*, edited by Laura E. Matthews and Michel R. Oudijk (Norman: University of Oklahoma Press, 2007), 102–26.

Matthews, Michael. *The Civilizing Machine: A Cultural History of Mexican Railroads, 1876–1910*. Lincoln: University of Nebraska Press, 2014.

McBride, George. *The Land Systems of Mexico*. New York: American Geographical Society, 1923.

McDonough, Kelly. "'Love' Lost: Class Struggle among Indigenous Nobles and Commoners of Seventeenth-Century Tlaxcala." *Mexican Studies/Estudios Mexicanos* 32, no. 1 (Winter 2015): 1–28.

McEnroe, Sean F. *From Colony to Nationhood in Mexico: Laying the Foundations, 1560–1840*. Cambridge: Cambridge University Press, 2012.

McNamara, Patrick J. *Sons of the Sierra: Juárez, Díaz, and the People of Ixtlán, Oaxaca, 1855–1920*. Chapel Hill: University of North Carolina Press, 2007.

Mentz, Brígida von, and R. Marcela Pérez López, eds. *Manantiales, ríos, pueblos y haciendas: Dos documentos sobre conflictos por aguas en Oaxtepec y en el valle de Cuernavaca (1795–1807)*. Jiutepec, Mexico: Instituto Mexicano de Tecnología del Agua (IMTA), 1998.

Mesolore. "Introduction to the Lienzo de Tlaxcala: Description." Accessed December 15, 2022. www.mesolore.org/tutorials/learn/19/Introduction-to-the-Lienzo-de-Tlaxcala-/53/Description.

———. "Introduction to the Lienzo de Tlaxcala: History and Publications." Accessed December 15, 2022. www.mesolore.org/tutorials/learn/19/Introduction-to-the-Lienzo-de-Tlaxcala-/54/History-and-Publications.

Meyer, Jean. "Haciendas y ranchos, peones y campesinos en el Porfiriato: Algunas falacias estadísticas." *Historia Mexicana* 35, no. 3 (January 1986): 477–509.

Meyer, Michael C. *Water in the Hispanic Southwest: A Social and Legal History, 1550–1850*. Tucson: University of Arizona Press, 2016.

Molina Enríquez, Andrés. *Los grandes problemas nacionales*. Mexico City: Imprenta de A. Carranza e hijos, 1909.

Montalvo Ortega, Enrique. "Revolts and Peasant Mobilizations in Yucatán: Indians, Peons, and Peasants from the Caste War to the Revolution." In *Riot, Rebellion, and Revolution: Rural Social Conflict in Mexico*, edited by Friedrich Katz, 295–320. Princeton, NJ: Princeton University Press, 1988.

Montaño, Diana J. *Electrifying Mexico: Technology and the Transformation of a Modern City*. Austin: University of Texas Press, 2021.

Morris, Nathaniel. *Soldiers, Saints, and Shamans: Indigenous Communities and the Revolutionary State in Mexico's Gran Nayar, 1910–1940*. Tucson: University of Arizona Press, 2020.

Mundy, Barbara. *The Death of Aztec Tenochtitlán, the Life of Mexico City*. Austin: University of Texas Press, 2018.

Musset, Alain. *El agua en el valle de México, siglos XVI–XVIII*. Mexico City: Pórtico de la Ciudad de México; Centro de Estudios Mexicanos y Centroamericanos, 1992.

Nava Rodríguez, Luis. *Historia de Huamantla*. Tlaxcala: Ed. Progreso, 1974.
———. *Historia de Nuestra Señora de Octolán: Su aparición milagrosa y su culto a través de los tiempos*. Tlaxcala: 1983.
———. *Tlaxcala contemporánea, de 1822 a 1977*. Mexico City: Editorial Progreso, 1978.
———. *Tlaxcala en la historia*. Tlaxcala: 1972.
Negretto, Gabriel L., and José Antonio Aguilar-Rivera. "Rethinking the Legacy of the Liberal State in Latin America." *Journal of Latin American Studies* 32, no. 2 (May 2000): 361–97.
Netzahualcoyotzi, Mariano. "Villa de Progreso: Desarrollo económico y estructura laboral en el Porfiriato Tlaxcalteca (1879–1892)." In *Las ciudades y sus estructuras, población, espacio, y cultura en México, Siglos XVIII y XIX*, edited by Sonia Pérez Toledo, René Elizalde Salazar, and Luis Pérez Cruz, 198–208. Mexico City: Universedad Autónoma Metropolitana-Iztapalapa, 1999.
Nickel, Herbert J. "Agricultural Laborers in the Mexican Revolution (1910–40): Some Hypotheses and Facts about Some Hypotheses and Facts about Participation and Restraint in the Highlands of Puebla-Tlaxcala." In *Riot, Rebellion, and Revolution*, edited by Friedrich Katz, 376–416. Princeton, NJ: Princeton University Press, 1988.
Nutini, Hugo G., and Betty Bell. *Ritual Kinship: The Structure and Historical Development of the Compadrazgo System in Rural Tlaxcala*. Princeton, NJ: Princeton University Press, 1980.
Ochoa Paredes, Cruz María. "Evolución histórico-geografía de las divisiones territoriales del estado de Tlaxcala (1519–1980)." *Boletín del Instituto de Geografía* 15 (1985): 211–53.
Offutt, Leslie S. "Defending Corporate Identity on New Spain's Northeastern Frontier: San Esteban de Nueva Tlaxcala, 1780–1810." *The Americas* 64, no. 3 (January 2008): 351–75.
Overmyer-Velázquez, Mark. *Visions of the Emerald City: Modernity, Tradition, and the Formation of Porfirian Oaxaca, Mexico*. Durham, NC: Duke University Press, 2006.
Pani, Erika. "Derribando ídolos: El Juárez de Francisco Bulnes." In *Juárez: Historia y mito*, edited by Josefina Zoraida Vázquez, 43–58. Mexico City: El Colegio de México, Centro de Estudios Históricos, 2010.
Pansters, W. G., and Arij Ouweneel, eds. *Region, State, and Capitalism in Mexico: Nineteenth and Twentieth Centuries*. Amsterdam: CEDLA, 1989.
Pastor, Rodolfo. *Campesinos y reformas: La mixteca, 1700–1856*. Mexico City: Centro de Estudios Históricos, Colegio de México, 1987.
Paxman, Andrew, ed. *Los gobernadores: Caciques del pasado y del presente*. Mexico City: Grijalbo, 2018.
Peña y Peña, Álvaro. *Estado de Tlaxcala*. Mexico City: Secretaría de Educación Pública, Subsecretaría de Asuntos Culturales, 1968.
Pérez Toledo, Sonia, René Elizalde Salazar, and Luis Pérez Cruz, eds. *Las ciudades y sus estructuras: Población, espacio y cultura en México, siglos XVIII y XIX*.

Mexico City: Universidad Autónoma Metropolitana-Iztapalapa; Universidad Autónoma de Tlaxcala, 1999.
Perry, Laurens Ballard. *Juárez and Díaz: Machine Politics in Mexico.* DeKalb: Northern Illinois University Press, 1978.
Piccato, Pablo. *The Tyranny of Opinion: Honor in the Construction of the Mexican Public Sphere.* Durham, NC: Duke University Press, 2010.
Pilcher, Jeffrey M. *Que Vivan Los Tamales!: Food and the Making of Mexican Identity.* Albuquerque: University of New Mexico Press, 1998.
———. *The Sausage Rebellion: Public Health, Private Enterprise, and Meat in Mexico City, 1890–1917.* Albuquerque: University of New Mexico Press, 2006.
Pineo, Ronn F., and James A. Baer, eds. *Cities of Hope: People, Protests, and Progress in Urbanizing Latin America, 1870–1930.* Boulder, CO: Westview Press, 1998.
Pitarch, Pedro. "The Zapatistas and the Art of Ventriloquism." *Journal of Human Rights* 3 (2004): 291–312.
Plunkitt, George Washington. *Plunkitt of Tammany Hall: A Series of Very Plain Talks on Very Practical Politics.* New York: Dutton, 1963.
Posada Carbó, Eduardo, ed. *Elections before Democracy: The History of Elections in Europe and Latin America.* Houndmills, England: Macmillan; New York: St. Martin's Press, 1996.
Postero, Nancy Grey. *Now We Are Citizens: Indigenous Politics in Postmulticultural Bolivia.* Stanford, CA: Stanford University Press, 2007.
Ramírez Rancaño, Mario. "Próspero Cahuantzi: El gobernador de Tlaxcala." *Historias* 16 (1987): 99–115.
———. "Próspero Cahuantzi en la contrarrevolución." *Revista Mexicana de Sociología* 57, no. 3 (July 1995): 177–90.
———. *El sistema de haciendas en Tlaxcala.* Mexico City: Consejo Nacional para la Cultura y las Artes, Dirección General de Publicaciones, 1990.
Razo, Armando. *Social Foundations of Limited Dictatorship: Networks and Private Protection during Mexico's Early Industrialization.* Stanford, CA: Stanford University Press, 2008.
Reed, Nelson A. *The Caste War of Yucatan.* Stanford, CA: Stanford University Press, 1964.
Rendón Garcini, Ricardo. *Dos haciendas pulqueras en Tlaxcala, 1857–1884.* Tlaxcala: Gobierno del Estado de Tlaxcala; Mexico City: Universidad Iberoamericana, Departamento de Historia, 1990.
———. "Paternalism and Moral Economy on Two Tlaxcalan Haciendas in the Llanos de Apan (1857–1884)." In *Region, State, and Capitalism in Mexico: Nineteenth and Twentieth Centuries*, edited by W. G. Pansters and Arij Ouweneel, 37–46. Amsterdam: CEDLA, 1989.
———. *El Prosperato: El juego de equilibrios de un gobierno estatal (Tlaxcala de 1885 a 1911).* Mexico City: Siglo Veintiuno; Universidad Iberoamericana, 1993.
———. *Tlaxcala: Historia breve.* Mexico City: El Colegio de México; Fideicomiso Historia de las Américas, FCE, 2011.
———."Una oposición reprimida: El caso de Andrés García." In *Historia y socie-*

dad en Tlaxcala: Memorias del 40. y 50. Simposios Internacionales de Investigaciones Socio-Históricas sobre Tlaxcala, octubre de 1988, octubre de 1989, 219–226. Tlaxcala: Gobierno del Estado de Tlaxcala, Instituto Tlaxcalteca de Cultura, 1991.

Restall, Matthew. *Seven Myths of the Spanish Conquest*. Oxford: Oxford University Press, 2003.

Reyes, Candelario. *Biografía de Juan Cuamatzi*. Tlaxcala: Difusión Cultural del Gobierno del Estado, 1961.

Riguzzi, Paolo. "Los Caminos de Atraso: Tecnología, instituciones, e inversión en los ferrocarriles mexicanos, 1850–1900." In *Ferrocarriles y vida económica en México, 1850–1950*, edited by Sandra Kuntz Ficker and Paolo Riguzzi, 13–98. Mexico City: El Colegio Mexiquense, 1996.

Ristow, Colby Nolan. *A Revolution Unfinished: The Chegomista Rebellion and the Limits of Revolutionary Democracy in Juchitán, Oaxaca*. Lincoln: University of Nebraska Press, 2018.

Rock, David. *State Building and Political Movements in Argentina, 1860–1916*. Stanford, CA: Stanford University Press, 2002.

Rockwell, Elsie. *Hacer Escuela, Hacer Estado: La educación posrevolucionaria vista desde Tlaxcala*. Zamora: El Colegio de Michoacán, 2007.

———. "Schools of the Revolution: Enacting and Contesting State Forms in Tlaxcala, 1910–1930." In *Everyday Forms of State Formation*, edited by G. M. Joseph and Daniel Nugent, 170–208. Durham, NC: Duke University Press, 1994.

———. "Todos tenemos la crisma de dios: Engaging Spanish Literacy in a Tlaxcalan Pueblo." In *Beyond Alterity: Destabilizing the Indigenous Other in Mexico*, edited by Paula López Caballero and Ariadna Acevedo-Rodrigo, 130–50. Tucson: University of Arizona Press, 2018.

Roniger, Luis, and Tamar Herzog, eds. *The Collective and the Public in Latin America: Cultural Identities and Political Order*. Brighton, England: Sussex Academic Press, 2000.

Roorda, Eric. *The Dictator Next Door: The Good Neighbor Policy and the Trujillo Regime in the Dominican Republic, 1930–1945*. Durham, NC: Duke University Press, 1998.

Rosas, Guillermo, and Joy Langston. "Gubernatorial Effects on the Voting Behavior of National Legislators." *Journal of Politics* 73, no. 2 (April 2011): 477–93.

Rosas Salas, Sergio Francisco. "Agua e industria en Puebla: El establecimiento de la fábrica textil la Covadonga, 1889–1897." *Relaciones* 136 (Fall 2013): 223–64.

Rozat, Guy. *Los orígenes de la nación: Pasado indígena e historia nacional*. Mexico City: Universidad Iberoamericana, 2011.

Rugeley, Terry. *Yucatán's Maya Peasantry and the Origins of the Caste War*. Austin: University of Texas Press, 1996.

Ruiz, Jason. *Americans in the Treasure House: Travel to Porfirian Mexico and the Cultural Politics of Empire*. Austin: University of Texas Press, 2014.

Sábato, Hilda. *The Many and the Few: Political Participation in Republican Buenos Aires*. Stanford, CA: Stanford University Press, 2001.

Salazar Exaire, Celia. *Uso y distribución del agua en el valle de Tehuacán: El caso de San Juan Bautista Axalpan, Pue., 1610–1798*. Mexico City: Instituto Nacional de Antropología e Historia, 2000.
Sánchez, Evelyne. *El Juez, el Notario, y el Caudillo: Análisis de un juicio verbal en Tlaxcala durante la Revolución*. Madrid: Casa de Velázquez: 2019.
Sánchez de Tagle, Esteban. *Los dueños de la calle: Una historia de la vía pública en la época colonial*. Instituto Nacional de Antropología e Historia; Departamento del Distrito Federal, 1997.
Sánchez Rodríguez, Martín. "La herencia del pasado: La centralización de los recursos acuíferos durante el Porfiriato, 1888–1910." *Universidad Michoacana* 7 (January–March 1993): 50–60.
Sánchez Sánchez, Jaime. *Los antirreeleccionistas de Tepehítec, Tlaxcala, y la Revolución en Tlaxcala, 1906–1915*. Tlaxcala: Congreso del Estado de Tlaxcala, LV Legislatura, 1999.
Santibáñez Tijerina, Blanca Estela. "Industria y trabajadores textiles en Tlaxcala: Convergencias y divergencias en los movimientos sociales, 1906–1918." PhD diss., University of Leiden, 2010.
Saragoza, Alex. *The Monterrey Elite and the Mexican State, 1880–1940*. Austin: University of Texas Press, 1988.
Sarmiento, Domingo Faustino. *Facundo; Or, Civilization and Barbarism*. Translated by Ilan Stavans. New York: Penguin Classics, 1998; Hurd and Houghton, 1868.
Schedler, Andreas. *Electoral Authoritarianism: The Dynamics of Unfree Competition*. Boulder, CO: Lynne Rienner Publishers, 2006.
Schmidt, Arthur. *The Social and Economic Effect of the Railroad in Puebla and Veracruz, Mexico, 1867–1911*. New York: Garland, 1987.
Schmidt, Henry C. "The Mexican Intellectual as Political Pundit, 1968–1976: The Case of Daniel Cosio Villegas." *Journal of Interamerican Studies and World Affairs* 24, no. 1 (February 1982): 81–103.
Scobie, James R. "The Growth of Latin American Cities, 1870–1930." In *The Cambridge History of Latin America*, edited by Leslie Bethell, 233–66. Cambridge: Cambridge University Press, 1986.
Shumway, Nicolas. *The Invention of Argentina*. Berkeley: University of California Press, 1991.
Simpson, Eyler N. *The Ejido: Mexico's Way Out*. Chapel Hill: University of North Carolina Press, 1937.
Simpson, Lesley Byrd. *Many Mexicos*. Berkeley: University of California Press, 1966.
Skopyk, Bradley. *Colonial Cataclysms: Climate, Landscape, and Memory in Mexico's Little Ice Age*. Tucson: University of Arizona Press, 2020.
Smith, Benjamin T. "Communal Work, Forced Labor, and Road Building in Mexico, 1920–1958." In *State Formation in the Liberal Era: Capitalism and Claims of Citizenship in Mexico and Peru*, edited by Ben Fallaw and David Nugent, 273–93. Tucson: University of Arizona Press, 2020.

———. *Pistoleros and Popular Movements: The Politics of State Formation in Postrevolutionary Oaxaca*. Lincoln: University of Nebraska Press, 2009.

———. "Rewriting the Moral Economy: Agricultural Societies and Economic Change in Oaxaca's Mixtec Baja, 1830–1910." In *Mexico in Transition/México y sus transiciones*, edited by Antonio Escobar Ohmstede and Matthew Butler, 81–110. Mexico City: CIESAS, 2013.

Sorensen, Diana. *Facundo and the Construction of Argentine Culture*. Austin: University of Texas Press, 1996.

Suárez Cortez, Blanca Estela, ed. *Historia de los usos del agua en México: Oligarquías, empresas y ayuntamientos (1840–1940)*. Mexico City: Comisión Nacional del Agua; Tlapan, DF: CIESAS; Jiutepec, Morelos: ITMA, 1998.

Sullivan, Paul. *Xuxub Must Die: The Lost Histories of a Murder on the Yucatan*. Pittsburgh: University of Pittsburgh Press, 2004.

Sumner, Jaclyn Ann. "The Indigenous Governor of Tlaxcala and Acceptable Indigenousness in the Porfirian Regime." *Mexican Studies/Estudios Mexicanos* 35, no. 1 (Winter 2019): 61–87.

Tannenbaum, Frank. *The Mexican Agrarian Revolution*. Hamden, CT: Archon Books, 1968.

Tenenbaum, Barbara A. *The Politics of Penury: Debts and Taxes in Mexico, 1821–1856*. Albuquerque: University of New Mexico Press, 1986.

———. "Streetwise History: The Paseo de la Reforma and the Porfirian State, 1876–1910." In *Rituals of Rule, Rituals of Resistance: Public Celebrations and Popular Culture in Mexico*, edited by William H. Beezley, Cheryl English Martin, and William E. French, 127–50. Wilmington, DE: Scholarly Resources, 1994.

Tenorio-Trillo, Mauricio. *I Speak of the City: Mexico City at the Turn of the Twentieth Century*. Chicago: University of Chicago Press, 2012.

———. *Mexico at the World's Fairs: Crafting a Modern Nation*. Berkeley: University of California Press, 1996.

———. "1910 Mexico City: Space and Nation in the City of the Centenario." *Journal of Latin American Studies* 28, no. 1 (February 1996): 75–104.

Tenorio-Trillo, Mauricio, and Aurora Gómez Galvarriato. *El Porfiriato*. Fondo de Cultura Económica, 2006.

Thomson, Guy P. C. "Popular Aspects of Liberalism in Mexico, 1848–1888." *Bulletin of Latin American Research* 10, no. 3 (January 1991): 265–92.

Thomson, Guy P. C., and David LaFrance. *Patriotism, Politics, and Popular Liberalism in Nineteenth-Century Mexico: Juan Francisco Lucas and the Puebla Sierra*. Wilmington, DE: Scholarly Resources, 1999.

Tilly, Charles. *Coercion, Capital, and European States, AD 990–1990*. Cambridge, MA: Blackwell, 1990.

Tinker Salas, Miguel. *In the Shadow of the Eagles: Sonora and the Transformation of the Border during the Porfiriato*. Berkeley: University of California Press, 1997.

Topik, Steven. "Entrepreneurs or Lumpenbourgeoisie?" *Mexican Studies/Estudios Mexicanos* 4, no. 2 (July 1988): 327–40.

Topik, Steven, and Allen Wells, eds. *The Second Conquest of Latin America: Coffee, Henequen, and Oil during the Export Boom, 1850–1930*. Austin: Institute of Latin American Studies, University of Texas Press, 1998.

Tortolero Villaseñor, Alejandro. "Transforming the Central Mexican Waterscape: Lake Drainage and Its Consequences during the Porfiriato." In *Territories, Commodities, and Knowledges: Latin American Environmental History in the Nineteenth and Twentieth Centuries*, edited by Christian Brannstrom, 121–47. London: Institute for the Study of the Americas, 2004.

———. "Water and Revolution in Morelos, 1850–1915." In *A Land between Waters: Environmental Histories of Modern Mexico*, edited by Christopher R. Boyer, 124–49. Tucson: University of Arizona Press, 2012.

Trejo, Guillermo. *Popular Movements in Autocracies: Religion, Repression, and Indigenous Collective Action in Mexico*. New York: Cambridge University Press, 2012.

Turits, Richard Lee. *Foundations of Despotism: Peasants, the Trujillo Regime, and Modernity in Dominican History*. Stanford, CA: Stanford University Press, 2003.

Tutino, John. *From Insurrection to Revolution in Mexico: Social Bases of Agrarian Violence, 1750–1940*. Princeton, NJ: Princeton University Press, 1986.

Valadés, José C. *El porfirismo: Historia de un régimen; El crecimiento*. Mexico City: Ed. Patria, 1948.

Vanderwood, Paul J. *Disorder and Progress: Bandits, Police, and Mexican Development*. Lincoln: University of Nebraska Press, 1981.

———. *The Power of God against the Guns of Government: Religious Upheaval in Mexico at the Turn of the Nineteenth Century*. Stanford, CA: Stanford University Press, 1998.

Vaughan, Mary K. *Cultural Politics in Revolution: Teachers, Peasants, and Schools in Mexico, 1930–1940*. Tucson: University of Arizona Press, 1997.

Vitz, Matthew. *A City on a Lake: Urban Political Ecology and the Growth of Mexico City*. Durham, NC: Duke University Press, 2018.

Wade, Peter. *Race and Ethnicity in Latin America*. Chicago: Pluto Press, 1997.

Wakild, Emily. *Revolutionary Parks: Conservation, Social Justice, and Mexico's National Parks, 1910–1940*. Tucson: University of Arizona Press, 2011.

Walker, Charles. *Smoldering Ashes: Cuzco and the Creation of Republican Peru, 1780–1840*. Durham, NC: Duke University Press, 1999.

Wasserman, Mark. *Capitalists, Caciques, and Revolution: The Native Elite and Foreign Enterprise in Chihuahua, Mexico, 1854–1911*. Chapel Hill: University of North Carolina Press, 1984.

Wasserstrom, Robert. *Class and Society in Central Chiapas*. Berkeley: University of California Press, 1983.

Wauchope, Robert. *Handbook of Middle American Indians*. Austin: University of Texas Press, 1964.

Wells, Allen. "Oaxtepec Revisited: The Politics of Mexican Historiography, 1968–1988." *Mexican Studies/Estudios Mexicanos* 7, no. 2 (July 1991): 331–45.

———. "Yucatán: Violence and Social Control on Henequen Plantations." In *Other Mexicos: Essays on Regional Mexican History, 1876–1911*, edited by Thomas Benjamin and William McNellie, 213–41. Albuquerque: University of New Mexico Press, 1984.

———. *Yucatán's Gilded Age: Haciendas, Henequen, and International Harvester, 1860–1915*. Albuquerque: University of New Mexico Press, 1985.

Wells, Allen, and G. M Joseph. *Summer of Discontent, Seasons of Upheaval: Elite Politics and Rural Insurgency in Yucatán, 1876–1915*. Stanford, CA: Stanford University Press, 1996.

Widdifield, Stacie G. *The Embodiment of the National in Late Nineteenth-Century Mexican Painting*. Tucson: University of Arizona Press, 1996.

Wolf, Eric. "On Peasant Rebellions." In *Peasants and Peasant Societies*, edited by Teodor Shanin, 264–74. Harmondsworth, England: Penguin, 1971.

Wolfe, Mikael. *Watering the Revolution: An Environmental and Technological History of Agrarian Reform in Mexico*. Durham, NC: Duke University Press, 2017.

Womack, John. "Mexican Political Historiography." In *Investigaciones contemporáneas sobre historia de México: Memorias de la tercera reunión de historiadores Mexicanos y Norteamericanos, Oaxtepec, Morelos, 4–7 de noviembre de 1969*, 478–92. Austin: University of Texas Press, 1971.

———. *Zapata and the Mexican Revolution*. New York: Knopf, 1969.

Wood, Andrew Grant. *Revolution in the Street: Women, Workers, and Urban Protest in Veracruz, 1870–1927*. Wilmington, DE: SR Books, 2001.

Wood, Stephanie. *Transcending Conquest: Nahua Views of the Spanish Colonial México*. Norman: University of Oklahoma Press, 2003.

Wright-Rios, Edward N. *Revolutions in Mexican Catholicism: Reform and Revelation in Oaxaca, 1887–1934*. Durham, NC: Duke University Press, 2009.

Yannakakis, Yanna. *The Art of Being In-Between: Native Intermediaries, Indian Identity, and Local Rule in Colonial Oaxaca*. Durham, NC: Duke University Press, 2008.

Yashar, Deborah J. *Contesting Citizenship in Latin America: The Rise of Indigenous Movements and the Postliberal Challenge*. Cambridge: Cambridge University Press, 2005.

Ybarra, Patricia. *Performing Conquest: Five Centuries of Theatre, History, and Identity in Tlaxcala, Mexico*. Ann Arbor: University of Michigan Press, 2009.

Zea, Leopoldo. *El positivismo en México: Nacimiento, apogeo, y decadencia*. Mexico City: Fondo de Cultura Económica, 1968.

Zoraida Vázquez, Josefina, ed. *Juárez: Historia y mito*. Mexico City: El Colegio de México, Centro de Estudios Históricos, 2010.

INDEX

absenteeism, 1–4, 54, 61–62, 102, 108, 110
agrarian reform, 54, 58, 92–98, 100, 102, 139–40; scholarship on, 177n3, 178n13
aguardiente, 41, 54–55, 75
Alarcón, Manuel (governor), 18, 21–22, 137
alcabalas. See taxes
alcohol. See aguardiente; pulque
Alzayanca, 60. See also Tlaxcala–Puebla region
Amatlán, 87–88
La Antigua República (newspaper), 27, 75, 116, 128, 135–37
Anzures, Rafael, 70
Apache people, 8, 49. See also racism
Apetatitlán, 85, 126
Apizaco, 55, 57, 67, 70, 122
archaeology, 24, 32–34, 39–40, 43. See also Cacaxtla; Chichén Itza; Plaza Mayor; Teotihuacán; Xochitécatl
archives, 10, 37, 40, 50, 62, 69, 82–83, 93, 97
Arellano, Juan (engineer), 123. See also engineers; bridges; Zahuapan River
Arenas, Domingo, 131, 139

assassination, 2, 68, 113, 131
Atoyac River, 54, 62, 74–89, 101–103, 106–11, 115, 119
authoritarianism, 3–5, 10–12, 15, 29–30, 46, 53, 65–73, 91–92, 98, 130, 133, 142–43; See also patronage; pragmatism; Porfiriato
Ayecac, 69–70, 101–103, 105, 110
ayuntamiento, 76, 109, 114–15, 119, 133, 141, 167n60; of Tlaxcala, 16, 60, 69–71, 103–105, 123, 125–30. See also elections: municipal; Tlaxcala (state); water
Aztec. See Mexica

Baerlein, Henry, 25
Balcázar, Amado, 67
Banco Central Mexicano (bank), 127
barley, 164n17
Beals, Carleton, 25
Bonfil Batalla, Guillermo, 142
Bretón family, 66–67
bridges, 10, 55, 72–73, 78, 116–21, 130, 138
Brigade Xicohténcatl, 140. See also Indigenous antiquity; Xicohténcatl (pre-Columbian leader)
broom root 94, 170n2

219

Cacaxtla, 159n45
cacique, 3, 12, 27, 53
Cahuantzi, Próspero (governor), 3–7, 58; career, 37, 47, 53, 64, 67, 71, 120; identity politics, 9, 12, 15–17, 21–22, 31, 33–34, 41, 44; Indigenous heritage, 25–28, 136–37. See also patronage; mediation; Tlaxcala (state)
camarilla, 15–16. See also patronage; Porfiriato
canals, 62, 75, 81–82, 101, 106–107, 110–13, 120, 122, 126–27
Cañedo, Francisco (governor), 18, 21
Carvajal, Melquiades (governor), 52
Carvajal family, 66, 109–10, 112
Caso, Alfredo and Bernardo, 81, 84, 106
Catholic Church, 8, 29, 35, 45, 49–50, 92. See also secularism
caudillo, 3, 11–12, 53, 146n14, 147n18. See also Porfiriato
Chacmool, 32. See also Indigenous antiquity; Maya
Chavero, Alfredo, 38–39
Chiapas (state), 20, 142, 165n29
Chiautempan, 122, 126, 167n60, 170n108
Chichén Itzá, 32
Chihuahua (state), 17, 20, 74, 139
científicos, 17, 20, 25, 33–34, 45, 49, 90, 129, 152n14. See also positivism
coffee, 3, 74
colegio electoral, 70
El Colmillo Público (newspaper), 23–24
colonial era, 29, 74, 94, 119, 121; law, 9, 63, 73, 96; legacy, 29, 38, 54, 76, 97; See also Spanish Invasion (1519)
conquest. See Spanish Invasion (1519)
Constitution of 1824, 6, 28
Constitution of 1857, 46–47, 92, 119, 168n63
Constitution of 1917, 112–14, 139, 141
Contla (village), 103, 121, 178n19; land dispute (1892), 96–98
corn, 41, 53, 164n17
Cortés, Hernán (conquistador), 8, 74. See also Spanish Invasion (1519)
cotton, 25, 67, 74, 174n53
Cravioto, Rafael (governor), 18, 21
crime, 56, 118–19
Cuamatzi, Juan de la Rosa, 96–97, 131, 139. See also Contla (village); protests; ejido
Cuauhtémoc (district), 57, 163n9, 165n27

dams, 3, 9–11, 62, 73–88, 106, 109–13, 117, 126–128, 132, 137, 141
debt peonage. See peones
Dehesa, Teodoro (governor), 18, 21
Desagüe General del Valle de México, 74, 173n27
Descuento Español (bank), 128
development, 2–4, 13, 17, 36, 74, 80, 90, 93, 95–96, 102, 105–108, 119, 133, 166n44. See also infrastructure; modernization; public works
Díaz, Porfirio (president), 2–6, 9, 17, 24, 31, 43–48, 56–57, 61, 73, 97–98, 118, 133, 138–39, 142; Indigenous heritage, 8, 28; paternalism debate, 11–12. See also camarilla; elections; military; Plan de Tuxtepec (1876); Porfiriato
Díaz Rubin, José, 62, 84
disentailment, 92–98, 100–102, 105. See also Ley Lerdo (1856); privatization
dissent, 3–4, 10, 30, 53, 65, 76, 112, 118. See also labor; litigation; protests

education, 40, 96, 120, 128–30, 152n18. See also literacy
ejidos, 96–98. See also Contla (village); land ownership; privatization

elections, 3–4, 11, 17–19, 27, 65, 132; clubs, 68, 136–138; municipal, 69–71, 115; objections to, 25, 61, 97, 140; state, 15, 67

electricity, 9, 13, 40–41, 75, 88, 100–101, 116–17, 122, 125–30

Eleventh International Congress of Americanists (1895), 32, 36, 42–46, 49

encomienda, 9, 29, 35

engineers, 20, 83–90, 102–106, 109–14, 117, 123, 127. See also mapping

environment, 4–5, 11, 35, 73–74, 78, 80, 105–106, 108, 111, 114; degradation of, 93, 126, 141. See also flood

Escandón, Pablo, 21–22

factory, 9, 11, 54, 57, 62–64, 68, 95; owners, 55, 60, 93, 105, 108, 121, 136, 138; water consumption, 73, 75–76, 80–90, 107, 112, 128; workers, 132, 135–37

faenas. See labor: forced

federalization. See Federal Waters Law (1888); Ley Lerdo (1856)

Federal Waters Law (1888), 12–13, 80–90, 100–105, 108, 111, 114–15, 141

flood, 105, 109–11, 113, 119, 121–23, 127, 137, 141; colonial era, 74; of 1888, 72–73; of 1893, 106; prevention, 76–79, 88, 107–108, 130. See also water

Flores Magón brothers (revolutionaries), 139

foreign investment, 52–55, 123, 127

foreign relations, 1, 23–25, 32–34, 152n16

forests, 55, 60, 94, 117, 126, 177n5. See also timber

Fortuño, Mariano, 122

French intervention (1861–67), 16, 38, 63

Gamio, Manuel (anthropologist), 22, 156n77; See also indigenismo

García, Agustín "el colgador", 56–57. See also rurales

García, Andrés, 131. See also assassination

García Cubas, Antonio (geographer), 44

geography, 42–44, 53, 82, 117, 143. See also Tlaxcala–Puebla region; water

González, Juan, 1–2

González, Manuel (president), 17, 19, 152n16

González, Martín (governor), 27

González de Cosío, Francisco (governor), 18, 21

Gutiérrez, Rodrigo. See El Senado de Tlaxcala

hacendado, 1–2, 58, 60–61, 66, 77–78, 82, 96, 98, 101–102, 110–11, 132, 137; funding public works, 118–20, 138; in political leadership, 16–17, 52, 67. See also absenteeism

hacienda, 21–22, 39, 53–55, 72–74, 81, 84, 94, 100, 106, 129, 140; foreign-owned, 1–3, 54. See also absenteeism; hacendado; hacienda–rancho distinction; labor; Ley de Hacienda (1897)

hacienda–rancho distinction, 163n8

henequen, 3, 24, 67, 74

Herrerias, Gerardo Emilio, 81, 85, 88, 175n59

Hidalgo (district), 61, 94, 163n9. See also hacienda; labor; Tlaxcala–Puebla region

Hidalgo (state), xv, 21, 53

Hidalgo, Antonio, 139

El Hijo del Ahuizote (newspaper), 23, 26, 131

Huamantla, 52, 55, 57––61, 66–67, 70, 122, 127

Huerta, Victoriano (president), 139

Huilopan, 96

Hunt Cortés, Agustín, 44

Ibarrola, Ramón de (engineer), 86–88. See also engineers
El Imparcial (newspaper), 45–46. See also journalism: Mexico City
Inca civilization 8, 33. See also Indigenous antiquity
Independence, 15, 33, 52, 63, 76
indigenismo, 5, 22, 44–45, 50, 116, 141–42. See also Gamio, Manuel (anthropologist)
Indigenous, 3, 9–10, 27–28, 31–32, 37, 44, 49, 141–42, 148n28, 157n20; cast as anti-modern, 6, 8, 50; foreign accounts of, 25–26; interlocutors, 5. See also indigenismo; Indigenous antiquity; racism
Indigenous antiquity, 8, 24, 33–34, 39. See also archaeology; indigenismo; patrimony
industrialization. See development
infrastructure, 3, 9, 55, 62, 105, 130; in modernization rhetoric, 10, 13, 73, 76, 80, 116–17, 13. See also development; modernization; public works; water
irrigation, 74–75, 78, 83–84, 86, 102, 120. See also water

jefe político, 52, 60, 66–67, 164n10
journalism, 27; Mexico City, 46–49, 131, 136
Juárez, Benito (president), 17, 47; Indigenous heritage, 8, 27–28
Juárez (district), 60. See also jefe político; Tlaxcala (state)

Kennedy, Diego, 84, 102, 138
King, Rosa E., 22

labor, 54; forced, 6, 9, 24, 45, 107, 121; rights, 2, 54, 132, 135–37, 140
Laguna (region). See Nazas River
Lake Acuitlapilco, 109–10, 113

Lake Rosario, 109–10
land ownership, 53–54, 131–32, 155n57, 179n33; communal, 4–6, 35, 72, 92, 97, 139–40; large, 11, 55, 71, 90, 137–38; small, 2, 103, 105, 112–14, 135. See also ejidos; hacienda; privatization; rancho
Larrea y Cordero, Pedro (geographer), 42
law enforcement, 62, 135. See also rurales
Lennox Kennedy, Carlos, 109–10
Lerdo de Tejada (president), 16–17. See also Ley Lerdo (1856); Plan de Tuxtepec (1876)
Ley de Hacienda (1897), 131–32. See also hacienda; land ownership
Ley Lerdo (1856), 13, 92–94, 100–103, 105. See also ejidos; disentailment; privatization
liberalism, 3, 16–17, 28, 34–35, 47, 66, 92–93, 95, 100, 119, 128–29, 142, 166n44; popular, 5
Lienzo de Tlaxcala, 37–39
Limantour, José Yves, 37, 113, 130
Lira, Pedro (engineer), 103–104, 127. See also engineers; mapping
Lira y Otera, Miguel (governor), 16–17, 60
literacy, 20, 25, 69
litigation, 93–94, 97, 101–103, 109, 113, 155n57; complaints, 86, 105, 112, 121–22, 136; letters, 65, 76–78, 107–108, 110, 119, 129, 132, 138; petitions, 82–83, 120, 133, 138. See also dissent
llanos de Apan, 53. See also pulque
local knowledge, 4–5, 12, 14, 22, 39, 53, 62–63, 71, 137, 140
López, Librado, 68, 85, 108–9, 112–13. See also assassination
Lucas, Juan Francisco, 27
Luis Velasco, Alfonso (geographer), 42. See also mapping

Macías, José N., 63–64. See also Tlaxcala (state); Tlaxcala–Puebla region
Madero, Francisco (president), 136, 139
Malintzin mountain, 53–55, 74, 95, 119
Manuel, Clement, 1–2, 4, 10
mapping, 83, 86, 89–90, 103–105. See also engineers
Mariano Grajales, José (governor), 17, 52, 77
Marquéz, Rosendo (governor), 61, 68, 98, 151n6
Martínez, Mucio (governor), 18, 21, 61, 68
Martínez López, Francisco, 107
Matienzo, Andrés, 111–12
Maya, 8, 96; civilization, 30, 32–33; racialization of, 45, 49. See also Chichén Itzá; Indigenous antiquity
mediation, 10, 13, 73–78, 91–98, 106, 108–11, 118–20, 138, 142. See also pragmatism; hacendado; water
Méndez, Juan N. (governor), 63
Mendizabal, José, 84, 107–108
Mercado, Aristeo (governor), 18
Mercenario, Antonio (governor), 19
mestizaje, 6, 22, 28, 30, 38
Metepec, 69
Mexica, 8, 24, 29, 32, 33, 35, 38. See also archaeology; Indigenous antiquity; Spanish Invasion (1519)
Mexican–American War (1846–48). See North American Invasion (1847)
Mexican Revolution, 3–4, 11, 13–14, 25, 28, 112–114, 133–42, 150–51n1
Mexico City, 6, 9, 17, 37, 40, 46–47, 50, 58, 66, 74, 113, 118, 123, 127; government, 1, 55, 68, 107, 138. See also Eleventh International Congress of Americanists (1895), 32; National Museum (Mexico City); railroads
Mier, Sebastian, 75, 83, 86, 88, 175n65
military, 4, 6, 16–17, 21–22, 31, 66, 128, 131, 137. See also Plan de Tuxtepec (1876); Porfiriato
Mitla, 43
modernization, 73, 79, 106, 116–18, 125; progress narrative of, 20, 33–34, 36–37, 136; scholarship on, 183n6. See also development; infrastructure; public works
monte. See forests
Montiel, Plutarco, 66–67
moral economy, 76–77, 173n26
Morales Benítez, Ignacio, 75, 84, 105, 112
Morelos (state), 21–2, 94, 96–97, 137, 139–40
Muñoz Camargo, Diego, 38

Nahuatl, 6, 9, 37, 49; bilingualism, 12, 25, 32, 34, 44–45, 50
National Museum (Mexico City), 32–33, 38, 44
nation-building, 33, 152n17, 160–61n70, 189n109; comparisons to western civilizations, 35–37, 48, 51, 117. See also indigenismo; patrimony
Nativitas Valley, 6, 60, 68, 71, 74–76, 98, 105–106, 112–14, 119, 122, 127, 129–31, 140
natural resources, 141–42; extraction of, 55, 94; usufruct rights, 10, 73, 76, 91, 98, 106, 112, 120, 140. See also environment; forests; privatization; water
Nava, Gregorio, 66. See also elections; hacendado; Huamantla; jefe político
Nazas River, 74, 174n53, 175n60
New York Times (newspaper), 25
North American Invasion (1847), 52

Oaxaca (state), 8, 17
Ocotlán chapel, 45–48
Ortiz, Isidro, 131

Panotla, 103–105, 109, 113–14
Partido Revolucionario Institucional (PRI), 70, 139, 143. See also Mexican Revolution
paternalism, 98
patrimony, 8–9, 12, 29–39, 41, 51; See also Indigenous antiquity
patronage, 3–4, 12, 53, 65, 67–68, 71, 131, 138, 140, 142. See also Porfiriato
peasants, 6, 16, 29, 54, 93, 96, 139–40. See also agrarian reform; ejidos; rural life
peones, 2, 54, 94. See also hacienda
Periódico Oficial (newspaper), 63–64, 72, 138
Petricioli, Concepción (Kennedy), 101–103
Petricioli, Plinio, 78–80
Petricioli–Kennedy family, 66, 78–79, 84, 101
Philip II (king of Spain), 38. See also colonial era; Spanish Invasion
Plan de Tuxtepec (1876), 4, 16–17, 22
Plaza Mayor, 24, 32
El Popular (newspaper), 136–37
Porfiriato, 3–6, 8–17, 47, 61, 74, 76–77, 136–37, 140–43; elections, 65–71; foreign view of, 20–21; Indigenous relations, 15, 23–24, 28–30, 32–38, 44–45, 49–50, 142; water disputes during, 110–14. See also development; Díaz, Porfirio (president); military; modernization; nation-building; Plan de Tuxtepec (1876)
positivism, 17, 33, 45, 49, 117, 152n14. See also científicos
poverty, 56, 97–98, 103, 105, 112, 131–33, 140, 155n57
pragmatism, 4, 11, 36, 98, 142. See also Cahuantzi, Próspero (governor); mediation
pre-Columbian. See Indigenous antiquity
prefect. See jefe político
privatization, 13, 55, 58, 92–98, 100–102, 105, 114–15, 125–26, 166n44; funding public works, 107, 118–20; of land, 17, 28–29, 35, 60, 64; of water rights, 76–82, 110, 112, 141; See also disentailment; ejidos; hacienda; rancho; water
protests, 2, 25, 56, 69, 71, 86, 97, 135, 137; in ejidos, 131–33; Indigenous, 45; over water, 11, 76, 111. See also dissent; elections; litigation; water
public health, 88, 109–10, 118, 125
public works, 10, 13, 86, 107, 116–28, 131, 133, 170–71n2. See also ayuntamiento; Tlaxcala (state); urban planning
Puebla (state), 21, 27, 66, 77, 98, 107, 111, 117, 136, 139. See also Tlaxcala–Puebla region
Puebla City, 57–58, 68, 125–26. See also Puebla (state)
pulque, 41, 53, 55, 57, 70, 94, 132–33

Rabasa, Emiliano (governor), 20
race, 5–6, 46
racism, 1–2, 22–23, 28, 35, 40, 49, 64, 142; anti-Indigenous, 8, 10, 12, 24–26, 30, 45
railroads, 3, 9, 33, 42, 52–58, 73, 83, 117–19, 121, 138–39
rancho, 62–63, 72 , 84, 94, 96, 103–104, 110, 113, 119. See also hacienda; hacienda–rancho distinction; land ownership
reform laws, 17. See also Constitution of 1857; secularism
resistance. See dissent
Reyes, Bernardo (governor), 18, 20–21
rice, 22
roads, 9–11, 13, 55, 78, 106, 118–22, 125–26, 128, 130, 132, 138. See also development; public works; urban planning

Romero, Manuel, 69. See also elections
Romero Rubio, Carmen, 47
rurales, 2, 56, 69, 118, 131, 135. See also García, Agustín "el colgador"; law enforcement; violence
rural life, 41, 46–50, 75, 93, 97. See also peasants

San Francisco River, 87–88. See also Atoyac River
San Francisco Tepeyanco, 109
San Hipolito (village), 103, 105. See also ejidos
Santa Ana Nopalucan, 112
Santa María Ixtulco, 6
Santo Toribio Xicotzinco, 107–108
Secretaría de Fomento, 80–88. See also development; litigation
secularism, 6, 28, 34–35, 46–47. See also Catholic Church; reform laws
El Segundo Círculo de Obreros Libres, 136. See also factory; labor; protests
Sela, Eduardo, 111
Sela, Francisco, 78–80, 111
El Senado de Tlaxcala, 35–36
Serdán, Aquiles, 139
Serrano, Rafael (engineer), 111. See also engineers
sisal. See henequen
Social Darwinism, 2, 6, 9, 22. See also racism
sociedad agrícola, 94, 177n4
Spanish Empire. See colonial era
Spanish Invasion (1519), 8–9, 29, 35, 38. See also colonial era; Tenochtitlán
Starr, Frederick, 25
sugar, 3, 21–22, 74, 94, 140

taxes, 21, 54–56, 62, 64, 71, 126, 130; alcabalas, 119; exemptions, 107, 136, 138; property, 2, 11, 96, 131–32, 137, 140

technocrats. See científicos
Tenancingo, 135. See also protests
Tenochtitlán, 8, 29, 35, 55, 74. See also Spanish Invasion (1519)
Teolocholco, 167n60, 170n108
Teotihuacán, 32, 43–44, 73
Tepeihtec, 103, 105, 109, 129
Tepetitla, 69–70, 110–11
terrenos baldíos, 94–96. See also privatization
textiles, 62–63, 135–36, 138–39. See also factory
threats, 97, 113, 129–30
timber, 28, 55, 72, 94. See also forests
Tlaxcala (state), 52, 83, 96, 117; administrative organization of, 57–58, 163–64nn9–10; economy, 13, 22, 36, 53, 98; municipal budget, 119, 127–28, 131; pre-Hispanic legacy, 8–9, 12, 29, 31, 35, 37–40, 140, 142, 152n17; sovereignty, 4, 9, 16, 45, 53, 56, 58–65, 73. See also ayuntamiento: of Tlaxcala; Cahuantzi, Próspero (governor); Tlaxcala City; Tlaxcala–Puebla region; water
Tlaxcala City, 54, 105, 122, 126, 130
Tlaxcala–Puebla region, 4, 9, 16, 45, 52–56, 58–65, 68, 71–72, 94, 108–10, 119–21, 138; water issues, 80, 83–86, 102. See also water
toma de agua, 82, 84, 90, 102–103. See also water
trade, 17; domestic, 53; international, 3, 6, 33, 67, 74, 81, 83, 118, 153n32
Treviño, Gerónimo (governor), 20
Treviño–Naranjas family, 20
Turner, John Kenneth, 20, 25
turpentine, 126. See also forests
Tzompantepec, 71

urban planning, 116, 130. See also infrastructure; public works

Valenzuela, Policarpo (governor), 27–28
Valley of Mexico, 74, 82. See also Desagüe General del Valle de México
Vargas, Melitón (bishop), 45–47
Vela Farfán, Trinidad, 68, 84, 103, 113
Veracruz (port), 52, 55, 139. See also railroads
Veracruz (state), 21, 117, 125
Villa, Francisco "Pancho" (revolutionary), 139
Villa Alta, 101, 110
violence, 1–2, 68–69, 71, 131, 135, 140, 143. See also assassination; threats
La Voz de México (newspaper), 116

water, 10–12, 53, 74–76, 85–86, 90–93, 110–12; communal use of, 4–5, 97, 100–105, 114–15, 140; infrastructure, 62, 106–107, 118, 120, 137; municipal control over, 13, 77–78, 94; potable, 88, 125–126, 130. See also bridges; canals; dams, Federal Waters Law (1888); flood; irrigation; toma de agua
women, 48–49, 69, 129
World's Fairs, 12, 40–41; Madrid (1892), 38; Paris (1889), 24, 33; St. Louis (1904), 40–41

Xaltitla, 60. See also Tlaxcala–Puebla region
Xicoténcatl (factory), 75
Xicoténcatl (pre-Columbian leader), 37, 116, 140
Xicoténcatl (theater), 96
Xipe Totec, 32. See also Indigenous antiquity; Mexica
Xochitécatl, 159n45

Yaqui people, 6, 24, 45
Yucatán, 6, 17, 24, 67, 96. See also Maya

Zacatelco, 77, 120, 132, 167n60, 170n108
zacatón. See broom root
Zahuapan River, 6, 54, 56, 72–75, 77–90, 99, 101–106, 109, 112–15, 120, 122, 124–27
Zapata, Emiliano (revolutionary), 22, 139
Zapatista movement, 21–22, 140
Zapatista National Liberation Army (EZLN), 142
Zapotec people, 8, 28
Zaragoza (district), 94, 163n9. See also hacienda; labor; Tlaxcala–Puebla region

The authorized representative in the EU for product safety and compliance is:
Mare Nostrum Group
B.V Doelen 72
4831 GR Breda
The Netherlands

www.ingramcontent.com/pod-product-compliance
Lightning Source LLC
Chambersburg PA
CBHW022008220426
43663CB00007B/1004